HINTON AMPNER
FARMING'S END

CHARLIE FLINDT

HINTON AMPNER
FARMING'S END

Text & images ©Charlie Flindt

ISBN 9781914615412

A CIP catalogue record for this book
is available from the British Library.
Published 2022 Tricorn Books, Aspex
42 The Vulcan Building Gunwharf Quays
Portsmouth PO1 3BF

Printed & bound in the UK

HINTON AMPNER
FARMING'S END

Foreword

For some years, my favourite farming phase has been "let's give 'em what they want!" It gets uttered after the latest agri-eco-lunacy has featured in the papers – even the farming papers. Experts tell us how we should be changing the English countryside to anything but conventional food production. We should be growing trees, introducing beavers and wolves, letting ragwort loose – and even if we are farming, we must revert to mediaeval methods, and have faith (like all religious converts) that it will be enough to feed an industrial world. "Madness!" we traditional farmers mutter. But how can we prove it's madness? Why, we should give 'em what they want, of course, and then sit back and watch. Trouble is, I can't see me ever getting that chance.

In the farmhouse
Charlie and Hazel Flindt - and Anthony, having a career break.

Not in the farmhouse anymore
Diana (working in Cambridge) and Jonathan (intern at the Bank of England)

Pets
Sasha – Malinois/GSD cross.
Bella, Evie and Tim – Flatcoat retrievers.
Cain and Abel - cats

In the farmyard
2016 Skoda Octavia Scout 2.0 diesel
2007 Hyundai Terracan (aka Tigger)
2017 Hyundai i20
1999 VW Lupo 1.4E
2022 Toyota Highlander (press car)

In the barn
2012 John Deere 6630 Premium (c/w Steinbauer chip)
2018 Massey Ferguson 5713S c/w front loader
2021 Claas Tucano 420 c/w 18ft header
2015 Kubota 400ci RTV – aka Pig.

Main farm kit
2006 Horsch CO3 seed drill
2007 Horsch Sprinter ST4
2018 FarmGem Diamond 3000 litre, 24m boom
2006 Kverneland 5 furrow plough.

Secondary farm kit
8.3m Dalbo rollers
3m Terradisc
3m mounted discs
Assorted haymaking kit
Assorted harvest kit

Introduction

When we join Manor Farm, on Michaelmas Day 2021, harvest is not long finished – and it was another thoroughly mediocre one. Crops had never really recovered from the wet winter ('20/'21) and conditions were unkind right through the year, right through to a summer that never really dried. A fresh farming year is about to start, and all we wanted was a routine and easy twelve months. Still, prices were good, the new combine had done half a harvest, and there's a brand-new tractor on the way – all signs of optimism and commitment to our farming future.

Dedication

Somewhat astonishingly, Hazel continues to be Mrs Flindt.
I count my blessings every day.

Five things we did* that we don't do now

1. Set fire to things. The most important tool in a farmer's pocket was a lighter. There were fields of straw to be lit (the ultimate in organic pest and weed control). You might be off to the old dell with a trailer load of rubbish and old spray cans – and a damn good bonfire got rid of them. At the end of a long day's drilling, what better way to relax than gathering all the paper seed bags and all the plastic fertiliser bags, and having a warm blaze in the sunset? And all accompanied by a last cup of tea – and, most importantly, a delicious cigarette.

2. Use guns a lot. A very effective way of keeping pigeons off oilseed rape was to load up the BSA with .22 hi-velocity bullets, and regularly let loose a volley of six shots (five in the magazine, one in the chamber) over the field. My treat for a day away from school was to adjourn to the old tennis court and go through a box of cartridges at clay pigeons. And I mean a box of 250, not of 25 – on a Sunday afternoon. The same BSA was lethal at up to seventy yards, and Dad and I would cruise around the farm thinning out rabbits and hares without any worries about walkers. And while it's true that we still have a little rough shoot, it's nothing compared to the grand shoots that once shared my fields, with teams of beaters, pickers up, convoys of Range Rovers and keepers keeping the woods free of folk.

3. Drive round the farm. The extensive network of tracks that once threaded round the farm - and constituted Dad's daily routine for checking on the men - has become overgrown and unusable. The reason is simple: rights of way are usually on tracks, so received wisdom is now that all tracks are rights of way. After the ten-thousandth fruitless argument with a walker, it became obvious that it would be simpler to let the tracks grow over, and enjoy correcting the Parish Council when they said I had to keep them clear. A similar change has happened to gateways. It was once possible to exit every field through a selection of gateways. Our hare coursing friends have seen to it that most gateways are blocked permanently, and the rest host a selection of hideous scrap in an attempt to keep the field safe.

4. Leave things unlocked. I hate to sound like a Monty Python sketch, but it's true. Nothing was locked. Cars, tractors, barns, and houses. At five to eight in the morning, we'd slide open the unlocked tractor barn doors, climb into tractors (with the keys still in the ignition) and set off. The barn door stayed open all day, until we got back at five past five. We now need chains and padlocks on pasture gates to deter campers, picnickers and livestock theft.

5. Farm unsupervised. We'd plough and plant a field, put fertiliser on it, spray off some weeds, combine it, and sell the product. And we had to tell no-one what we'd done.

*Back in 1984, when I started on the farm.

Contents

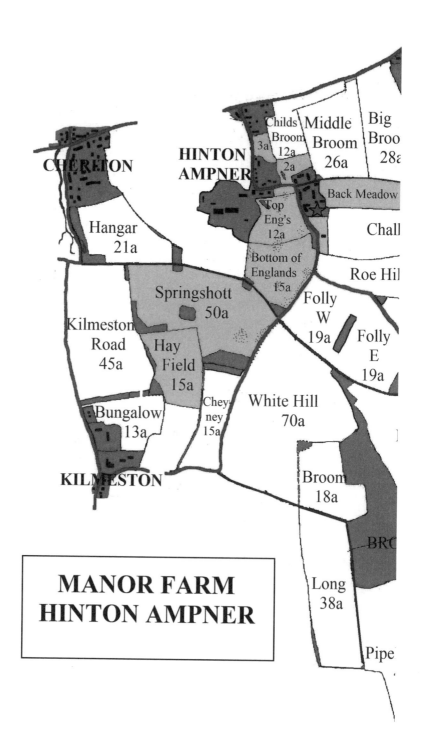

CHERITON

HINTON
AMPNER

Childs
Broom
3a
12a
2a

Middle
Broom
26a

Big
Broo
28a

Back Meadow

Top
Eng's
12a

Chall

Hangar
21a

Bottom of
Englands
15a

Roe Hil

Springshott
50a

Folly
W
19a

Folly
E
19a

Kilmeston
Road
45a

Hay
Field
15a

Chey-
ney
15a

White Hill
70a

Bungalow
13a

KILMESTON

Broom
18a

BRO

**MANOR FARM
HINTON AMPNER**

Long
38a

Pipe

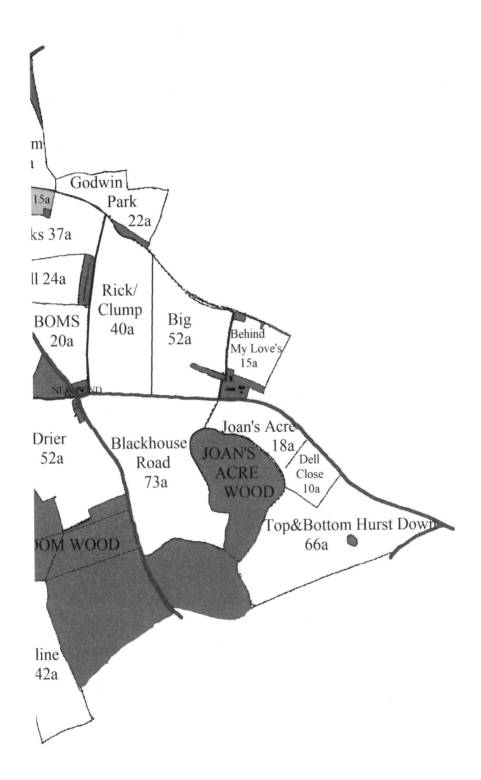

m
l

Godwin
Park
22a

15a

ks 37a

ll 24a

Rick/
Clump
40a

BOMS
20a

Big
52a

Behind
My Love's
15a

NEW POND

Drier
52a

Blackhouse
Road
73a

Joan's Acre
18a

JOAN'S
ACRE
WOOD

Dell
Close
10a

OOM WOOD

Top&Bottom Hurst Down
66a

line
42a

Field names (sort of) explained

Back Meadow – The pasture at the back of the farm buildings. 'Horse meadow' in the old days, according to the old farm maps

Behind My Love's/BML's – I could explain it, but probably best not to.

Big – It's big. Probably the biggest at one time, although it isn't now.

Big Broom – the biggest of the three 'Broom' fields in the Godwin's block.

Blackhouse Road – The field next to the road to Blackhouse Farm

BOMS – Acronym for 'Behind Old Man Simpson', who used to live in New Pond Cottages just south of it.

Broom Field – Next to Broom woods, but unrelated to the Godwin's 'Brooms'.

Bungalow – There's a bungalow next to it, although the old boys called it 'dog kennel'.

Chalks – Mostly very chalky.

Cheyney – A Mr Cheyney farmed it in the 1950s.

Child's Broom – The smallest of the Godwin's 'Broom' fields.

Dell Close – The smallest field, with a dell in the middle.

Drier – Field next to the drier buildings. It was enlarged in the 80s, after we took on the meadows belonging to Joan Dutton. Many historic hedges were bulldozed out – but that's what you did. It was briefly two fields, with the old meadows area being named Violin Field, as Granny Flindt's violin teacher was Joan Meadows.

Englands (Top and Bottom) – Not a clue

Folly – Supposedly after the long narrow copse in the middle of it.

Godwin's Park – Not sure why. It's part of Godwin's, but that's about it.

The Hangar – After the big Saxon boundary bank at the top of it

Hay Field – The best bit of grass for making hay.

Hurst Down (Top and Bottom) – No idea – apart from the usual query why we call high ground 'downs'.

Joan's Acre – Opposite, and once connected to, Joan's Acre House. It's not an acre, and it was never farmed by Joan Dutton. So I don't get it, either.

Kilmeston Road – The field next to the road to Kilmeston

Long – It's long.

Middle Broom – the middle of the three Godwin's 'Broom' fields.

Pipeline – It's got a pipeline in it. No idea what it was called pre-pipeline.

Rick/Clump – The lower bit was often where a straw rick was built, the upper bit was next to a clump of trees.

Roe Hill – 'Rough Hill' according to the old maps, but Grandpa Flindt pronounced 'trough' as 'troe', so probably Rough' as 'roe'. No idea where the original 'rough' came from.

Springshot – A big pasture where the springs rise at the end of the winter.

White Hill – Another chalky field.

HINTON AMPNER
FARMING'S END

HINTON AMPNER FARMING'S END

September 30th

Year thirty-one didn't get off to the brightest of starts. The 'poachers' were round again last night, and the kitchen was cold. It turned out that the Aga had gone out when we turned the central heating on for the first time last night. I bet the heating oil has run out; we're due a load imminently. And my first job after a slightly cold and clammy breakfast was to drive round to see what damage the 'poachers' had done last night – apart from wrecking my night's sleep.

There was nothing to be seen. No piles of feathers where birds had been catapulted from the trees, no fresh wheel marks across fields. But it was still hugely frustrating. We've had a remarkable year almost free from these bastards. I cheered myself up by clearing out the faithful Deere 6630P in preparation for the arrival of the new tractor. It's amazing what you find under the debris on the floor, and in the bottomless pit behind the seat.

October 1st

We were woken by rain – really heavy rain, hammering against the windows from a depressingly dark sky. It was just like last year. And the year before that. You can go off farming, sometimes.

The rain had stopped ("rain before seven, dry by eleven") when the home phone line rang. It was our ten tonnes of winter barley seed being delivered by a charming and chatty Latvian, and he was an hour early. Still, I made him welcome, thanked him profusely, and congratulated him on sourcing some diesel.

He wasn't long gone when the distinctive sound of a John Deere straight six could be heard coming up the hill; it was my new tractor, a Deere 6155M, being delivered by the salesman himself. It was a relief to hear the noise – the engine note is one of my favourite features on the old 6630P.

A quick tour of the 6155M confirmed that many other features of the old tractor have been carried over. Little things like opening side windows, proper old-fashioned gearbox and easy to use side steps. Mind you, it was no surprise; Hunt's lent me a demo tractor last spring to do some cultivating and drilling, and I very soon felt at home in it, and agreed the order. That was six or seven months ago now, and the long delay has been caused by phenomenal demand; an interesting point in the current doom-filled farming climate. I can't help thinking that I'm not the only farmer looking for a 'traditional' cab in which to spend my time. I wasn't convinced about changing the tractor; the old 6630P had years in it. I think there's some tax advantage in it somewhere, so that might explain it.

Fired up with a new enthusiasm for farming (seed! A new tractor!) I finally got the latest FonF done – the 'Michaelmas grumpy moment' seemed perfect, and, even better, they seemed to like it.

I was checking the oil level in the central heating tank – to see if that was behind the Aga giving up again (it wasn't) – when Policeman Ian called in, keen to discuss the surge in poachers (as we must call them). My 999 call the other evening had got mixed up with a frenzy of other calls, so no result had been achieved. In the batch of rural-related 999s was a mugging/camera theft in Southampton; not sure how that can happen, but there we go. He said that we are not alone, and the issue is getting flagged up further up the police ladder. In the meantime, he said, keep ringing them in. Bastards.

Then it was time for my favourite job: installing your old kit in a brand- new machine. Once again, it was a great advantage that I was moving control boxes from one old cab to a near-identical one. Ten minutes prising off pristine plastic trim and then attacking it with the cordless drill (not quite so pristine after that, of course) and I could get my M10 mounting bolts in.

I'd asked Hunt's to install a ¾" free-flow return in the back axle – for the Sprinter ST4 hydraulically driven fan – but 'male' and 'female' had got lost in translation (a metaphor for our time, in many ways) and the 6155M had a female coupling – as does the Horsch. I jumped in the test Highlander and popped up to Gaskin's to get a male. I passed the West Meon Hut petrol station, which had fuel – and queues and men in high-viz jackets sternly directing traffic. It looked relatively calm, though.

Rod's dealership was back to normal anyway. No masks, no barriers, no stress. Very refreshing. I pick up my coupling, exchanged lots of insults with the team up there, and agreed that, yes, I do fully expect Jeremy Clarkson to take over my column in *Farmers Weekly*. He is, after all, Britain's most famous farmer.

By the time I'd got the coupling in, it was getting dark. I realised I could have got out and done that last bit of Roundup that's needed on White Hill. It would probably have been too wet on the clay end, and I hadn't finished wiring in the control boxes completely. Nice to know I've still got the excuses handy.

With the Aga still out, we had fish and chips from the Alresford chippie, and only just managed to polish off three children's portions. We Flindts are letting our standards slip. And Facebook announced that the West Meon Hut service had been shut by police due to the traffic chaos. Curious times.

October 2nd

The forecast suggested that yet more big weather was on the way, and I had an inkling that the Aga's problems were down to something blocking the fuel. Ten minutes hacking away at the ivy near the back door tap revealed the aluminium filter casing, and a couple of minutes later we had the filter out; it was full of what looked like black tar.

I got a fresh filter out of the 'Aga odds and sods' box, fitted it, and got everything relit. An easier job than I thought it would be.

The deluge arrived just as Hazel set off with Evie for some veterinary inspections of hips and joints – just in case we decide to have a litter of pups from her. I brought one duvet down from the bedroom, settled down on the sofa (with Sasha joining me under the duvet) and had a proper snoozing Saturday. I nearly lit a fire, but it wasn't quite cold enough. Just bloody wet.

The Aga got almost up to full heat, but was still being noisy. We might just have to put up with it.

October 3rd

Hazel was off at some silly hour to do her dog training up at Mullenscote. I saw her off, had some porridge, went back to bed for a bit, watched last week's BTCC highlights – and that was about it. We had some warm sun and some showers. I did a long walk to Big Field with Sasha. It was all very mundane and very dull. A perfect Sunday. The forecast's dramatic improvement suggests we're going to be quite busy enough in a few days' time, thank you very much.

October 4th

Caine was yowling outside my room at about six fifteen. He was drenched, but I still made him welcome on my bed. This suggested two things: first, we'd had another bucketload of rain, and second, someone was up very early on a Monday morning. This time it was Anthony, getting ready for Day Three down at the flower-packing plant next door. If he lasts the day, he'll beat my brother Ian's record, which was three days at Marwell Zoo before being mauled by a llama and handing in his notice. And Dad had bought him a Suzuki GT185 specially for it.

It did mean we were all up in time for the central heating oil delivery, which was flipping early. I often wonder if we get marked for sparrows' fart delivery times because our address has 'farm' in it. As I tipped two bottles of 'Topanol' additive into the tank (the drivers aren't supposed to do it, apparently) I asked if he had been followed by car drivers desperate for fuel. He said that he was very sceptical of the story of drivers chasing anything that looks like a fuel tanker – especially a mortar tanker, as the Sunday papers tried to claim.

It was nice to have a full diesel tank and a full central heating tank, all set up for a busy and cold autumn. Just in time for the heatwave that starts later this week, apparently.

Time for our ACCS inspection. This normally happens in the final weeks before harvest, but everything is cockeyed at the moment. The good news is that our favourite inspector is back on the circuit, and it was a firm but friendly run-through of all the questions. Quite different to the humourless virtual version we had fifteen or so months ago.

We probably spent more time moaning about the state of the world than we did actually checking up for those vital dates ('when did you wash the combine?' etc.).

It was still a relief to pass, and we could then face the NFU pensions advisor with a clear mind. Rumour has it that our years of piling stuff into pension funds have been wise. But he still insisted that we should keep going, and pile even more into them. "And get on with the accounts, you idle sod!" was his main message.

I had a phone message promising another lorry-load of seed late tomorrow or early Wednesday, and it rained a lot. Again.

October 5th

Very, very wet again last night. It seemed odd to be taking delivery of more seed when we haven't turned a wheel on the ground in weeks, and aren't likely to for some time yet.

The ex-Editor rang mid-morning to suggest a visit to his favourite clay pigeon ground; he knows I've yet to pull the trigger of the brand new Rizzini BR110 I bought myself with the proceeds of Book One and thinks we ought to see it in action before our first pheasant day on the farm. Why didn't we pop up there shortly? I said I'd check the seed lorry times and ring him back.

It all went a bit bizarre from there. The transport manager took my call and was quite clear. The lorry hadn't been loaded yet; when he was about to set off, she'd get him to ring with detailed plans. She suspected it might be late afternoon, or perhaps first thing in the morning. But I could be sure of one thing: he'd be ringing soon with his plans.

That would suit me just right; I needed some new 12V plugs to fit the curious 'socket bar' in the new Deere. And I hadn't driven the Toyota Highlander enough, so a high-speed trip to Chilbolton would be perfect.

The phone rang, and it was indeed the delivery driver. "I'll be with you in an hour," he said. "About ten thirty." Left hands and right hands, eh? Still, these days we have to be grateful for HGV drivers, and their diesel, and their loads of precious seed.

After I'd unloaded him and got his enormous machine turned round, I had lunch and then set off to the Deere dealer for the electrical plugs. It was a delight to see all 'virus'-related stuff done and dusted, with only the '2m spacing' stickers looking a bit tired and jaded on the floor. I was collared by a young lad who excitedly explained that the new tractor was fitted with wonderful telematics. Thanks to an app on my smartphone, I'd be able to check on performance and fuel consumption and maintenance details and locations and a hundred thousand other things. "What's an 'app'?" I asked.

Once home, Sasha and I did a long walk round TBHD, and pondered the state of the world. Well, I did; Sasha stalked Murph's pheasants.

The last job was to drop the Octavia Scout off at North's for a new clutch. I haven't put a clutch in car since the one in my Alfasud – and even that was a bit of a con by the garage. But the pedal is playing up and there's a terrible 'death rattle' when stopping and occasionally when starting, which suggests the dual mass flywheel is in trouble. It won't be cheap, but the Scout is one hell of a bus, and worth looking after.

October 6th

The latest and last lorry- load of seed arrived on the dot of eight o'clock. He'd rung about forty minutes earlier, so I was ready for him, and had 8½ tonnes of 'Gleam' wheat unloaded by half past. All very efficient. The barn is officially full.

That meant I could take the block of wafer weights off the Massey loader and leave it on the little stand round by the calf pens, ready to be hitched onto the front of the new tractor, ready for drilling. Once I'd sorted out how to fold down the front linkage on the Deere, I got the weights on, came back to the main yard and hitched onto the drill. All very exciting.

Another hour's worth of wiring was needed, installing the new plugs and trying to get the mass of cables into some sort of order. Give it six months and it'll be chaotic spaghetti again. A couple of minutes checking the drill itself showed that the points were on their last legs, and even though the yard is littered with semi-worn points, I thought a new set would be in order. A quick text to the Toyota man, checking when he would be here to pick up the Highlander, showed I had time to shoot up to Olivers and pick up a fresh set.

Back home, I grabbed a couple of 19mm spanners and had the whole new set on in about an hour. All very satisfying, and I was feeling quite sunburnt when the man from Toyota finally arrived for his vehicle. He'd been dropping huge hints about me picking him up from Petersfield station, but I had declined. He arrived at 'Peef' just in time for the schoolchildren to hoover up all the taxis, and the poor fellow had had to catch a bus and walk up the hill.

We had our first band rehearsal of the new farming year, and it was not good. Ian the drummer couldn't make it, and the rest of us weren't really in the mood to be serious. Not sure why; possibly the fine forecast that means we'll all be out drilling tomorrow. Possibly me telling 'em all that *Farmers Weekly* had genuinely expressed interest in using us as the band for the 2022 FW Awards. The 2021 Awards are tomorrow – John is going (his company, Germinal, are sponsors), so we told him to do a recce of the whole event and see if we're anywhere near good enough. After this evening's chaos, we'd have our work cut out. We were struggling with a three-chord Quo.

Just before bedtime I texted the ex-Editor and said I'd be too busy to go clay shooting in the morning.

October 7th

It was wet. Not heavy, but just enough to be a bloody nuisance. Still, it's an ill wind and all that: I texted the ex-Editor again, changing my mind, and suggesting we do go shooting after all. Not surprisingly, he was up for it.

I got the next FonF done nice and early, and then pondered which car to take shooting. The Skoda is having its clutch done, the little i20 is almost out of fuel (and buying fuel is still a lottery) and that leaves Tigger. I checked over the tyres (must get them replaced) and cleaned it up a bit. By 11 o'clock, the ex- Editor and I were on the way to Andover.

The Lains shooting ground was a bit of a revelation: fantastically well organised with DIY stands, a card that you pick up at reception that kept track of where/how many you've shot (at), deserted, lots of hard standing and some challenging targets.

It was the very first trip out with my new Rizzini BR110 – my first brand-new gun since the mid-1980s. I didn't shoot terribly well with it, and the double discharge that it did once didn't help concentration. I'm on good terms with the gunsmith at the importer, so I might drop him an email. On the way back, all the petrol stations were open as normal.

After a late lunch, I set about the Horsch's tyres and wheels with a grease gun and a compressor, and was on the cusp of doing a calibrate and even a trip out to Godwin's when an outbreak of laziness put paid to that idea. It took some persuading to get me off the sofa to give Hazel a lift to North's to fetch the newly clutched Skoda.

October 8th

The phone started buzzing quite early – but not with birthday greetings. It was John reporting from the *Farmers Weekly* Awards that the band was a proper pro unit, way out of our league. There were lots of birthday messages, too, for both me and Hazel. Jonathan rang from London to say he'd love to come down for a birthday lunch tomorrow, but those nice people at the Bank of England have decided to exploit the placement student somewhat, and he has a mountain of genuinely urgent work to do. You never heard anyone so happy about it, though. Pigs in shit spring to mind.

After a final calibration and a check over of the drill, I could think of no more excuses not to go and make a start in Godwin's drilling wheat, and set off, rather gingerly, in the new tractor. I marked out three sides of Big Broom and started down the hill next to the hedge.

The 'fan speed alarm' went off; the fan was apparently running too low. An hour or two of phone calls to Hunt's (was it the new tractor's hydraulics?), Olivers (should I change the Horsch's hydraulic motor settings?) and a contact I have at Horsch UK (ditto) resulted in me tightening up the pressure relief valve on the fan drive motor, and finally all seemed OK. The fan didn't sound right, though; it sounded far too fast now, even though the control box said it was running at just over 3,000 rpm.

I pressed on anyway. Down the hill (bout number three), up the hill (bout number four, overlapping half to set up the tramline correctly in a minute or two), down the hill (bout number five) and up the hill (bout number six, tramlining).

It should have been tramlining, anyway. It wasn't. The number '6' on the control box resolutely refused to flash – which is how it shows that some spouts have been shut off and the pre-em markers are down. Another 'oh, for goodness sake' moment. I had visions of rat-damaged wiring that would need repairing, tramline-free fields that would need marking out, calling in contractors, switching to the faithful Horsch CO3 parked in the yard but now set up permanently as a bean machine.

At the top of the field, I lifted the machine out of the ground, and the control box went to '7' instead of back to '1'. Ah. It all made sense. The ST4 doesn't go to '7' (to paraphrase Spinal Tap); it goes to six, because six times four metres is a tramline set. The little CO3 goes to '8' (3m x 8 = 24m). I had forgotten to swap control boxes. Hence the confused fan speed signals – the CO3 has a different sized PTO fan, not hydraulic.

Only one thing for it: drive home, swap boxes, recalibrate, have a cup of tea. Basically – start again. So I did. By four o'clock, I was back out there with everything as it should be (and pressure relief valve screw wound out to where it was) and managed a couple of good hours. The new tractor was similar enough to the old one to feel right, although it did seem to struggle a bit coming up the hill. I think the untouched ground is pretty tough, and the engine is straight out of the box, so let's give it time.

Diana came down from Cambridge quite late, ready for our belated birthday lunch tomorrow. Good thing Anthony was available to do the ten thirty pick-up. We could hardly stay awake till then.

October 9th

Very foggy and damp to start, and the early drilling was quite slippery. The view was stunning, though, and it would have been a very long productive day in Godwin's were it not for the monumental (late) birthday lunch. A magnificent bit of lamb with all the trimmings.

And then it was time for presents: socks, a desk diary for 2022 (already?), slippers – all very mundane but no less welcome for it. Hazel and I had organised a proper ABS case for the new Rizzini, which looked very smart, and she had a new shooting/picking-up/beating coat.

We should have broken open a bottle or two of something, but the tractor beckoned again, and I got out of Big Broom and made a good start in Middle Broom. Any ideas of cracking on well into the night were wrecked by Diana's sponge cake – cream 'n' strawberries and everything – which was really quite unnecessary after that lunch, but four Flindts made very short work of it.

I didn't dare stand on the scales after my shower.

October 10th

Hazel was off early to her gundog training near Andover – in the dark. I would say I long for the clocks to change, but all that does is make the evenings horrible instead. I had a long morning in Godwin's, warming to my task, and got back just in time for the first BTCC race.

Anthony took Diana back to Peef station for her trip back to Cambridge, and I kept going in the tractor, finishing all of the Godwin's block. With a bit of luck, I'll get the Folly done tomorrow, and then have to decide where to go next: get the winter barley done nice and early (Drier/White Hill/Cheyney) but risk the weather breaking before we get to the heavy land at Stanmore? Or get the heavy land done first and risk the winter barley going in too late? I've got a day to think about it.

I brought the tractor and drill home for a fuel up and a session pumping up those bloomin' awkward tyres – but decided to do it in the morning instead.

October 11th

Another good productive day. I had an online argument with Emma at FW about the headline on the latest *FonF*, and sulked virtually because she wouldn't go with my suggestion.

Drilling was more satisfying. I gingerly eased the Deere/Horsch back out of the yard and down to the Folly, and got the whole lot done in a day. It helps that I've gone up a gear, and am now cruising along at 10 kph. The Folly is one of the lightest fields on the farm, so doesn't present much of a horsepower challenge. It's one of the fields we should be leaving till last, when the weather is catchier, but I'm sticking to my plan.

Hazel rolled all of Godwin's and did seed support, and then took Tigger up to Long Field and walked back with a pack of dogs (and a slightly groggy Anthony who appears to have caught something). Once I finished Folly (inch perfect on an eighth turn of headland) I took the drill up to Stanmore and came home in Tigger. Perfect logistics.

An artisan burger and chips from the legendary burger van went down particularly well on a Monday evening.

October 12th

Hazel went off early with Bella for her first day picking-up, this time at Barrow Hill. I loaded up a trailer of wheat seed and set off to Stanmore.

The race is on to get in and out of that 100-acre block of heavy land before the weather breaks. And, to speed things up, I thought I wouldn't bother spending an hour calibrating; I'd just put a bag of Skyscraper into the drill and see how long it lasts.

I marked out the headland of Broom Field, and then made a start next to the northern boundary, curling my way round the huge fallen oak, and then straightening up once I started the land work. It was on the very edge of being too sticky – especially where the crop had rotted away in last winter's deluge – but conditions got better as I worked my way across the field. The first 500kg of Skyscraper ran out too early, but not by much, so a slight tweak to the rate should get it back on track.

Broom Field finished rather well, and right on the expected area – and I had the seed rate running spot on by now. It was time for Long Field, with its (duh) long turns and several sinkholes. After marking out, I started next to the west edge, and thought I'd stick with the curves this year.

The best bit was where the seed had rotted last year and I'd sprayed off the weeds in the spring when I was doing shoot strip preparations. It was bare soil. The worst bit was where the seed had rotted last year and the weeds had got away, and only just been sprayed off. That was a bit of a lumpy challenge. The rest of the field – where there had been a reasonable crop of Zulu – drilled well enough, helped by the new chopper on the Claas Tucano; it actually chops straw into tiny pieces, rather than just apologetically push lengths of straw about, which is what the New Holland used to do.

By the time I was getting tired (the new Deere's cab suspension isn't as comfortable as the old one's), I'd done about half of Long Field – without getting stuck once. Another respectable 38-ish acre day. Most of the sitting room was sound asleep by nine thirty.

October 13th

Blimey – it's a long time since we had a run of autumn drilling like this one, although the forecast suggests it'll come to a crashing wet end on Monday. So we must push on.

Hazel loaded two more bags into the drill in Long Field, and then went rolling in the Folly for the rest of the morning. And for the afternoon – because she hadn't been busy enough – she went off to the stables for a session doing their accounts. That's what she says she does, but I think they sit round and drink tea with ITV racing on.

I finished sowing Long Field and popped through the game strip into Pipeline. By evening, I'd done a very large chunk of land work, and it was all going rather well. God, the years we've had sowing nightmares up there. Too many to think about. Just keep going.

October 14th

Same again, really. More wheat drilling in perfect conditions. Pipeline finished perfectly, with only a few pounds in the bottom of the drill after six turns of headland. I ran that bit out on the heavily used tramline round Long Field on my way home.

Then it was the long haul back to base – once I'd taken off the side harrows and folded up. All the way back through White Hill, through the Folly (dry enough to drive over,) and back to the yard for a top-up of diesel and Adblue.

It was tempting to bucket a bit of winter barley out of a 500kg bag into the drill, and do a calibrate, ready to start sowing it in White Hill, but I thought I'd treat myself to an earlier evening finish, and contemplated having got Stanmore sown in such fine conditions. It doesn't happen often, and it's nice and early. But it's a second wheat (in most places) and I still have terrible memories of dreadful takeall-ravaged continuous wheat up there. One-ton crops of Haven spring to mind.

October 15th

A morning in the office was bizarrely welcome after all that drilling, but tractor work beckoned after lunch, and I headed out to White Hill with some winter barley. By the time I'd got started, and put the first 500kg through to confirm my in-yard calibration, Hazel arrived in the field with a trailer full of bags. She topped me up, and then went off to roll Pipeline. I had another 30 acres done by evening.

We went down to the ex-Editor's garden shed for a few Friday beers and a catch-up on life. Unfortunately, I was so tired I was pretty poor company. Seeing double vision after only two pints didn't help. Still, it's a small price to pay for one of my longest continuous drilling spells ever.

October 16th

A morning out of the tractor was in order (beer, this time), so after Hazel and the two brown flatcoats had set off for a day's picking-up in Hambledon I grabbed a pad of A4 paper and made a bold (and early) start on the accounts. First job: a simple list of what was grown last year in what fields. Even though it was only harvested a couple of months ago, I still had to give it some thought to remember the cropping plan. It's amazing how quickly you forget. A distant rumble, not unlike a Chinook on the wrong fuel, meant that neighbour Robert was on his way into the yard in his more-battered-by-the-week Defender for a coffee and a catch-up. That was a couple of hours wasted (not 'wasted' at all, of course; such things are vital). The next interruption was the contract sprayer, conveniently available on a Saturday morning to put yellow and smelly pre-emergence weedkiller on the nicely sown and rolled Gleam. That meant another half hour of 'old man moaning' with George before we could even contemplate the day's spraying instructions.

Neighbour Robert Jnr was on the phone next on the hunt for a hundredweight

of winter barley seed to finish his sowing – nice to know tha
miscalculate sometimes. I told him to help himself from one
outside the barn. Half an hour later, with a sound that al
made by his father-in-law's Defender, he arrived outside t
Deere and even more mega Väderstad drill. I had thought
up, but there we go. It made the day for several National ⅃.
on their loop around the farm.

After an early lunch, I finally got back out to White Hill, and had a good afterno
almost finishing the land work. Another hour doing the rapidly shortening turns in
Rough Field and I can get on with the vast headland.

Hazel and the two dogs came back slightly sunburnt, George finished the
spraying without incident (even though the footpaths were busy) and White Hill
looked a treat. A good day.

October 17th

I was late up – I was only just starting my morning in the bathroom when I
heard the Skoda set off. It was Hazel on her way to Mullenscote for a day's gundog
teaching, and she'd taken Tim to give him a bit of a workout between sessions.

After a quiet morning, I did yet another long afternoon in the drill, finally
finishing White Hill – seeming to get through the haunted Rough Field unscathed;
Sub-Lt Daley decided to leave us alone this year. Mind you, let's see if the barley
grows first.

Hazel popped out for an hour's rolling once she got back, and I did a shuffle
over to Cheyney and made a good start in that one. There's talk of rain tomorrow. I
quite fancy a quieter day.

October 18th

The weather muppets were right about the rain: it arrived just after lunch, just as
I was finishing Cheyney. What they didn't predict was the shower which did an
early recce, and rendered the ground that was rolling so well yesterday evening
unworkable. Hazel abandoned the rollers and did some trailer shifting.

It did mean that she was available to do a precautionary diesel run up to Cheyney
just as I was finishing. Just a couple of three-quarter full jerry cans (full ones are too
heavy these days), and possibly a tad overcautious on my part to send for them, but a
new tractor with a fancy digital gauge is not necessarily to be trusted. The last thing
I needed as the horizon got blacker and blacker was a dry engine.

I had a flashback to a Ford 6610 – the 'B' reg one – that was one of the worst
machines we ever had. It was too loud to use, and tractor driver Ernie very quickly
opted to revert to using his 'old' X-reg 6600. We even summoned Curtis Padwick
(the Winchester Ford agents) to check out the timing, but they found nothing. But
it didn't clock up many hours, and sat unloved in the corner of the barn. These were

...nties, remember, when we had a fleet of seven tractors in the barn for ..., so it was perfectly possible for one not to be used for ages.

... poor build quality didn't stop at clattering pistons, though. My brother Ian ...ed on the farm for a few years, and had the misfortune to be many miles away ...m base in the 6610 when it ran out of diesel. No phones in those days, of course, so it was a major job to get home, get a supply (probably in an old Add-F drum), fuel up, and bleed all the pipes to get going again. As usual, Dad considered it operator error, and made that thought plain – but it wasn't. The fuel gauge read just under half full. I remember buying a permanent red marker and enlarging the 'red' zone on the gauge. That's probably why I'm over cautious about these things.

It was mild and muggy as well as wet in the afternoon, so I grabbed a duvet and a wet cat (although it was his idea rather than mine) and had a long-overdue sofa session. The steaming cat didn't make it any less muggy, but at least I was feeling a bit better by the time the Old Gits had a rehearsal. A very good one it was, too, what with talk of two local gigs – including New Year at the Fox – and the fun but 'unlikely to actually happen' concept of us playing the *Farmers Weekly* Awards next October. We sounded somewhat less shambolic than usual, if you ignore the chaotic scenes as 'Caroline' collapsed into a right mess. It's not as if we haven't been playing it for thirteen years or anything.

October 19th

We didn't get that much rain in the end, which meant that the cess pit man didn't have too wet a job clearing ours out. It helped that one of Anthony's jobs over the summer was to clear the shrubbery which used to make access to the multiple lids a nightmare. Mind you, Anthony being home has boosted the rate at which the cess pit fills quite considerably.

The forecast suggested that bigger rain was on the way, so Hazel went and retrieved the rollers from White Hill; I don't think they'll be back in action for a day or two. I did my first walk for ages – just a loop round the Chalks dell – and was astonished to see the early wheat up and away, after only ten days. It's always a relief to see that the markers seem to be set right and the tramlining modules are successfully shutting off the right spouts every six turns. It was also astonishing to realise just how unfit I am. That's the trouble with sitting in a tractor too much: no exercise. (That and eating too much, of course.)

The first shoot of the season takes place on Thursday. This means a round- up of all the kit (radios, batteries, Pig trailer, earmuffs, select right chokes on new Rizzini BR110) for me and a frenzy of cooking for Hazel.

Trouble was, the phone kept ringing all afternoon. I had the Trust's building manager wanting access to the bungalow on Monday to measure   up new windows, the gang in charge of putting the new pipeline through the farm wanting to discuss which trees and hedges they'd be ripping out when work gets going, the Alresford

Show secretary wanting Hazel to take her old job back (Trade Stand Secretary) because her replacement had handed in her notice, and – my favourite – the machinery dealer from whom I bought the Horsch Sprinter leaving a message to ask if we had any kit to sell.

This was so intriguing that I rang him back. Was he really cold-calling clients on the look-out for kit? Indeed he was. The trade is extraordinary at the moment – mind you, we know that after hearing the prices of mundane but 'honest' farm kit at the West Meon Crap Sale last month.

The most crucial call was from me to neighbour Robert, double checking our Tuesday evening in the Pots. I had to drive myself as Anthony is still catching up with chums in London. I was quite restrained as a result, and the fact that one of the new co-owners of the pub bought us a round made it a fairly cheap evening. Even so, I was quite pleased that they're saying very wet tomorrow morning.

October 20th

Another wet night, so I could treat myself to a brief lie-in. Not for too long though, as the central heating engineer was due reasonably early. The trouble with central heating is that you always feel awkward paying someone to service it when it appears to be going fine, but the man didn't take long and gave it a clean bill of health.

He seemed to be taking a heck of a long time to pack up and leave, though, and when I got back from assorted pre-shoot jobs (cleaning the old table down at the Drier and bringing the Pig trailer over from Godwin's barn) he was still in the kitchen.

It turned out he'd spotted our beast of an Aga, complete with non- functioning Agamatic on the end, and getting old Agas up to speed is his obsession. I filled him in on the state of play. The main block is a solid-fuel to oil conversion, I do the servicing myself, and have done for twenty years. It could probably do with a proper reconditioning, with new copper pipes and a better base for the shallow 'well'. As for the Agamatic: the hot water jacket cracked and flooded the house for the second time in about 1989, and Dad never replaced it. I said it would be fantastic to get it up and running, with gravity-fed and electricity-free hot water supplied in copious quantities as a result. He said anything was possible.

Shoot preparation was interrupted once more by the ex-Editor, on the hunt for beating sticks. Mrs ex-Editor has signed up as beater on a couple of local pish-posh shoots, and he had promised to scour the woods for coppiced hazel of the right length and thickness. We sent him off to Blackhouse Road, where there is plenty – but not before we'd had a cuppa and a good natter.

Anthony arrived back from his long weekend in London. He was full of news of job applications and interviews – he has chosen the right time to be looking again. I thought he'd headed up to town to party for a few days.

October 21st

Another major downpour in the small hours – perfect for keeping me out of the tractor for the day's shooting, and perfect to be the scapegoat for the lack of pheasants. Just like the old days with the traditional keepers.

Hazel had been up for some time when I got up, and she was not in a good mood. For some reason, one of the main two trip switches had blown on the fuse box, and all the sockets were out of action. And included in that were the freezer, the fridge, the electric kettle for high-speed pre-shoot teas and coffees. Not a great start to the day.

A quick look in the back larder showed another flood had come in – probably via the back shed (which happens when its drain can't handle the volume of water) – so I jumped to the immediate conclusion that the freezer (now standing in an eighth of an inch of water) was to blame. Probably. I turned it off at the wall.

But it was worth doing some more methodical testing. I turned off all the other small fuses and reset the main RCB. One of the 'downstairs sockets' fuses set it off again. I was about to work my way round all the lamps, computers and (most important of all) the internet router when I spotted a hand-written addendum on the fuse's label. 'Boiler' it said. Ah. Surely not.

Sasha and I piled down the cellar steps (one day Sasha will catch the baddie who's down there – he seems to get away just in time every single time) and found more flooding. No surprise really, after last night's rain. But the boiler sits on a raised pedestal and should have been unscathed. I isolated the electricity, came back up to the fuse box and gingerly tried the RCB. All was well. We had all our sockets back.

My text to the heating engineer was remarkably succinct, but he was on the doorstep forty minutes later. We only just had time to do the 'Tigger drop off' at the Drier Yard through the flooded New Pond. The engineer was slightly sheepish, but vanished down the cellar and emerged half an hour after that wielding a 'dodgy control box', and promising that all was well now.

By now the shoot team were arriving, so I saw him on his way, promising to have a chat about the Aga at some stage. The kitchen filled with four guns and five beaters – everyone very cheerful and studiously not mentioning the news that another lockdown is being demanded by the leftie scientists.

Everyone was dressed for the weather – lots of waterproofs and, for the first time, sweaters. By the time we made it to the Drier Yard to empty Tigger of its vast supplies of sugar-based snacks, we were all jolly warm. The wind had dropped, the sun had come out spectacularly, and the bag, after only four 'home S' drives, was already 22. The maize strip at the top of Chalks (sown with the leftover seed after doing the huge Big Field strips) had been brilliant. Mind you, its ability to trip beaters up and send them flat on their faces was worth much more than any number of pheasants. Unfortunately, we guns couldn't see all this – the maize was too thick. Bodycams are in order, I think. Everyone seemed happy with the idea of only doing one more drive, so we headed out to the Big Field strip. You realise why grown-up shoots use maize; the birds coming out were fantastic, and poor old Graeme, who'd drawn the south-east gun position and was walking up the hill, was treated (subjected?) to a flow of towering birds – the highest and fastest we'll ever see on this shoot. He missed the lot. OK, he got one, but only after a third barrel while it 'helicoptered'.

(Probably unkind to mention that I got a left-and-right on two similar birds. So I won't. The new Rizzini BR110 was lovely, and I forgot I was using a brand-new gun.)

We called it a day, and all made our way back to the house in dribs and drabs, some walking, some in Tigger, some in Pig. By the time the next shoot comes round, we'll be in a bit more of a hurry as the clocks will have changed. And the day after COP26 has finished, and all the private jets have flown home, we'll be in lockdown again.

I aired this last theory at a very noisy shoot tea, and got roundly shouted down. We'll see. But it was an utterly joyful day. Hazel said that on the other shoots she's been to this year, the mood was the same: people determined to get some fun back. And we'd done well to avoid walkers in this fine weather and curious two-week half-term that the local schools are having. Not in our day, you know.

The house was like an oven. The heating had been on all day. And none of the fuses had blown.

October 22nd

Too much wine yesterday – the early headache was a bit of a giveaway. I was into the paracetamol nice and early, and my head had cleared by the time I remembered I was a day late with Flindt on Friday. I had an idea that had been brewing for several days, and they were happy with it

They were less than happy at my nonchalant request for yet more free publicity for Book One. "No, Charlie, you've had quite enough!" They did agree to mention Book Two (being polished up at the moment) in the Christmas Gift guide in the middle of November. I'd better get a move on with the polishing.

During yesterday's shoot, I'd noticed that Drier Field had greened up again. I sprayed it a month ago, but there's a new flush of volunteer wheat coming, and it's due for the last bit of winter barley. I drove down rather optimistically to see if it might possibly carry a tractor after all that rain. The rain had all gone; the pond was dry – yesterday morning it was full to the brim – and the field had drained astonishingly, too.

I rang Tod to check how low we could go with glyphosate, and he said one litre per hectare would be enough for young volunteers. I've got a very precious supply of sixty litres in the store, so enough for that field at least.

It did mean hitching the drill off the new tractor and replacing it with the sprayer for the first time. It was no problem at all. I did struggle to get the PTO set to the right speed (the selection lever is now tucked down in the depths of the cab instead of a push button job) and the dead man's seat no longer lets you turn the PTO on and then get out for some sprayer filling – not unless you've gone through a reasonable safety routine. I got there in the end.

Drier Field worked out just right, with only a few litres to run out on the headland, and that'll be ready for barley in a day or two – the forecast is still quite good. The big debate is whether to put my last forty litres of Roundup on the brome-filled stubble of Chalks and BOMS, giving it plenty of time to take effect before spring barley, or do I use it in TBHD/JA/DC to tidy up more wheat volunteers up there, even though it's going into second wheat? I'll have a think about it.

Anthony rang from London to say that his job 'trial' with a gardening maintenance company had gone very well. The 'company' turned out to be a husband-and-wife team and one employee who manage gardens for a handful of hideously huge houses. I had visions of him joining a team of a hundred and having to sleep in a Portacabin. He seemed delighted – it'll be perfect while he gets his head round a career. I can hear Granny chuckling with glee from the urn over my left shoulder.

October 23rd

That's it. All the Roundup's gone. No more in the store. No more till the new year, apparently. I made the decision to put my last precious forty litres on Chalks and BOMS, where the brome was terrible before harvest – so bad that I went out and topped it with the flail mower. Not sure it did any good, but it was certainly spectacular. The rate was about 1.8l/ha, and on fast-growing grasses (and volunteer winter barley) it should be enough.

It was a bit of a challenge avoiding the Trust Saturday walkers, but I only had to pause for a bit at the top of Chalks. BOMS was much simpler, of course, and I had dregs enough to run out on the thickest bit of brome in the middle. That'll do me for a Saturday. I drove home and hitched off the sprayer.

October 24th

Hazel had only been gone half an hour (she was off to dog training near Andover again) when the phone rang; it was ten to eight, and a number I didn't recognise. "My truck's been stolen!" was the first thing said.

"I'm sorry, but who are you?" I asked.

"It's Julie!" Poor old her. Sometime in the early hours her manky but much-loved Shogun Sport had been taken from her drive. She was not pleased. I tried to cheer her up by pointing out that she usually has at least a dozen spaniels in it, but to no avail. We both marvelled at the thieves making off without waking half the county; the Shogun doesn't have a single non- screaming belt. She wanted some police numbers to ring, and I directed her to the Police Countrywatch 'Rural Times' pages on the internet. Not sure she'll raise anyone on a Sunday morning, but she should have a go. Anything is better that stupendously useless 101.

No sooner had she hung up than Hazel rang to see what the latest was – Julie has obviously rung her, too. What can you do? Julie said her road had had late-night white-van visitors some time ago, so they should have guessed that a follow-up was imminent. Doesn't make it any less depressing.

The weather was cheerful, though. We have five dry days ahead – perfect for (perhaps) getting the winter barley finished (today and Monday), and then three long days in TBHD/JA/DC with the rest of the Skyscraper – and that would be autumn 2021 done. Let's get on.

I loaded up the last seven bags of Hawking onto the old bale trailer, pausing only to pop into Godwin's to shut the barn doors which were mysteriously a couple of feet open. Was it related to Julie's job this morning? There was no sign of anything else amiss. Everything seemed to be where it should be. I shut the doors, unloaded the bags in the left-hand lean-to down at the Drier Yard, and hitched the Deere back onto the drill. I thought it would be wise to turn the rotor over first, to check the barley hadn't jammed in the bottom of the hopper – I'd left the best part of a bag in there now for a few wet days. Always a risk.

It tried, and then jammed. There was much cursing, swearing, undoing of bits, and swapping of rotors from the CO3 (very handy to have an almost identical machine the other side of the yard). The seed seemed to flow OK, but I could get neither rotor to turn. Some careful reconnecting of cables (and the inevitable 'turn off/turn on') did the trick, so I could at last head out to Drier Field.

I went down the road, across Roe Hill and BOMS, and along the short stretch of road into Drier Field at the pond corner. A quick mark out twenty metres in, an unfold (after pumping up a few tyres with my fabulous new Makita 18V tyre pump), and I was ready to start in the short corner, at a slight angle to last year's work.

The part-bag of seed ran out a bit light, but not too far out. I might just bucket out the very last bits to check there's not a clump of green something in the way and slowing the flow – but that's for tomorrow. I tucked the tractor and drill out of the way (I hoped) behind the Conder bins, and walked back through a very healthy Folly.

There was enough time and daylight to take the Nissan Qashqai (delivered during the Thursday shoot) out for a spin, and very nice it was too. It helped that it looks stupendously bland, so that the fact that it's a bit of a cheeky little number comes as a great surprise. Don't think I'll put that in the final article though.

October 25th

Not a good night. I was awake at three, fighting off another blasted mosquito, but not before it had at least two bites of my forehead. Still, I could hardly wait to leap out of bed and get Operation Finish Drilling 2021 restarted.

A rather unexpected deluge at 6.30 put a stop to that. I thought I heard a rumble or two of thunder, so turned over and went back to sleep for a bit.

It wasn't long before all the phones started ringing, though. Robin the Beeman's shed had been broken into, and thoroughly messed up, but it seemed that nothing had been taken. That might explain why our barn doors (just thirty or so yards away) were open on Sunday morning. Nothing anyone can do, of course, except look nervously around all the other buildings in anticipation of seeing doors smashed open. It seemed that Robin's was the only one to have been hit - this time.

Now that drilling was off the menu, it was time for a plan B. I was on the Screwfix website shortly after breakfast and found a 240V insect zapper for forty quid. That'll get the busy little bastards. I ordered some cement, too, as part of a plan to redirect the rainwater back into the drain in the middle of the yard rather than it coming across what's left of the gravel and out of the rapidly deteriorating drive entrance.

They had both in stock in Aldershot and I had a test car. Perfect. I had a lovely drive via Farnham and came back using the M3. There was a lot of half-term traffic, as well as the now-compulsory middle laners causing chaos. I got nostalgic for lockdown traffic levels.

Back home, I took Tigger down to the Drier Yard and set off for a proper walk – across Drier Field, into the woods, out into Pipeline, along Long Field, through Broom, across White Hill and back to the Drier along Dark Lane. It was hard going. That nice Mr Google told me it was about two miles, but I doubled that distance to take in the mud. The crops looked fantastic in the evening sunlight, though.

Sadly, there was no band rehearsal, but after that yomp I needed an early shower, and I had an early bed to the warm purplish glow of UV light from the insect zapper. I put up with that for all of ten minutes then had to get up and turn it off. Just then, a car sped down the hill and stopped at the bottom of the hill. There were voices, slamming doors, and then it sped off to Kilmeston. It sounded like a serious machine – possibly a Plod BMW, but now that we're all under siege again, it took me ages to sleep, listening for the roaring that would be more hare coursing. Still, I had plenty of plans of high- speed drilling all formulated by the time I did doze off.

October 26th

Wet – again. Unforecast – again. But we grow used to it these days. I was cheered to find a gruesome selection of insects in my zapper. There were at least two mosquitoes, but it was hard to tell exactly; they seem to explode in contact with the high-voltage grid. That'll learn 'em.

Too wet for drilling, and Hazel vanished off picking-up again, to Barrow Hill with both brown dogs. There's only one thing for it: clear the kitchen table and start on the accounts. By late morning I was surrounded with spray records, fertiliser records, invoices for seed, and had just finished writing out the blank form for the field-by-field fill in when the phone rang. It was the Colonel.

"Where's your tractor?" was his very odd opening line. It turned out he was in the yard. He'd driven up from Dorset in his precious Outback to take it to North's for a new exhaust. He'd borrowed a courtesy car and thought he'd come on up for a cuppa. Of course, he hadn't thought to ring us first, but thought he'd track me down somewhere. Silly sod.

I explained that the tractor was still tucked away behind the barn down at the Drier Yard, waiting for some dry weather. He said he'd been down there and looked. My 'tucking away' was obviously working. We wasted a couple of hours over tea, although the new exhaust took all of twenty minutes. And he was gone again. Bizarre. But lovely to see him anyway.

Policeman Ian rang for a chat and to apologise; he had planned to get over and make the right noises to Julie and Robin the Beeman, but it was all hands to the pump to help execute a warrant in the north of the county, where an unbelievable cache of Land Rovers, UTVs, trailers and all sorts had been found. Mustn't elaborate any further on the case, of course.

Hazel and two dogs arrived back from Barrow Hill, suitably knackered, and with Evie having performed brilliantly. A relief, as Evie has spent most of her life being a git. And I made the most of Anthony's last Thursday at home to cadge a lift to the Pots for another evening of beer and peanuts with neighbour Robert.

Curiously, I didn't get very far with the accounts.

October 27th

We have a very long list of stuff marked 'Things for Anthony to do now he's back at home'. But now that he has found a job back in London we have had to cull the list to just the one of two things we can persuade him to do before he goes.

There's the harvest dregs, for a start – the three or four tons of wheat lining the back of the main Drier barn. It's the feed supply for the pheasants, and will be much needed over the harsh forthcoming winter, but it really should be in a trailer, out of vermin's way. (That's rats and mice, by the way, not men in white vans. Although if wheat prices go on as they are, wheat will be the new scrap metal.)

I remembered how to start the combine (not always easy with a brand-new machine), carefully reversed it out of the barn and parked it round the back, out of harm's way. Hazel and Anthony then set off with a green trailer and the loader, and soon had the barn floor clear. I was still in 'harvest' mode when they got back, instinctively asking if it was a good lorry-load.

What else could we do with him before he leaves the farm? We sent him over to the empty bungalow with the loader to retrieve as many of the loose but unused bricks that litter the garden. They're left over from the extension job that Dad did (out of his own pocket) when he reluctantly moved in in 1997. They'll be handy for something.

Dad's set of green cast-iron table and chairs went too – picked up by St Cross

Hospital in Winchester, who had advertised on Facebook that they were looking for just such a set. I think they're hideous and uncomfortable, but there we go. Dad would be happy to know they've gone to such a good cause.

By now, I was getting itchy drilling feet. The weather is due to break big- time on Friday, and it would be lovely to get the rest of the barley in, even if my plan to get all the drilling done has crashed and burned. A couple of turns in Drier Field went well enough, so I kept going. The chalky soil was drying nicely in the wind.

The bloody central heating packed up again – for the second time since its service. We should have left it alone. I sent another curt text to the engineer.

October 28th

It was a very busy morning – but out of the tractor, Book Two is – we think – ready to go. We've read it, and read it, and sent it back to Dan the publisher, who read it and sent it back and we read it… Finally, we think it's done. Or as done as we can get it, and paying another proofreader is pribably two expensive.

Dan was ringing round his assorted printers, looking for the right combination of price and delivery dates, and reckoned he'd found the right one. A good price, and a promise to get it here in time for the *Farmers Weekly* Christmas gift guide, which is out on 19th November. Go for it, we said. All very exciting.

Nissan were on their way to pick up the Qashqai, which had turned out to be a huge hit. You can see why SUVs are taking over from hatchbacks, and why the Qashqai is the new Golf. I sat in it and made the traditional copious notes. It was now late morning, and time to get back in the tractor. Drier Field continued to go well, and I couldn't help but think that it might even roll OK, with the strong dry wind blowing across it. Hazel volunteered to have a go after lunch, and it did go well. I finished drilling, doing the long wide headland last, and had about 50kg in the bottom of the tank. Not bad, after starting with ten tonnes. I ran that out on an eighth run of headland, hitched off the drill in the left-hand lean-to, and took the tractor home for a refuel (man and machine).

I took over rolling from Hazel and just as it was getting too dark to see, I finished the last turns of headland. It looked fantastic, and although it's very late for winter barley, it's all in. The early stuff in White Hill is storming ahead in these mild temperatures. One hundred and thirty-three acres of it is a lot, but this is not a normal year – and the forward prices for winter barley are extraordinary. The last hundred acres of wheat – well, that can wait. One thing we've learnt from the last few years is that late wheat can do well if it's sown well. The forecast suggests that we won't be rushing up to Hurst Down any time soon.

A rather sheepish central heating engineer arrived and replaced yet more parts on the boiler, which seemed to run OK for the evening. After some complicated logistics of getting all vehicles home, we were all set up for the deluge due tomorrow. The house was too bloody hot, though.

October 29th

It was a good thing that Hazel and Suzi set off for their dog walk nice and early, when it was only just getting light. It meant they were safely back indoors tucking into tea and buns when the heavens opened – big time. A real gutter-bursting, yard-flooding deluge. No drilling today. It did mean I could get on and do my FonF – which was a) late and b) not very inspiring. For some reason, I'm short of ideas at the moment.

A walk across White Hill and into Broom Field (once the rain had stopped) revealed lots of surface water (of course) but reasonably healthy crops – except in the south-east corner of White Hill, where it seems that the slugs have got to the seed already. We didn't get it all rolled, which might have made a difference. It may just be late, and winter barley shoots are so big and dramatic that the rest of the field is now a lurid green. I could hardly stand up in places, so slug pelleting is not an option.

A parcel arrived from New Zealand. It contained a short letter, some spices, a bag of 'beer-flavoured gummi bears' and a dramatic photo of a girl in her twenties. It took some explaining, particularly to Anthony, who wasn't in on the early stages of the story.

A few months ago, almost exactly forty years after I ended my mid-gap-yah three-month hitch-hike round New Zealand, a message arrived via Facebook. "Are you the Charlie Flindt who stayed at Hamilton Youth Hostel in 1981?" I replied that I was indeed. "Do you remember the warden? She was my best friend, and I've been going through her letters, and you get a mention!" I did remember the warden, and the fantastic days I stayed there, when it was more like a gentle hippy commune than a hostel. Why the sudden contact about her? "I've been clearing out my stuff, and we wrote long letters to each other all the time. I re-read hers, and she talks about the hostel, and the party, and you playing the piano." Blimey, that brings it all back. What happened to her? "She took her own life in December 1981." Ouch.

We then had a long exchange of memories and photos, and I transcribed some of my first 'tour' diary, which featured the Hamilton Youth Hostel heavily, and sent it to her. The story of my roommate being cross because the warden had rejected his wine-fuelled amorous advance neatly matched her entry in a letter saying she'd had to fight off this drunk bloke, and nearly given him a black eye.

Because we were discussing diaries, I offered to send her a copy of Book One in exchange for B&B when I go back to New Zealand to find my soul, which got left there – if the country ever gets out of lockdown, of course. The parcel was a lovely thank you from her.

Funnily enough, I'd been in the attic recently, thinking that no one would ever be interested in all my New Zealand stuff, and it should really head for the skip. I'm glad it didn't. The second tour diary got left on the Cathay Pacific jumbo when we changed planes in Hong Kong on the way home. I hope that never surfaces.

October 30th

We'd done our best to persuade Anthony to stay at home as long as he has, but the time finally came for him to go back to London, and I volunteered to do the long drive. Not 'long' as in hundreds of miles (Mr Google said just over seventy from Hinton to Camden) but 'long' as in time. Two hours and ten minutes from door to door.

It's a heck of an eye-opener to venture into that part of the world, especially as the years creep by and you feel slightly more ill-at-ease with every trip into an urban environment. Anthony was navigating in the Skoda (tempting as it was to take the mud-splattered Terracan to avoid being bullied – or even the tractor) and the early bit was easy. Pick up the M3 at Aldershot and head straight in. The junction with the M25 was solid, but once we'd got through that there was a surreal stretch of deserted motorway – almost lockdown levels of emptiness.

The M3 morphed into the A316, and then we took the A307 to pick up the North Circular. If I'd been in charge, we would have kept on it, but Anthony directed me off, down the A40 into Central London – something I would never do on my own. But in the end, it's just another bit of tarmac, if a rather busy one.

Some of the architecture is stunning – old and new. There are the million billion squid mansions (Anthony rating each one in millions per bedroom as we passed them) and the new residential tower blocks that seem impossibly narrow for their height. Tomorrow's weather might put them to the test.

Turning north, we were in Camden, and there was Anthony's squat block of flats. After parking immediately outside (free at the weekends) we carried his stuff into and up in the lift. His flatmate was sitting in the warm sun flooding in through French windows, watching live football on TV. The view out past trees filled with magpies (I offered to pop back and get my Anshütz 22LR) was of a deserted school playground. It was all very nice and peaceful. We'd promised Jonathan that we'd call in on him, and it was a short walk through unbelievably picturesque streets to get to his flat, tucked at the end of a tiny one-way street which was lined with film-set two-storey pastel-painted houses. I half expected Hugh Grant to pop into frame at any moment.

His flat was tiny, but on the top floor, with great views. I'm not sure I'd last any time in it, though. My bedroom is probably bigger than the whole flat. Mind you, he had a fantastic 6ft by 3ft balcony from which he'd already made friends with the similarly elevated neighbours. A pair of his boxer shorts had blown off his drying rack over to one old dear's place. Great chat-up line there.

On the walk back to Anthony's, we passed through a tiny park – what was once the garden of a sizeable villa. It now has a small play area, a bit of grass, and some benches. A toddler was playing rather forlornly on a tiny roundabout, his mother sitting on one of the benches, watching him. "This is as much green as some people get," said Anthony. One hell of a comment. I thought about it a lot as I set off home. That's my excuse for missing a key turning and having to thread my way through the narrow streets of Richmond and Twickenham to finally get back to the M3. I don't think I've ever seen so much 'country' wear.

I was so tired that the thumping music from a party in Kilmeston (outdoors – at this time of year?) didn't keep me awake.

October 31st

As usual the change in the clocks caused chaos, and I had no idea what time it was when I got up. It didn't help that it was raining stair rods again. I promised Hazel that by the time her dog-training classes got going at Mullenscote it would have blown over.

The only things that blew over were the trees up at the training ground; I had a rather plaintive phone call saying that she'd got there OK, but a whole line of trees had been felled as they watched, and everyone was trapped. Sounds like a bit of a squall line tornado on the back edge of the storm. I also felt sorry for the storm, as the Met Office had neglected to give it a dramatic name.

I got the Sunday papers, watched the BTCC highlights from last week, and probably ate too much. The rain cleared – although heavy showers continued to blow in for most of the day. The trees also got cleared, so Hazel made it back safely – if somewhat windblown and wet. She put out a call for chocolate, and since I am now the only other one in the house, I volunteered to drive down to the West Meon Hut – Tigger needed a refuel, too. I had to buy two bars of chocolate; the fuel bill was so close to £100 for sixty-seven litres of diesel that it seemed wrong not to push it over three figures somehow. Unbelievable.

To round off an interesting weekend, the mice moved into the attic, and were running round like a herd of elephants as I tried to doze off. You've got to hand it to them; we always say that they wait until the clocks change, and they've nailed it to the day. That's tomorrow's job sorted.

November 1st

New month, new moon (nearly), new weather (they're promising a bit of a settled spell). There was a massive pile of dog poo in the kitchen which put a stop to poetic musing about the passing of the year. I blame Bella; she spent most of yesterday with her head in the dog biscuit bag, having recovered from being very off colour earlier in the week. And I'm blaming the clock change, which meant we were late getting up.

It was a monumental dump – visible from space, big enough to warp the space-time continuum etc. etc. – and sat stodgily across the ridges of an unusually ridged kitchen rug. I attacked it with a paint scraper, some rags and a bucket of hot water, but soon gave that up for a game of soldiers and carried the whole rug out onto the lawn. At last, I could get on and have some breakfast in relative comfort.

The first of the month also means the next car review has to be in at *The Field*. The Qashqai was full of stuff to write about, so I had that done and sent off in no time.

Finally: mice. I found an old nutty chewy cereal bar, just the right consistency to be pressed onto a mousetrap, and worked my way round the house. I put three traps in the attic room above my bedroom, two in the one above Diana's old room, two more above Hazel's and one above the kitchen. That'll get them. Bastards.

With the weather definitely on the up, and the fact that we'll be out getting the rest of the wheat in as soon as I can travel, I cracked on with the accounts. (aka, I sat in the kitchen drinking coffee and pushing assorted field records around, trying to look productive.)

November 2nd

I did more accounts while waiting for the 'proof copy' of Book Two to arrive. Dan the publisher had promised it today, and it was touch and go as to whether we'd get it approved and then get the order for a squillion copies in on time for the *Farmers Weekly* Christmas Gift Guide; they've promised to feature it as yet another freebie.

Hazel set off with Sasha in Pig to do the pheasant feeders. She was braver than me; the first proper frost of the winter had arrived – and it was cold enough to dig out a sweater for the day and put the electric heater on in the office – and that's not a cheap option anymore. Bloody global warming. Sorry – it's 'global heating' now.

The book finally arrived while we were having a catch-up across the kitchen table with the bank manager, smiling sweetly and asking for the usual overdraft facilities. She was happy to oblige, and very positive about farming in general.

We checked Book Two at high speed and rang Dan the publisher to give the go-ahead. We decided we'd need to get 2,000 copies in ASAP. Christmas is coming. I'll feel a right chump if we sell twenty.

November 3rd

It was another fantastic November morning (and we haven't said that for a couple of years). Unfortunately, two large owls were sitting in the huge sycamore tree just outside the window, arguing noisily about something. Their intense debate managed to get all the blackbirds shouting, and every pheasant for miles decided to chip in their penny's-worth too. Add the roar of traffic coming from the A32 – the wind had swung to the east – and it was a bloody noisy wake-up call.

Still, it's good for you to get up too early every so often. I tried to get some video of the two owls shrieking at each other with a magnificent dawn erupting behind them, but they promptly adjourned to one of the ash trees further along the Back Meadow's hedge line, where they picked up just where they'd left off.

With another shoot tomorrow, it seemed wise to get the next FonF column done, and the trip to London was perfect fodder; how we should all be counting our blessings rather than moaning about fertiliser prices.

Tod was round for an update, suggesting that a pre-em herbicide on all of Stanmore and the winter barley in White Hill and Cheyney would be wise, as soon as either my or Tosdevine's machine can travel. The forecast continues to be fine – once again, a delight for November.

When Book One was launched, I spent a few months getting the right combination of packaging and posting options sorted out – and got it wrong more than once to start with. With 2,000 copies of Book Two now firmly on order, I thought I should crack on and order everything we'd need once sales start. That means lots of printer ink, lots of A5 sticky labels, and a mountain of strong cardboard envelopes. It was a pricey afternoon (especially the printer ink) and a walk round the fields was definitely in order. White Hill looked a bit better, although the slugs and waterlogging have had a good go at the south-east corner. Broom and Long looked fantastic, and driving back via the Godwin's block was also very rewarding. There's yet another phrase we haven't used for the last few Novembers.

An evening of shoot preparation, with all the associated butterflies, rounded off the day nicely. I should really be doing more accounts or the last bit of drilling – but not yet.

November 4th

We're just getting stuck into our eighth season running the little rough shoot here, and I don't think we've had a day as good as today. It was cold and dry with a fairly stiff northerly – perfect for minimising any friction-filled encounters with walkers and persuading the pheasants to fly better.

As usual, we were late out, but by the time we'd done three of the four drives of the Home 'S', we were well ahead of the 'bag schedule'. It helped that we had a crack team of guns out, but it was still astonishing to see the number of birds out there. We like to finish the day with a bag in the mid to high twenties, working on the rule that the vast majority of the birds must be taken away by guests, leaving Hazel with only a handful to be turned into a casserole or dog treats.

There was a bit of a policy discussion after we'd finished Clump, and we agreed we'd be more selective over pheasants, and concentrate on pigeons, which were swirling round in huge clouds in the wind. As a result, shares in Eley/Hull Cartridge/CCI surged as we blatted away at them, mostly without success. The ex-Editor suggested we change our beating policy for Big Field, and instead of doing two teams of two guns/two beaters who start at each end of the maize, we should send all the beaters to the top, and all the guns, with Suzi as stop/picker-up, to the bottom – almost like a proper drive.

It worked – with birds screaming out of the notches that Hazel cut in the maize some weeks ago, and flying, mostly untouched, over the two 'guest guns'. A joy to watch – or would have been if I hadn't had to answer my phone mid-drive.

There was a time when answering a phone mid-drive was the worst possible thing you could do on a shoot – the very height of bad manners. Stories abound of keepers/shoot managers snatching phones off yuppie guests and blasting them to smithereens. Things are different here. We're a working farm. There's only us managing it – no staff. The world is full of idiot delivery drivers. We're expecting lots of deliveries after Tod's visit and after deciding to press 'go' for Book Two. If a mobile phone rings constantly on a day full of deliveries, you answer it, mid-drive or not. The fact that the highest hen of the day soared over me while I was trying not to lose my temper with the idiot delivery driver is irrelevant.

It was indeed an idiot delivery driver, trying to drop off some spray. He'd found the sheeted gates shut (he could have come in the main drive) and the padlock was still on the spray store door (he should have looked more closely at it). As a result, several hundred quid's worth of spray had been dropped off in the corner of the yard. Oh well.

It was nice to get out of the wind for elevenses in the Drier Yard, with ten million calories and lashings of hot soup to wash them down. We agreed that we'd do George's and Barracuda, which boosted the bag by another ten or so, but left everyone properly satisfied with the day, and ready for a monster lunch. One guest went home early with a sniffle, which was very responsible – and we're happy with that. If you can use a mobile mid-drive, you can come and go as you please.

It was dark and cold when the house emptied, but we'd had a fantastic day. The new Rizzini had behaved impeccably, and Hazel didn't believe me when I said there were only half a dozen birds left in the Pig trailer – thirty had indeed been taken home by the assorted guns and beaters. Good job.

Once again, everyone was in bed and out for the count well before ten.

November 5th

It's a good thing I'm not in a proper job. After yesterday's overindulgence (physical, mental and dietary) I wasn't fit for anything. I could sit at the garden table, enjoying the warm sun burning off a surprisingly hard frost, and generally feel pleased with how the day went.

Hazel, thank goodness, is incapable of such idleness, so fed cattle, walked dogs (again) and went off to the racing stables for an afternoon working on their accounts.

November 6th

The morning started with the very odd sight of Hazel and Nessa preparing for their day picking-up at Murph's by sticking cotton buds up their noses. Murph has asked that everyone does a thingumabob test before coming along, and Nessa, being NHS-linked, had all the right kit. Hazel is not a fan of having things stuck up her nose, but bravely managed a swab (should have had a 'well done' sticker to hand) which tested negative. They could all pile into Tigger and head off, leaving me to my feast of rugby.

Mind you, it's all very well there being a feast of rugby going on out there – but we have to find it. The BBC is far too busy chasing agendas to cover 'A' list sport, so we have to delve into the mysterious regions of the internet if we're going to make the most of another lazy day.

I should have been drilling or spraying, but the wind got up too much for the latter, and the forecast suggests that we can leave the late Skyscraper ground for a few days yet. It'll probably change to 'three months of rain' come Monday, but hey ho. We've navigated two winters like that in the last two years, so we can probably survive another. It certainly doesn't do the 'food supply' equation any harm.

So where is the rugby? Amazon have pretty-well cornered all the broadcast rights, with Channel 4 picking up the scraps, and it took all of five minutes to log in and agree to a £7.99 monthly subscription, suspended for the first month.

It did mean I spent the best part of ten hours watching it on assorted computers – it is possible to link it to the main TV, apparently, but we're short of young people who could show me how. The quality of picture was a bit iffy, but the commentary was good, and France vs Argentina, which rounded off the day, was stunning – one of the best games I've seen in ages. It was worth the fee on its own. Hold on – that's what BBC sycophants say when they write into *Points of View*.

Team Picking-up got back mid-afternoon, all suitably windblown and chilled. I was glad I'd got the heating going early (after yet another 'lockout'). They'd had another great day, with challenging birds going mostly untouched. Hazel snoozed her way through a feast of racing from the USA, this time brought to you by ITV. Not – again – by the BBC. They're too busy.

November 7th

A nice routine sort of Sunday. Hazel went off to dog training at Mullenscote, the wind was too strong to do any spraying, and I got the papers and had a lazy day. It was nice to see a letter I'd sent to the *Sunday Telegraph* in support of ploughing get top spot, with bold print and a picture of a horse-drawn plough in action. It was in reply to yet another piece by yet another woke farmer claiming that ploughing was 'catastrophic' – even though we've been doing it successfully for 5,500 years. I must become a woke farmer – I'd never have to stick to the truth ever again.

I cleaned up all the flapjack and drizzle cake left over from Thursday's shoot, and generally felt ill as a result. Australia vs Scotland was excellent (thank you, Mr Amazon), although it was interrupted by a white van in the yard. Sasha went ballistic at the window, which is never a good sign.

It was a dodgy looking lad selling 'gourmet food', door to door. I declined his offer to see his wares. Any chance of him changing my mind vanished when he called me 'bud'. His company seemed kosher – it had a valid-looking website, anyway. Mind you, we once lost stuff in a van that had been bought by some ne'er-do-wells who had kept the signwriting on it just for that reason.

A quick drive out to Hurst Down showed that the ground was dry enough to drill. I hadn't got round to spraying off the green regrowth, but it'll have to do without. I met a tractor towing a beaters' trailer along the lane – odd, on a Sunday afternoon. The driver seemed very reluctant to catch my eye. Very odd. We had our 4t Warwick grain trailer nicked a few months ago – and it vanished into thin air. I might drop Policeman Ian a text.

November 8th

Restarting drilling was never going to be a case of 'jump in tractor and off you go', but I really had hoped to be on the move before 1.30pm. Mind you, I had to go down to the Drier Yard in the Massey to move the poacher block into Blackhouse Road, and then move the telegraph poles blocking the route between Blackhouse Road and Joan's Acre. I managed to drop one pole right into the anti-poacher ditch opposite Joan's Acre House, which I couldn't have done more neatly if I'd tried. God knows how we'll get that out, but that's for later.

Back home, I switched to the bag loader and put four tonnes of Skyscraper on the old bale trailer. The rats had had a bit of a party in the stack of seed in the barn; the quicker we get it in the ground the better.

I refuelled the Deere and took it down to the Drier Yard where the drill had been parked up since finishing the winter barley, pulled it out and pumped up the two of the three flat tyres that will hold their pressure for a few days. After a drive through Blackhouse Road, Joan's Acre and Dell Close, I reached the Bottom of Hurst Down, where I marked out a headland and rang for a lift.

Hazel got held up looking for the spare key for Tigger, which appeared to have gone missing in the end-of-shoot chaos on Thursday, when one of the beating team had driven it home. No matter – she arrived in the Skoda and picked me up.

Calibration in the field is slightly more awkward than when it's done in the yard, mainly because you need a flat surface for the scales so that all   four little feet (where, I assume, the strain gauges live) have to be firmly grounded. The bed of the trailer was the best I could come up with, and it may have been flat but it was at a slight angle. I toyed with the idea of tangents and slopes, but decided to just get on and do a standard calibrate, for 227kg/ha. With a tgw of 51g, that gives a respectable early-November seed rate.

Finally, flaps were shut, engine was warm, all connections seemed fine, and I could go drilling; the clock on the little cab radio said 2.30 – and I haven't bothered finding out how to reset it after the change to GMT.

I started next to the road and worked my way up the hill. It was sticky but passable, and infinitely better than the quagmire this time last year. By the time it got too dark – only minutes after Hazel had kindly brought out some tea – I'd managed three bags over seventeen acres, which worked out just right. November days are short days. Luckily, the forecast is good.

Ian the Drummer cried off tonight's band rehearsal with the sniffles, but it would be unkind to say just how well it went. There are gigs firming up, and that always helps.

November 9th

Hazel was off picking-up (again) early, and I had a morning in the office. Then an early lunch, and another short afternoon in Hurst Down, finishing the bloody awkward bits round the dell, and finally getting onto some long turns on the best soil. It was very tempting to do one more bag at about four fifteen as it got horribly dark, but the forecast is good, and another trip to the Pots beckoned with neighbour Robert.

Just as I was heading off for my pre-pint shower, Sasha was hopping up and down at the back door, desperate to get out to the garden. What was bugging her? A fox? A badger? I let her out, and she ran out onto the lawn – and stopped, eyes fixed in the dark distance towards Roe Hill. Sure enough, lights could be seen, and cars could be heard revving furiously, spinning wheels on the loose road surface. Oddly, at the same time a dog could be heard barking furiously on the road outside the house; I walked out to check, and could hear footsteps, but these was no torch or anything. It was all very odd. There were two cars on Roe Hill, revving and roaring. I popped back indoors to get Tigger keys and Sasha, and quietly drove down the hill from the farmhouse. Parked next to the Folly gateway were two cars, both Fiesta- sized. One shot off towards Brockwood as I slowly approached, the other stayed. Two up, both scruffy-looking Herbert's in hoodies. It was hard to say, though, if they were of the hare-coursing fraternity.

I wound down the window and asked if all was well. "Yeah, mate, we're looking to park up somewhere." I didn't ask why. I did ask who was doing all the hooning up and down the road. "No idea, mate." Of course not. I asked if the one that had shot off was his mate. It was, apparently. I thought I'd try and get at least one numberplate, so went off after that first one. As soon as I set off up Roe Hill, the second car did a high-speed U-turn and headed up farm hill. Funny couple of mates.

There was no sign of the first car, of course, and the second was nowhere to be seen by the time I got back to the village. All very odd and unsettling. Were they linked to the dog-walking? Were they trying to drag telegraph poles out of gateways? Who knows?

It all meant I was late getting to the Pots, but my reasons provoked a fantastic bar discussion, and not a lot of it would be welcome in the BBC canteen. "If you say you've got a gun, you get a proper police response," was one helpful suggestion.

"You'll also lose your licence faster that you can say '999'," I pointed out.

November 10th

It was wet all day, a hideous continuous drizzle. I was buggered if I was going to head up to Hurst Down and do a skiddy wet turn or two, so I did office stuff and went for a huge yomp. I parked at the Drier, walked up to Pipeline, along Long, through Broom, then Rough Field and into Folly, then along Dark Lane back to the Drier. Most crops looked well – only the heavy land in White Hill and Rough Field looked waterlogged and slugged. My flippin' hip hurt though. I must walk more to try and toughen it up a bit. Or lose two stone.

November 11th

A much better drilling day. Neighbour John had commandeered our blue bale trailer for his Christmas tree trade, but, as is traditional, has lent us Mac's massive four-wheel version. Hazel and I loaded it up with the rest of the Skyscraper and I got stuck into Hurst Down again. Not literally 'stuck', of course – it's a lovely bit of soil, and drilled well despite yesterday's rain.

The weather was unbelievably beautiful, and I spent as much time taking artistic photographs as I did drilling. Come eleven o'clock, I paused the tractor on the headland, and raised a bottle of mineral water to all those poor lads and lasses. Not much of a tribute, but it'll do.

A long lunch sorting out some bizarre water pipe queries from the Trust meant that I was late back out there, and a sharp shower (unforecast, of course) had been through in the meantime. I cracked on anyway, and finished the long headland at about four o'clock. In a fit of enthusiasm, I marked out Dell Close and did a few turns to empty the drill. It was sorely tempting to load up with two more bags, and not bother bringing the seed home – they reckon there will be some spots of drizzle overnight, and I'll be able to crack on tomorrow. Nonetheless, I left the drill empty and parked the huge trailer in the left-hand lean-to on the way home.

November 12th

After some light drizzle designed to convince us that the forecasters had got it right, the heavens opened, to prove that they hadn't. I was cross – but relieved that I'd put the seed away last night, and that the drill only had dregs in the bottom to start growing. It also meant I could get on and finish Flindt on Friday, which was a day late.

I had to ring Crop Advisors (our buying group) and place the order for fertiliser first, as that act was to be the last paragraph of the article. We'd had quotes which were up 150% on last year's (admittedly bargain) prices, and I'd held off ordering after reading reports of the price of gas coming down a bit. This morning, however, I decided to get on and place the order. The news was full of stuff that suggested that price was going to do anything but go down. The Russians are – apparently – massing on the border with Ukraine, a proper winter is coming, and, most importantly, the wheat prices are on the way up big time after the US WASDE report. This last one should pay for the extra fertiliser costs. Well, it's enough of a theory to get on and book my tonnage with almost total conviction.

Funny old week. On Monday I was sure that we'd have everything done and dusted by yesterday. Mind you, that's what happens when you listen to the weather forecasters.

November 13th

Almost exactly forty years ago, I staggered up the stairs to my new room in Eustace Percy Hall at Castle Leazes halls of residence. I had two huge suitcases, and the long journey from Hampshire (via Waterloo, the Underground and King's Cross) to Newcastle University had been a bit fraught, ending a glorious 'gap yah' of idleness, part-time jobs and hitch-hiking round New Zealand. "Blimey," I thought as I sat on the bed for a minute or two. "What now?"

There was a knock on the door. "Hi, I'm Peter." It was my next-door neighbour. A good start. Within a week or two a gang of six had formed. Chris from a few doors down the corridor, another Chris from the floor below, Carol (who was from further afield in the halls but was on the same course as Chris No 2), and her chum: some fabulous red-headed Ulster girl whose name escapes me. In the second year, we six moved into a house in Benwell (192/4 Ellesmere Road) which I still use as my address when subscribing to things I don't want mail from.

A couple of weeks ago, Peter's wife got in touch via Facebook, asking if we could gather at their huge house in the New Forest to celebrate his 60th birthday. As luck would have it, we all could, but I was quite nervous as we turned off the M27 and headed into the Forest towards Fordingbridge. I think we've occasionally met in twos and fours since the end of uni in 1984, but this would be the first total gathering since then. What do you say to each other? Hazel's only thoughts were that it would be better if I didn't get onto Brexit or the Virus. Fair point.

There was no need for nerves. Once we picked our jaws back off the floor on seeing Peter's house (the boy's done well), it was as if we were back in the flat. Some of us were a bit fatter, a bit greyer, a bit balder, and Chris No 2 was battling a rare cancer – even though he looked the fittest of the lot. Four of the original six had formed two couples, and I felt a bit sorry for the 'non-flat' wives of the two of us who had married 'outside' the group. They bravely sat through the reminiscences for a bit and then headed for the kitchen. Can't blame them.

On the way home up a phenomenally busy A31, Hazel joked about how conventional we all were; four couples, all still married after relatively early marriages, all with two or three children who had all done university, too. Hazel and I were the only ones not retired, though. We drove the rest of the way in thoughtful silence. Forty years. Fuck me.

Sister-in-law Heather had done a great job housesitting for the day, looking after all the dogs and checking livestock. She'd also let the new lady chimney sweep in so that we can finally get on and have some roaring fires with clear flues and clearer consciences. Unfortunately, she reported that the sitting room fire was going to need some serious de-tarring, and recommended a friend who did this complicated operation. Let's hope the cold weather doesn't get here till we've done that.

November 14th

Remembrance Sunday. Hazel and the dog-training gang all paused up at Mullenscote, and I sat back in the office chair and pondered for a minute or two.

Meanwhile, a car full of bombers set off for the Remembrance Parade in Liverpool, but were somehow foiled – initial reports suggested that the taxi driver managed to scupper their plans.

The BBC unbelievably put this as item two on their ten o'clock bulletin, running the inevitable failure of the COP26 jet-fest as the lead story. The BBC is beyond belief.

November 15th

Damp and yucky after more unexpected rain yesterday. After proofing the next Flindt on Friday ("Don't you dare use 'was sat' in the standfirst!") I had a drive round. The winter barley in Drier Field cheered me up, coming on really strongly in the mild weather, and Dell Close felt like it wouldn't take much to dry enough to drill.

A large silver double cab was in the yard when I got home, which meant that at least an hour was due to be wasted; Mac was in for a chat. As usual we covered a million things, but the 'how I lost a lot of money recently' competition was the best bit. Me, when I didn't take and save the last order of cheap fertiliser last spring; him, when he thought he'd do just a bit more work with an already-traded-in tractor that was sounding a bit rough, and it sounding a lot rougher when he'd finished. The dealer knocked ten grand off the original trade-in price, which was just how much I'd lost by not ordering that lorry of fertiliser. A draw.

The flatmate meeting in the New Forest the other day has provoked some odd reaction. Today, we started blitzing the attic in the farmhouse, home to a lifetime's worth of junk – and not just mine. I emailed my siblings to check if we had carte blanche to throw stuff out. The reply was an unsurprising 'yes, but…', so we'll keep an eye out for anything of importance.

It would be nice to make it a bit more inhospitable for whatever is crashing round like a herd of elephants – and eating the mice that die in the traps. And dragging the traps themselves away to God knows where.

The weather forecast suggested more dry weather, so I topped up the fuel bowser and refuelled the Deere in Dell Close. Given a long day, I reckon I could get everything done, so it's worth having a tankful.

We had another drummer-free band rehearsal; the Fox in Bramdean has confirmed we're a concrete booking for New Year's Eve. I hope Ian gets better before then.

November 16th

Frosty but suddenly – and oddly – dry. Dry enough to decide that today was the day to get the rest of the wheat in. And about time too.

First things first, though. *Farmers Weekly* emailed to say that Book Two is indeed to be featured in Friday's Christmas Gift Guide, but the subs were querying my claim that it was available through all the usual sources. They had had a good look but found nothing. I pointed out that there was a very simple explanation: it wasn't online yet, but would be on Friday, after (I hope) we'd had them delivered.

That was my cue to sign into Amazon and try to list Book Two alongside Book One. Blimey, what a nightmare. All sorts of odd questions, all sorts of incomprehensible statistics needed – but in the end, I got it up on the site. I had a small panic when I saw it had already gone 'live' – ready for orders. I edited the stock level to 'zero' before ten thousand (yeah, right) orders were placed.

Dell Close drilled really well before lunch, and Joan's Acre was as good in the afternoon. I finished the six turns of headland in the gloom, running out of seed perfectly. I was very pleased with myself.

I checked the area meter, dug out the drill record book, and jotted down all the details. Funny to think that the first time I drilled that field it was with a hundredweight-and-a-quarter per acre of Klaxon spring barley and 1½cwt/ acre of No 11 (fertiliser, kids) in 1987. Thirty-five seasons ago. Blimey. Quite a moment.

It didn't help that the scene was stunning; a curious red glow as the sun set behind incoming cloud, and a large moon rising at the other end of the sky. My lines looked straight; and the seedbed look pretty good for a mid- November finish. Fantastic.

After parking the Deere/Horsch combo in the top corner of Joan's Acre, I bundled the seed bags into the ladder frame of Mac's huge trailer. Thirty-five years ago, I'd have had a nice fire with paper and plastic sacks, lit a Rothman's to go with the dregs of my Thermos, and contemplated life by the flames. I headed home in the Massey, winning a head-to-head with a high-speed Waitrose delivery van who didn't want to back up along the Joan's Acre Road. Neither did I, but I won. Never had that problem thirty-five years ago.

November 17th

Not a great day. I logged onto Amazon and found that my listing for Book Two had been changed from the carefully chosen description that I'd sent in, to something else completely. Somehow, the lovely photographer who did the back cover was co-credited as author (which was slightly awkward) and the dimensions of the book were suddenly wrong. If and when the book goes 'live', it will cause chaos, because Amazon will choose postage based on those dimensions; it will not be enough. I got onto Dan the Publisher as quickly as I could. He wasn't impressed either. He's in Sicily at the moment, but promised to try and sort it from there. Something to do with some central information service that Amazon assumes is a better source of info. Yeah, right.

A nice walk out to Joan's Acre to pick up the drill and the tractor seemed like a good way to calm down, and indeed it was. I'd told Hazel to keep an eye out for the 2,000 copies of Book Two that were dead-cert never-fail due to be delivered today, and set off. Godwin's looked fantastic, and from the top of Clump and across Big Field the world looked magnificent in the low November sun. God, we deserve a November like this after the last two. We're drilled up and the sun is shining.

More book envelopes arrived, but no books. Hazel and I did shifts so one of us was always here to unload the lorry when it turned up. But by late afternoon, I thought it was time to make some enquiries. Dan gave me the number of the printers, who were very apologetic and said there had been a glitch, and the books would not get here till tomorrow. I confess I had a bit of a rant. Another walk round Drier Field calmed me down. It, too, was looking magnificent. I'm quite good at farming. Sometimes.

Much of the evening was spent polishing up my speech, ready for the after-dinner season which starts on Friday. It'll be nice to be back on the road telling my joke.

November 18th

Had it not been for the continued lack of 2,000 books, it could have been described as a productive morning. Sprayerman George was in early to put weedkiller on the Stanmore block; we'd decided to hold off the White Hill and Cheyney winter barley until it's clearer how much has survived the slugs and the waterlogging.

Tod arrived at about the same time for a catch-up, and to discuss whether we should move our version of 'get by with a little help from my friends' (done a la Joe

Cocker) from A to E to help the vocals hit the high notes. He then set off for some cropwalking.

I tried one more call to the book printer, who promised that the pallets were imminent, but I couldn't hang around any longer; it was time to head into Alresford and get a haircut, ready for the start of the speech season. I tried my venerable jokes – one clean, one filthy – on the hairdresser, and she seemed less than impressed. I suspect that a room full of pissed farmers might be more inclined to guffaw.

The books had arrived when I got home – three pallets lined up neatly outside the Colonel's empty container. Which reminds me, I must agree a price to buy it off him, now he's done with it.

Hazel went off to the stables to do their accounts, I threaded the books into the container, got the willies about having ordered far too many, and polished the speech up a bit. I left both jokes in.

November 19th

Of course, what I really needed on a big day like this was a long and restful sleep. The dogs decided that that was right out of the question, and started their tumble of barking just after four thirty. Four thirty, for goodness sake. I'd given up trying to get back to sleep by five and got up. I tried to give the speech a bit more polish, but it wasn't in the mood to be polished. Hazel was up shortly after six, and I went back to bed to try and catch up a bit. Unfortunately, two cups of tea – or it might have been three – wrecked that idea. As did Cain, who was delighted to find me returning to bed, and proceeded to knit my armpit. Time to get up again.

I ended up setting off earlier than I'd planned, but it was lucky that I did. The A34 was clear, including Winnall (which was nice), and even Oxford was free-flowing. Things got a bit stickier once off the M40 and onto the M42, then clear again on the wonderful M6 Toll. I was actually relieved to reach the toll road, having had a mini panic that I'd missed the turning for it. But for a few miles, we could relive a bit of 80s-style empty motorway. Expensive, but worth it.

Then, the M6 proper. It was now getting dark, and two lorries had had a monster shunt on the southbound side, and it was getting on towards rush hour. The twelve-mile queue behind them was quite a sight, and made me feel grateful that we northbounders were moving at all. I found myself longing for an automatic gearbox as we crept north, past signs that should have been read out in an Eddie Waring voice.

The satnav kept suggesting I turned off left onto minor roads for some reason, but I ignored it, picked up the M55, and then the old A6 towards Garstang. After a few more miles, I arrived at the smart hotel/entertainment venue shortly after five forty.

My host, a senior farmer of four-score-and-a-bit-more years, was waiting in reception, and made me welcome. He gave me a tour of the hotel, a few beer vouchers for petrol, and agreed that jacket and tie was acceptable. I'd brought the suit, but it still didn't fit properly, so that was a relief. I adjourned to my room for a much-needed shower and a ten-minute snooze.

The dinner went well – there were about 140 farming folk, all keen for a good night out after all these months, all well warmed up before I got to my feet. I think they liked the speech, but you never can tell. I got a lovely engraved fountain pen for my troubles, and assorted charities got nice cheques. And I sold a pile of books. Perfect.

November 20th

How odd. I was in a strange bed, in a hotel full of guests, with a building site outside the window, and I slept right through until eight forty. It is definitely all about personal space: if the world beyond the duvet doesn't concern me, I can sleep like a baby. If I'm in the middle of 'my' 910 acres, sleep eludes me.

I was forty minutes late for breakfast as a result, but the restaurant didn't seem to mind. I chatted with two guests from last night's dinner as we ate and watched the faithful golfers going through their warm-up routines – the first tee appeared to be just outside the window. I thought we pheasant shooters invested in a lot of daft kit until I saw what the keen golfers bring. The best moment was when a golf trolley (if that's what you call it) took off down the fairway on its own while its owner was doing practice swings and had to be hurriedly rescued.

Any chance of making a quick break for home was scuppered when Old Tom (my host) arrived in the restaurant, ready to fulfil his promise to give me a tour. Mind you, it was worth it. We climbed into his BMW X3 and trundled round the lanes of the farm, which is now a business-like combination of golf course and building site. No sentimental obsession with old-fashioned farming for him. "That's where the farmhouse was," he pointed out as we rounded the last corner on the way back to the hotel. A dozen smart new houses now occupied the site.

The drive back was as easy as the drive up was difficult. No crashes, no roadworks, and the lovely M6 Toll being almost deserted. Bits of the M40 were, as usual, being used as racetracks by blacked-out Mercs and BMWs with curious private plates, weaving from lane to lane with absolutely no lane discipline. I had two near misses on my nearside as yet another gleaming German beast flew up the inside lane just as I was pulling over. God knows the 'smart' motorways are dangerous enough without these idiots clogging them up.

The MacDonald's magnet struck again at Winchester services, just as I was beginning to flag; that's my excuse, and I'm sticking to it. I was home by four, just in time to log onto Amazon to watch some great rugby and start packing the Book Two orders which were piling in. I was in bed by nine, though, 500 miles in two days is quite a lot for me.

November 21st

Not a lot of sleep – again. The burger/chips/milkshake combo was sitting pretty heavily, so when a rally car came screaming through the village just before 2am, I was wide awake at once. I heard it go up Roe Hill, and accelerate away down towards the Drier; but then there silence. An ominous silence. Sure enough, my phone rang a few minutes later. It was Darren from New Pond. "You've got a car in your poacher ditch." I said I'd be there in a moment or two.

Sasha was furious not to be invited, but I didn't think she was needed. I was right – they weren't poachers. They were rally enthusiasts in a Micra Mk 2. Darren and I formed a bit of an unrehearsed but synchronised team of grumpy locals. The two lads were quite well-spoken and very apologetic, and we gave them a right earful for a good half hour. It made me feel better for getting out of bed, anyway. They promised that a mate was on the way to rescue them. I gave them another oral blast and went home. Sure enough, a car sped past the window ten minutes later; obviously their rescuer.

The 'rescuer' failed miserably in his one and only task – to pull them out of the ditch. That's why they were hammering on poor old Darren's door half an hour later, asking for more help. They'd obviously spotted his 4x4 van earlier. I missed this part of the evening, having finally got to sleep.

The day was dull by comparison. It suddenly got very cold, I packed lots of books and Hazel went off to dog training. The business with the rally cars will make good FonF material, though.

November 22nd

Two important things needed doing today. First, it was time – with some proper cold weather forecast – to get some antifreeze into the sprayer. Our barns are so small that it's far easier to flush it with something than to try and back it into a warm corner of a barn. And our barns are far from warm, anyway.

A couple of years ago I bought lots of official bright blue antifreeze, and put that in. That left me with the awkward problem of what to do with it when the winter was over. I think I sprayed it onto a field and rather hoped it wouldn't affect the following crop.

It's far simpler to pop down to the Drier Yard and suck out a few litres of liquid fertiliser, run in through the system and spray a bit out. Inevitably, this wasn't as simple as I'd hoped. When I drained the last of the season's fertiliser back into the tank in the early summer, I'd done some 'transfer pipe management' with a hacksaw and a flask of boiling water. The pipe that goes with the fertiliser tank had its coupling cut off, and I'd never got round to replacing it. I'd left the coupling itself inside a pile of car tyres that act as supports for the pipe when it's being used.

I thought it worth checking that it was still down there, and, of course, it wasn't. Some bugger had had it. That meant bringing the water transfer pipe from the yard down with the sprayer once I'd hitched it on. After a few hundred litres had been successfully sucked out, I drove into the winter barley in Drier Field, unfolded on a corner of headland and did about 100 yards of spraying – enough to get the liquid fertiliser down the booms.

And then I had a chilling thought. What was the last job I did with the sprayer? Oh Lord, I think it was Roundup, and I think I didn't bother to flush out the booms with clean water. There will have been dregs of Roundup in the tubes. I have a horrible feeling that I've just wiped out an eighth of an acre of respectable winter barley. Luckily, it's just out of sight, and I can always claim it's early blackgrass control. Why I didn't flush out on some stubbles, I don't know.

The second job was done with rather less incompetence – although, once again, it was an act of incompetence that needed sorting out. Opposite Joan's Acre House we have a poacher ditch, and across the open gate we have a telegraph pole. When we started drilling that field a few weeks ago, I carefully lifted the pole with the loader, and set it down next to the ditch. It promptly rolled neatly into the ditch, rendering both methods of barricade utterly useless.

The solution: ratchet straps. Come to think of it, they're the solution to almost anything on the farm, second only to baler twine. And duct tape. So, make that 'third'. I had the pallet forks on the loader and positioned them over the middle-ish of the pole. I dug down under the pole in two places, threaded the straps through – ooh, ow, bloody nettles – tightened them up and Bob's yer uncle. Five minutes later, Joan's Acre field was secure – or as secure as we can make it, anyway. When I was walking over the field, and driving over it with a heavily loaded tractor, I couldn't help noticing how dry everything was. It has been a remarkable November, made even more remarkable by comparing it to the last two Novembers; both of them were hideous washouts. If this goes on, we'll be looking to put more wheat anywhere we can. Where's my farm map?

November 23rd

Lovely, cold and clear. Hazel set off to Barrow Hill for a day's picking-up with the two brown dogs, and I stayed indoors and generally felt under the weather. Tosdevine came in with the slug spreader and gave the south-east corner of White Hill a good dose (probably a stable door job, though) and I packed more books. Sales are going well. An evening pub trip with neighbour Robert and the ex-Editor made for a vintage November day.

November 24th

It was worth doing all that faffing about with the sprayer the other day – we had a serious frost this morning. It was hard work getting out from under the duvet, and when I did, Cain was waiting outside the door; obviously, I had to go back to bed for a bit to keep him company. It's the law.

Much of the day was shoot preparation and book packing. In among all that I wrote the next FonF, based on the incident with the rally drivers the other day, and thought I ought to get the oil leak on the loader's grab sorted out. It was quite bad when I was using it to rescue the telegraph pole from the ditch the other day, and it was never going to get better on its own.

Five minutes with some spanners got the offending pipe off, and once Tigger had reluctantly started and warmed up a bit, I went up to Gaskin's. My timing was perfect – Rod was just showing a brand-new salesman the ropes. I was able to give the lad some advice. Don't forget the front linkage when selling a tractor (Rod did just that with a Massey 6465 nearly twenty years ago, although he claims it was my fault. He's probably right) and never call a potential customer 'bud'. Not never, no way, no how. While these pearls of wisdom were being dispensed, Verity got the new pipe made up, and the loader was once again fit for use.

I say 'my timing was perfect', but it was nearly fatal. On the way up, I turned off the main bit of road and set off up Rod's little lane, only for a fish wholesaler's van to emerge from the 'Pub with No Name' and head straight towards me. He'd looked right, but had failed to look left and not seen me at all. I slammed on the brakes and leant on the horn – and we had a bit of a shouting match.

He said he'd looked left and it was clear, and I'd 'just come flying round the corner'. I pointed out that Tigger doesn't fly, and there is no corner. I suggested we ask an oncoming van for a second opinion, and he wound the window up and sped off. It was a genuinely scary moment.

A few days ago, I dropped a copy of Book Two at Oxley's, the book shop in Alresford, for their perusal and approval. I rang them up today, nervously checking if it was fit to grace their shelves as Book One has done successfully for some time. "Well, we've sold it, so you better send more!" was the encouraging answer.

November 25th

We had another fantastic shoot. The bag was far too high – 37, which left the Head Keeper tutting about leaving birds for the rest of the season – and we stayed dry. Dry, but freezing cold, in a wind that got stronger as the day went on. A fantastic day.

November 26th

We all felt a bit sorry for ourselves after yesterday's efforts in the wind. As a result it was a quiet day, eating leftover sweets and flapjack. By evening, I'd recovered enough to head off to Itchen Abbas for the much-delayed Growmore Club Quiz final. We – Petersfield Wey – had qualified for it last spring but Kung Flu was still (apparently) rampant back then. The world has moved on, of course, and we all seem to be accepting that there's a nasty flu doing the rounds, as nasty flus have been doing since the dawn of time. The world is gradually coming to its senses.

We lost the final, as is traditional.

November 27th

A typical early-winter-themed Saturday. Hazel set off with two brown flatcoats to Murph's, and I sat indoors and packed books – and chuckled at the ferocious north wind (with occasional sleet) that was inflicting itself on those who had ventured outdoors. Far better to be sitting indoors, packing books and drinking tea.

To no one's real surprise, and a tad ironically after yesterday's thoughts, Boris announced that a scary new strain of the virus had been found, and started preparing us for the much-predicted Christmas lockdown by reintroducing masks in certain places, but not in others. I must say, these viruses can be very choosy about where they get us. But at least it waited until all the private jets got home from COP26.

November 28th

The sun was back out, but the north wind was strong, and it was just above freezing. Full marks to Hazel who set off for another session of dog training up at Mullenscote. I packed books and drank tea – again. Sasha and I ventured out to Hurst Down to check for slugs in the late wheat. It's dry as a bone up there, and the cold is keeping the slugs down a bit – although some warmth would be handy to get the wheat on a bit.

The afternoon seemed to get colder. Puddles in the yard that had been mushy froze by teatime, and then the west went cloudy. Not long after that, Cain yowled his way through the cat flap covered in snowflakes, and we were indeed witnessing some November snow. If there's ice in November and all that...

November 29th

Another disturbed night. We decided that the reason the dogs start baying at five thirty is that there must be something running around on the kitchen ceiling. And Hazel said that something huge had been lolloping around above her room, too. Right. I asked her to buy a Marathon bar (look it up, kids) while she was in Alresford handing in huge bags of packed books to the Post Office and paying in the huge piles of cheques from my adoring public. I then set about every bloody trap in the house: mouse, rat and squirrel. Above my bedroom, above Diana's, above Hazel's and above the kitchen.

All this frenzy meant that we nearly missed the stunning snowy morning with a delicate sunrise. Hazel said the untreated roads were lethal – she was grateful for the Scout's 4WD. I managed a photo or two among the snapping of fingers in the traps.

There was lots more book packing, and some emails exchanged with *Farmers Weekly*, who are kindly giving Book Two a huge free plug in next week's issue. They wanted to check I was happy with the artwork they'd knocked up for a quarter-page advert. It was so generous, I felt slightly rude suggesting changes – gift horse in the mouth and all that.

Mac is threatening to come in and muck out the back barn for Hazel tomorrow, so we had a session moving hurdles and the crush. Only a couple of days ago we agreed that now would be perfect, as the ground was incredibly dry. It's funny how a small covering of snow seems to leave everything drenched. I made a mess with the Massey, and I suspect it will look awful by the time Mac has finished.

Sasha and I did the Clump loop, finding the ground suddenly pretty sticky out there, and fresh hare-coursing wheel marks in Roe Hill; the recently rolled-down tyre tracks showed up clearly as lines of snow in the untouched stubble. It was a bit of a mystery how they'd got in. I followed the tracks back to the bank opposite the entrance to the Folly. It wasn't easy for them to get in; they'd taken quite a lot of the bank with them as they drove over. More lumps of wood will be needed.

November 30th

Some mornings start bad and get better. This morning started bad and got worse. In the brief time between heading downstairs for porridge and coming back up for ablutions, Cain had settled down on my duvet, made himself extremely comfortable, and then thrown up. Really thrown up. Not just cat biscuits and some parts of a mouse, but some long strands of spaghetti, too. Odd (I thought as I swept the little heap into a dustpan). Spaghetti?

I then noticed that the 'spaghetti' was in fact moving. It was a couple of roundworms – possibly the most revolting things I've ever seen. The idea that these things – about five inches long – had been happily living inside the cat was too horrible to think about. And all that time he'd been taking any chance possible to snuggle up as close to me as he could. Suddenly, cuddling the cat didn't seem such a good idea.

The curious complete broadband failure didn't seem quite so bad in comparison after all that, but it soon turned into the traditional phone call nightmare. But I eventually got through to two sensible human beings – one at Fleur telecom, and one at Openreach – who agreed that everything was up the creek, and that something should be done ASAP. The Openreach man promised an engineer in the morning, which was good going.

I gave up packing books (internet-ordered ones, anyway; there were plenty of letters with cheques to be dealt with) and went and 'helped' Mac with mucking out the back barn. This involved me leaning on the gate and watching, claiming that my back was far too fragile now to even risk picking up a prong.

It was a good thing Mac didn't see me chainsawing one of the massive telegraph poles that were left in the yard by Openreach some months ago; they're delighted when a farmer requests them, as they haven't got to haul them back to base to be disposed of. We were sawing this one up for the new gap the coursers have made into Roe Hill, and I felt quite guilty; it was a relatively new one, and should really have been saved for seven-foot lengths as gateposts and strainers.

Curiously, just after eight, the broadband came back on – and faster than it has been for ages. I had a pre-bed frenzy of packing.

December 1st

The Openreach engineer was here just after eight, and within an hour had mended the junction box on the pole outside the office, tested everything indoors, heard the crackle on the line, been down to the exchange at Bramdean and changed what he called a 'dodgy connection'. It was all very efficient – and the internet seemed to behave itself. He tested it at eight megathingies per whatsit, which is unheard of up here, miles away from the exchange. It might even keep the children happy if they're allowed home for Christmas.

On the shoot the other day, Hazel lost Tigger's spare key, somewhere in the frenzy of penknives and string. Easily done, but very frustrating after over a dozen years of careful key management. It didn't help that it's a single black key, with no fob or garish red John Deere keys attached. Mind you, if we'd lost a whole bunch of keys, it would have been even more inconvenient.

Andy at North Motor recommended a little electrical company in the suburbs of Southampton. I pumped up the tyres (not really needed) and checked the fluids (all fine – we love Tigger) and drove down the M3. After five minutes, I realised I'd forgotten the printed-off map, but reckoned I'd memorised the route.

"It'll take an hour," said the man behind the counter. I asked for recommendations for how to waste an hour in the suburbs of Southampton, and he recommended a café round the corner. I set off, pretty well at random, past the Thai massage parlour, past the vegan barbers (huh?) and past a proper old school pub – the Wellington Arms. This looked a lot more attractive than a café, so I did a U-turn and went in. I chose the weakest beer, added a packet of peanuts, and adjourned to a quiet corner to play with my phone – the modern equivalent of unfolding a newspaper.

There were a few proper old boys in there, too. It was probably the most unimproved pub I've been in for years, and all the better for it. It smelt of a good few fantastic evenings, there was a dart board, and posters for quiz nights. It felt like home.

The best thing was the music – and I usually loathe pub music. A series of songs, each one leaving me thinking "That's good – who is it?" I asked the girl behind the bar who was in charge of music. "Me!" she said, waving her phone. I asked her to go back through the recent songs, until we found the one that had provoked one of those 'where was I when I first heard this?' moments. It was Arcade Fire singing 'Everything Now'. I was sure it was Errol Brown singing an Abba song, but there we go.

The key gang had had no luck. There seemed to be a certain amount of confusion and blustering about why they couldn't do it, but I didn't want to press things (except another key, of course), and drove back in a bit of a grump.

December 2nd

Tonight's dinner – the next of a busy winter - was in Woodhall Spa, a part of the world I've never been anywhere near. I think I bought a sprayer from a dealer up there some years ago, but that's about it. It was one heck of a drive for me, but at least it didn't have the jams of the M6 which were such a nuisance a few weeks ago. It got dark horribly early in the drive, which doesn't make for easy navigation to a strange hotel.

I was a guest of the Horncastle Fatstock Society, who put me up in a very smart room in an annexe of the hotel, and then filled the dining room to the brim with farmers and their wives all wanting a good time. Of course, the Fatstock Society no longer have fatstock, and where they once used to guess the weight of someone's animal as part of the evening's entertainment, they now needed to guess the weight of the speaker. I decided that this wouldn't present enough of a challenge, and so suggested that it should be multiplied by the mileage from Hinton to Woodhall Spa. That got them thinking.

I had a lovely dinner, sitting between a fellow agricultural engineering graduate from Newcastle, and a Bradfield old boy – from 'B' House, too. He was a good few years older than me, but it was amazing, as we compared notes, how little Bradfield had changed from his time to mine, before the huge modernisation programme swept through the college in the late 1970s. I also had time to chat to the professional Liverpudlian comedian who had been booked to speak after me.

My speech went OK, but I was, of course, blown out the water by the pro comedian. I sat feeling slightly deflated. Still, I could have been following him, and that would have been much worse.

December 3rd

Once again, I had a fantastic night's sleep in a hotel bed. There's a theme developing here. It meant that I had an early breakfast, packed up all my stuff and was on the road back south just after ten.

But not until I'd done my traditional random stroll. I hadn't realised – until I threw open the curtains – that the hotel was surrounded by woodland. I'd assumed Lincolnshire was nowt but vast flat horizons. In fact, it was in lovely if slightly spooky woodland. By the time I'd done my forty-minute constitutional, I'd read up on some of the wartime history of Woodhall Spa (found on roadside boards as you walked), discovered a bizarre little cinema in the depths of the woods and greeted countless dog walkers. It was lovely. I said my thanks to the hotel staff, threatening to sneak one of their lovely mattresses into the back of the Skoda while they weren't looking.

It's always fun driving a route that you've only done once before, and that was in total darkness, concentrating hard after a four-hour drive and on some roads that were, frankly, terrible. In daylight, the roads were no better, and it was even harder to concentrate, gawping at all the new sights. All that premium dirt, great heaps of sugar beet, bizarre machines for loading it, airfields, radar installations, huge beet-processing factories belching steam – and then being buzzed by something indescribably loud near RAF Coningsby.

It was actually a great relief to get onto the A46 – which is now officially my favourite road: great long lengths of dual carriageway, and almost deserted. True, some of it was concrete sections that fed a stream of ba-donks through the car, but I made fantastic progress to the M1 at Leicester.

It was all going rather too well on the complicated roundabout-filled link road from the M1 to the M40 – I think I may have been snapped by a speed camera while hastening to the next roundabout. I think I was doing about 75mph at the time. I await the buff envelope.

Consolation for my misdemeanours came in the form of a burger at Winchester services, and I was home packing just the right amount of book orders (FW had given it a plug at the end of today's column) by three o'clock.

December 4th

Very quiet. I packed books, drank tea and generally recovered from the trip to Lincolnshire. Hazel did some gardening, having no shoot to go to. It was cold and bleak, so the fire was lit all day.

December 5th

More of the same. Hazel went off to dog training and came back frozen solid, and I lit the fire, put the heating on early, and packed books. All very mundane.

December 6th

Huge excitement in Hinton Ampner: a road was closed! Someone – the Council, I assume – is quite methodically and brutally felling all the ash trees anywhere near a road – part of the horrific dieback thing that's going on at the moment. We've had signs up for some time, and even a leaflet through the door from the contractors, warning us that the road to Kilmeston was due to shut today.

It may have been another cold and wet day, but the lanes echoed with the sound of chippers and chainsaws as they got to work. The lucky ones sat all day in a Transit at the entrance of the Folly, orange lights flashing. All day. I mean it. All day. We're in the wrong job, everyone. At least it meant that when the man from Claas came out to do a mod to the new combine, he was in no doubt which way to turn when he reached the bottom of the hill.

It's a nice little glimpse of summer when there's work to do on the combine. I went and opened the roller shutter doors early for him and enjoyed a brief bit of nostalgia for harvest – such as it was. I must get the winter list of gripes and gremlins written up for the service proper.

A walk over Hurst Down with Sasha brought us back to the right season. It was wet, cold, but the wheat out there is trying its hardest. Curiously, the worst slug damage was up on the top – in theory, the best soil, although it was sown just that bit later, and doesn't seem to have cracked on so much.

It was good thing I'd turned the heater on mid-afternoon in Shed 3b: the band were meeting up for a much-needed rehearsal. Trouble is, Tod's lad Jesse was back in the country from Poland, with his fiancée, and proceeded to gatecrash the whole rehearsal with his talent. We eventually put him on the drum kit and once we'd taken all the noisy bits off him and told him to not hit things so hard, he was quite handy. Drummer Ian, you understand, was back at the music shop where he works, preparing for the imminent storm. Or that was his story, anyway.

December 7th

It was also a good thing that drummer Ian did spend the day at his music shop, battening down the hatches for the storm, because when it did get here, it was quite something. It had a name, of course, as all storms must do these days ('Barra') and it blew and rained from late morning onwards.

Hazel set off with two brown flatcoats to Barrow Hill again, wearing all the right kit. It wasn't rain that worried her, she said, but flying branches. Good point. The back end of the rain featured quite an impressive squall line on the rainfall radar, and I ended up with a big towel over my head digging leaves out of the drain in the yard, in a successful attempt to stop water pouring through the back door.

I texted the ex-Editor to ask if he too was out in the rain and wind, but he was pleased to reply that he was tucked up indoors. No chance of taking the mick there, then. And when Team Flatcoat got home, they were so bedraggled that I couldn't really laugh at them either. Not even Evie, who was crying in discomfort, with a right-angled tail that looks so painful on a flatcoat. Limber tail, I think they call it. And a flatcoat's sole job in life is to wag its tail, and if it can't, it's tragic to watch.

Neighbour Robert and I had a couple of beers in the Flowerpots, pleased to note that on a hideous cold December Tuesday, it was nicely full. I expected a silent house when I got home, but somehow Hazel was still up. Evie's tail was still a terrible shape, though.

December 8th

I'm not going to even mention the Ashes.

You never heard so much noise out there. There's a tree-felling gang attacking the ash just below the entrance of the Folly, and up in Hurst Down, there's another gang clearing the hedgerows for the new pipeline that's due next summer. It's a proper celebration of fossil fuels, with chainsaws and huge chippers going flat out.

Sasha and I did our yomp across Hurst Down (my favourite walk at the moment) and she was quite distracted by the din – although they were still one boundary away from getting to our field. She hardly had time to stalk Murph's pheasants out of the dell. The wheat seemed to have crept on a bit, but still looks terribly vulnerable.

Out in the real world, the virus mayhem is unbelievable. There are reports of illegal parties, sobbing spokespeople who have been sacked, warnings of another ten million billion deaths per minute, and a growing feeling that we're just going to ignore whatever they tell us to do this time. Hazel certainly adopted this attitude with the Christmas shopping – blitzing the internet shopping sites and heading to Tesco for a load of food that had the Scout sitting pretty low on its axles. Our children will be coming home for Christmas, they will need lots of food, and that's it and all about it, as Dad used to say.

December 9th – 31st

A very odd and scary few weeks. What happened? The chimney de-tarring team said they didn't think they could sort out our fireplace. I tried another independent auto electrician for a new key for Tigger – and failed. Oh, and we agreed to surrender most of the farm back to the landlord. How did this happen? The best way to explain is to use the Flindt on Friday I wrote in September 2022, when I announced to my adoring reader that I was quitting the column. Forgive me for reproducing it here, but it's the best summary I've got.

Two very significant things happened at the end of 2021. First, our youngest set off for his placement year in the City, and within a matter of days, it became blindingly obvious that he had found his vocation. Obvious – but no surprise; he's simply returning to the Flindt roots. He's working a few yards away from his Uncle Ian, a couple of buildings away from where his great-grandfather spent his working life, and not far from where Gustavus Flindt set up as a foreign exchange broker after arriving on these shores from Germany at the very end of the 18th century. Jonathan was simply following his brother and sister away from the farm.

It's sad in many ways, not least because the two boys are the most instinctive tractor drivers I've ever come across, and Diana is the only person to come close to having Hazel's supernatural affinity with livestock. All three of them should really be putting wellies on every morning. But that's it and all about it – as Jonathan's grandfather would often say when debate is done.

Hazel and I had a bit of a moment when the truth dawned on us: we have no third generation to take on our tenancy. I'm sixty, she's twenty-one (again), and time is creeping on. Bits of me (some of them mentionable, some of them not) don't work anymore, and another ten or fifteen years aren't going to improve things. The farm is in dire need of infrastructure overhaul, and the money involved (all from our own pockets, of course) would need far longer than a decade to pay itself off.

Then the second things happened. There was a phone call from the landlord. They said they'd like to come and see us. Curious, we thought. "Come on round," we said. "We'll put the kettle on."

Out came the tea and Hobnobs, and the Trust got straight to the point. "We've made a very public promise to plant a million trees and rewild a billion acres, and we're looking for farmers who might be interested in helping us."

"Hmmm," I said, trying not to sound too enthusiastic. "Nice idea, but where would we live? We're tenants with no savings and nothing to sell to raise funds. I'm content to stop arable farming after 38 years, but Hazel can't live without her cattle and sheep."

The next few weeks were a frenzied blur of negotiations, suggestions and countersuggestions – all of which are highly confidential, of course. I think I'm allowed to say, however, that both sides emerged content with the outcome.

The sacred AHA is intact, although the farm itself will shrink to about a hundred acres come Michaelmas. Hazel is now the third 'generation', and we're secure in the house where I was born. We are keeping barns and fifteen acres of permanent pasture, and the arable land we're retaining will be grassed over for assorted environmental schemes. And I can sell the sprayer.

Meanwhile, the Trust can press ahead with its very public promises, most of which involve overuse of the word 'nature'. What exactly will they do? Who knows? It's their land, and they can do what they want. We will watch with interest. It would be mischievous of us to add to the rumour mill that's outraging the neighbouring White Settlers by suggesting wind farms, solar panels and car parks, so we're making do with 'free-range beaver' and 'organic wildebeest'. "Really?" ask some White Settlers, whose smart accents cover up bottomless stupidity.

Meanwhile, spare a thought for the Trust's agents (and there's a phrase I never thought I'd write) who are being summoned to explain themselves to local Parish Councils, and being harangued by frightfully important people who have lots of money demanding land for their llamas. (And there's Hampshire in one sentence.)

Don't go thinking (and I have had to make this clear to my wonderful landlord who was keen to suggest otherwise in press releases) that I have had some Damascene conversion to eco farming, and now worship at the shrine of St Greta. Far from it. I think all forms of reducing food production – including tree planting, rewilding, organic and regenerative – are lunacy.

What we're doing is borne of pragmatism, not green dogma. We'll have a front-row seat as land into which I have (literally) shed blood, sweat and tears enters a new phase in its centuries-old agricultural journey, and I will watch (and, I hope, report) with great interest. My little package of 1,800 annual tons of stuff will be off the market. The more farmers who are in the lucky position to do what we're doing, the sooner the cry will go out for a return to food production. Don't laugh; consider how public opinion on rewilding has changed in a few short months – as the Trust is finding out on its social meeja pages. Who knows – farming's golden days may be on the way back. Too late for Anthony, Diana and Jonathan, of course. But that's it and all about it.

Where did that leave us as New Year arrived? Remarkably, drilled up. Book Two published and selling well. We'd just had a short but enjoyable Christmas with the children, and a retirement plan has been realised. Momentous.

January 1st

Now that's how New Year should be welcomed in: sitting in front of my new Roland RD-88 (thank you, Santa) banging out a high-tempo version of 'Auld Lang Syne' for the benefit of a crowded and not inconsiderably drunk pub in Bramdean. As usual, no one knew the words ("Should old acquaintance be forgot, and blah de dum de dum, da dum de blah be dum de dum, for the sake of auld lang syne?") but that didn't detract from the occasion. It was a gig with the band in a pub, and everyone was determined to have a good time.

We finished at about one, stood around and chatted and drank, and then set about the long process of packing up all the kit. By the time we'd unloaded it all in Shed 3b again, it was well past two o'clock. The inevitable post-gig bowls of Frosties meant I was in bed just before three.

Hazel, of course had missed all this, preferring to settle down in front of the television with a two-hour DVD of gundog championships. Probably a far more sensible option. At least she could get out of bed brightly and breezily the next morning. I was somewhat late out of bed and somewhat worse for wear, and, after hauling down a duvet to the sofa, snoozed through the usual selection of films.

In fact, in all felt just like pre-Covid days; but all the while, we know that there's every chance we'll be locked down again immediately after we've been allowed out to have some fun. The Omicron variant is sweeping through the nation, thrilling the lockdown fans. Jonathan had it just before he went back up to London after his brief Christmas stay, and Hazel was coughing and sputtering a bit a few days ago. My distant memories of animal health lectures tell me that it's the best way to get herd immunity – exposure to a mild but very infectious variety – but the voices of doom are crying out for more population control. What a surprise.

There was a late morning phone call from Australia to my mobile, from a chum who returned to his homeland in the late 1980s. It's funny to think that phones are now catching up with the internet, which itself had displaced expensive and unreliable long-distance phone calls as the means of round-the- world communication. I was chatting away on the phone while filling up the kettle for yet another cuppa while I could hear Tom, as clear as day, with only a slight delay on the line. I might have been calling Bramdean.

Even the Ashes didn't get much of a trans-global gloat. We were too busy chatting about the virus and, more importantly, the Big Plan. I told him the situation, and he was yet another one who pondered it for all of a couple of moments and said it sounded 'right'.

Puss in Boots was an hour too long, *The Mask* was still fun, and *Indiana Jones and the Last Crusade* was beginning to look a bit old. Mind you, 1989 was a third of a century ago, so it is old.

January 2nd

A much-needed good night's sleep, and yet another quiet day to recover. It rained a lot – as it has for the last few weeks constantly, but there's no crop work to do. I kept on packing copies of Book Two, and then had a good long walk with Sasha around Hurst Down, Blackhouse Road, JA and Dell Close and back to the truck at the entrance to Hurst Down.

Suddenly it all looks different; not because there's a very healthy shade of green growing out there, even though it was late drilled into iffy conditions, and we've had a run of winters with most fields unsown. No – it's different because I will never sow those fields again. I've been putting crops in those fields since 1984, and I've been at the wheel of the drill tractor almost continuously since 1987. A couple of years have seen contractors in, but it has been predominantly me.

And now, that bit of English farmland faces a different farming future under the Big Plan. I know the Trust are planning huge areas of trees, so will it be part of their new forest? Or will they recognise that the Top of Hurst Down is the only quality soil on the farm and keep sowing it? Letting it to a local farmer? Bringing in new farmers? Who knows? Hazel and I swore that whatever the Trust do, we are going to smile sweetly and make approving noises. To do otherwise would start a death spiral of cynical negativity. We've done a deal with them, and we must approach the consequences with enthusiasm. Watch this space, as they say.

Anthony arrived back from London after his low-key New Year celebration. He and three friends sat round a table and played cards, apparently. Not much to shout about, but still an improvement over full lockdown, I suppose.

January 3rd

The last day of the Christmas break. I'm sure that in my youth the world stopped for two distinct breaks – one for Christmas, one for New Year – and worked in the middle bit. Nowadays, the break goes on for the best part of a fortnight. Still, in these times, that's maybe a good thing. Returning to work seems somewhat more alluring – if you're able to, of course. In the days when we employed people, I made sure that a five-day holiday was threaded among the bank holidays so that we enjoyed a long break. I must have been a bit of a trendsetter.

The 'old days' theme continued when I thought it was time I checked out the bungalow. It has been empty since our tenants moved out unexpectedly in the autumn, and it has since returned to National Trust as part of the Big Plan. Even so, we still hold the keys, and I feel sort of responsible to keep an eye on it. I popped over in Tigger for an unlock and a walkaround, and turned off the water while I was there, ready for the cold weather that we're being promised.

Saying goodbye to that little cottage is going to be as hard as saying good-bye to the majority of the farm. It was where Hazel and I moved to in 1984, just after arriving in Hinton fresh from university. We did a summer in the farmhouse with the parents and then started a gradual transfer (including a minimum-fuss registry office wedding to quench the flames of outrage at both Manor Farm and Jerrettspass) in the autumn, once Dad's last 'assistant' had moved out.

We stayed there until 1997, starting a family in 1995. My parents moved in when we did a house swap – somewhat reluctantly, it must be said – and they were there until he died in 2011, and she went to a lovely care home in Alresford. "Someone scrubbed my back in the bath the other day!" she announced triumphantly on one visit there. I suspected that that was a first for her. She was gone in the mind by the end of 2012, and the body followed in 2013. Bless them.

Since then, the bungalow has hosted a selection of families, some more successfully than others, but the time is right for us to release it back to the Trust. We did wonder if keeping it for our old age would be better, but the days of opening up the southern flank of the garden to enjoy the view to the hilltop above Riversdown House are well gone; a thousand times a day you'd get a Trust walker watching you back from the exceedingly popular footpath. Everything seemed in order in there; I wandered from room to room, imagining I could hear the echoes of children playing, or Anthony crying after tumbling out of his cot, or Dad reading *The Tiger who came to Tea* from his armchair, or Mum playing cards on the kitchen table with an entranced six-year-old. It was Don Henley 'Deadhead sticker' time; I locked up and headed back to my present home.

The next car review for *The Field* was due in today, but with all the press cars suddenly vanishing in December as Omicron arrived, I was in a bit of a hole, with nothing to review. I'd been mulling over an article on the insane world of second-hand car prices for some weeks, and that seemed perfect for the mad mood of the times.

January 4th

That little thing that fell out of the cot in the bungalow is 27 today. Where do the years go?

I was well behind with the accounts. Something else somewhat bigger came along in the late autumn (when I should have been doing them) and all our mental energies were diverted. Today I put the finishing touches to what might generously be called our 'valuation', packed up all the invoice and income files, threw in some bank statements and the crop records, and drove down to Havant in a now well-practised routine. I took the Hyundai i20 for a change. If the seat wasn't so narrow for my huge arse, I'd give it five stars.

There was a dramatic sleety/snowy storm as I approached Petersfield, and for a brief moment I spared a thought for Hazel and Bella who were somewhere behind the hedge picking-up at Barrow Hill. It was very brief, though, as you can bet they were having a fantastic time.

It being Tuesday, Robert and I had our Flowerpots trip, and I managed to persuade Anthony to give me a lift down *and* come down to pick me up a bit early so he could join us for a pint – it being his birthday and all that. Which he did, and a very jolly half hour we had, too. I think I had one too many, and Robert swore a lot. I should have warned Anthony.

January 5th

Another quiet day, but one with a stunning cold start and lots of much needed sunshine. There's just a hint of the days getting longer, and, inevitably, thoughts turn to spring cropping.

One thing we won't need this year is spring break crops. We abandoned oilseed rape a few years ago after the neonicotinoid ban (although those who have stuck with growing it have got magnificent fields and jaw-dropping forward prices) and I grew weary of winter beans (although the kind autumn might have meant that they would have gone in on time for the first time in three years). Tod and I had been mulling spring options: spring beans and/or peas – and that's about it. Soya continues to fail to take off; we did look into it a few years ago, but the growing regime was too prescriptive and on-farm drying and storage was needed.

One thing we did check with the National Trust when the Big Plan was agreed was cropping; if they've got farming tenants lined up to start work on our land, then we'd be happy to plant break crops so that the new occupiers could start with first wheats. The Trust said 'thanks, but no thanks' which worried us a bit; will they actually be bringing in 'new' farmers? Anyway, that's no longer our worry.

Planting no break crops means an awful lot of spring barley on the unsown acres. Still, the forward price for barley is good, and we can bale and stack the mountain of straw. Hazel pointed out that after this harvest, we're going to have to buy straw for her cattle – unless this harvest yields a lifetime's supply. The next order was for glyphosate to clean up the stubbles. Ouch. There's not a lot we can do about the price of it – except dig out the rusty ploughs and spend a fortune on diesel to plough it all. And then buy a power harrow/drill combo. Far better to pay the money for spray to do the job.

Sasha, Tim and I had a walk in the weak winter sunshine to contemplate it all. Good thing we've got another shoot tomorrow, to take our minds off things.

January 6th

I usually make a great song-and-dance about shoot weather; "As long as it's dry," I'll tell anyone who might be listening, "we can endure anything!" Today put that claim to the test. There was a stunning frosty sunrise, and the clouds came in from the west, accompanied by a strengthening south-east wind.

We did indeed stay dry (except for one brief sleet shower at about eleven o'clock), but it was as cold as I have ever been. The hot soup at elevenses was a life saver.

The shooting was moderate; we've had four very successful days so far this season (and stayed dry on every one) with bags in the thirties, so we knew that numbers were likely to tail off a bit in the new year. We had good shooting in the maize strips and copses, but the other cover crops were flat and deserted. As the day got darker, we headed into the Folly with a bag still in single figures, and we do like a few more than that. Both the Folly trees and Bob's Wood produced some excellent birds (and some challenging pigeons, just to keep everyone's barrels warm). We've been pondering the wisdom of keeping Folly in the Big Plan just for the shooting, but today confirmed that it was a good call.

Anthony was shoot bunny for the day, being in charge of putting assorted pies and puddings in the Aga on time, and they all went down very well. Suzi went home before lunch, but we inherited two 'other halves', meaning eleven of us sat down at the huge round table and behaved like ten-year-olds. My niece, who had driven down from London to join her husband (who had bravely joined in as the one stranger in a chummy shooting party), later texted a lovely thank you with the small complaint that there were too many willy jokes. What did she expect? Proust? And to think that I was predicting another post-Christmas lockdown. Boris is going to come out of this shit smelling of roses. Again.

January 7th

Sore heads all round this morning. It didn't help that I'd been trawling the house for Rennies in the wee small hours, with chest pain that was on the verge of being scary. I didn't find any – but the pain died after a bit of walking about, and the dogs took no notice of me, which is unusual; normally they'll leap around and bark at the slightest provocation. Bella, after two hard days' work in three, wasn't going to move for anything.

Anthony caught the train back to London to restart work, this time as a contract gardener. He's bravely given up the world of offices and computers, sales targets and grumpy hire-car customers, and just wants to spend the day gardening. He is doing it on a 'self-employed' status, and has had to learn the intricacies of tax returns and invoices. That in itself is a good thing for a 27-year-old to know about.

Hazel got back from dropping him off at the station just in time for Chris the Land Agent's visit. We'd called him in for a post-Christmas chat about the Big Plan – what's next? As it happens, lots. An hour later, we had a long list of things to do, people to notify, officials to be written to – it certainly made worrying about a lack of straw seem fairly trivial.

Next stop before hitting the sofa for the afternoon was the doctor's surgery in Medstead for some blood tests. It's always worth getting blood tested at this time of year; the wonderful life-changing Questran has a habit of draining you of vitamin D, and around Christmastime all the joints start to ache. There's also a lot of torso itching going on, too, and after a lifetime of crop spraying, I do worry a bit about liver function. Blimey, we're all getting old.

The surgery was, of course, empty, but it was cheerful and punctual, and I was in and out in moments. We await the results with interest.

In the meantime, I grabbed a duvet and hit the sofa. Some restored Westerns from the 1950 were perfect for the occasion. *The Tall T* – what a cracker.

January 8th

"Yeah, you might get a shower or two," I promised Hazel as she and Bella set off for Murph's Saturday shoot. What she got was six hours of hideous freezing rain – although there was an hour's break in the deluge during which I got the other three dogs walked. The heating went on very early, and the log burner about half an hour after that.

January 9th

A good hard frost this morning, and locks and gates were frozen when Hazel set off at some unearthly hour to Mullenscote dog-training centre, which is where she is now a teaching assistant. She very quickly got 'spotted' and promoted after a few weeks of being a client up there last year.

I dozed for much of the day, having been awake for much of the night listening to the end of the fourth Test match in Sydney. We showed 'em. Oh yes. We bravely managed not to lose. Still, a good advert for Test cricket when the result depends on the last ball of the last day.

Neighbour Robert dropped in for a cuppa. He was particularly kind about last Friday's Flindt on Friday, which was all about the stupidity of trying to recreate a medieval countryside while worrying about food self-sufficiency. It's true that the timing of the article couldn't have been better. The government's rewilding plans were published on Thursday, and have been all over the media since then. I wrote it on December 20th without any idea that it would be published at exactly the right time. It will, of course, provoke an angry flurry of letters in *Farmers Weekly* from the wokefarmers.

Just like yesterday, the heating and the log burner were on all day. The forecast is quite cheerful, though. I might finally get back in a tractor soon.

January 10th

The slight problem with our plans for Dead Dog Farm (as I, and no one else, am calling the bit of farm we're keeping) is that we will have no arable income, but will still have rent to pay. But we do have a farmyard surrounded by barns and stables, most of them untouched and in a very poor state of repair. The Trust have promised that they'd make the old stable block and the tractor barn safe to walk in (they aren't at the moment) and therefore safe to let out.

The time has come to start thinking about what we should do with them. Up to now, we have never done any form of diversification other than let neighbour John park his taxi minibuses in the old calf pens.

We've been mulling ideas: self-catering holiday lets in the old stable block, industrial units in the tractor barn and the calf pens, a car service bay in the diesel barn, rehearsal room in Shed 3b, and Pilates studio in the old shoot shed. Many of these ideas have been prompted by existing enquiries.

Jeffrey the Building Guru called in for lengthy discussion of such matters. I'd like to say that the result was a crystal-clear plan of action which promised a dozen easy-peasy years of rent pouring in to refund the investment. In reality, we were left somewhat befuddled by procedures and planning, and some of the projected costs involved would need many decades to recoup. And while the idea of self-catering flats in the old stable block sounds lovely, someone has still got to change dirty sheets.

Suddenly the idea of letting out a run-down but safe barn for someone to store logs seems a lot more practical – if less lucrative.

I went to Wickes in Winchester to buy a much-needed rim lock for the back door. Three screws and a bit of chiselling later, it was fitted, and, for the first time in years, the door shut properly. That's my barn conversion for the day done.

January 11th

It's all very well ordering a small mountain of Roundup to start on the spring stubbles, but no one's looked in the chemical store for months. And, sure enough, when I did, I noticed that a bit of work was in order. The rats had found the bags of slug pellets, and bit of a session sweeping and re-bagging was in order – once I'd found decent masks and gloves. It was a bit of a messy job, but it wasn't long before all the pellets were out of harm's way in the tin bin. I also set about the heap of empty boxes left over from the autumn herbicide programme, all of which left a nice clean and empty floor ready for the delivery.

Halfway through re-bagging, I remembered the curious slug damage out in White Hill that we spotted while out shooting the other day. Along with the 'expected' damage in the heavy land in the south-east corner and over at the far side of Rough Field, the tops of the Bronze Age mounds near the northern edge had vanished too. They looked like the bald bits on a monk's head.

I thought I had better walk out and check them – not least because in the depths of the night, I'd thought it might be something else: nighthawkers.

Those historic mounds are easy to find on the maps and in the flesh (as it were) and we have stopped men with metal detectors in the past, just unloading their vans after initially and nonchalantly claiming to be 'going for a walk'. I couldn't help wondering if these illegal metal detector teams had been giving the mounds a good workover – hence the bare tops.

The tops were untouched. Bare as babies' bottoms (or monks' heads) but no sign of any digging. The drill marks and the occasional tramline marker were still perfectly visible. The very edges of the bare patches showed slug grazing. There must be something unique about soil conditions this year that means those little patches of different soil, hand heaped by unknown hands thousands of years ago, have harboured legions of slugs. Mind you, it's perfect slug conditions: mild and heavy drizzle. No fun to be out and about in.

It did mean that neighbour Robert and I could adjourn to the Pots and moan about the weather with proper justification.

January 12th

Too many peanuts last night, and I was rather late up. There was sudden change in the weather, to cold and dry. A stunning winter morning. I can't see anyone rushing out to do any fieldwork quite yet, though.

Our favourite WPC called in for flapjack and dog cuddling, and to have a good chat about the latest on the hare-coursing battles. She was very positive, with several recent 'ops' proving very successful. I asked if it was all down to our PCC – but apparently not, although she has already developed a reputation for taking no nonsense. She 'won' the battles with the folk who wanted to close the A33 dual carriageway for trap racing. She decided it was not going to happen, and it didn't. Full marks on that one.

Perhaps it was down to the new harsher legislation on hare coursing that has been featuring in the country press; once again, no. That has some way to go until it takes effect. It just seems that our wonderful Countrywatch Police have been in the right place and at the right time. Our WPC did say that there's a new enthusiasm in the public to spot and ring in such activities – and they're hugely grateful for it.

Our first load of liquid fertiliser sneaked quietly down to the yard and was delivered. I was half expecting it to come with an armed escort at the price we've paid for it – 150% up on last year. Still, what can you do? You either buy it or don't have it. The driver did the job perfectly, right down to the half-hour notice phone call with Google maps open, so he could actually look up where the tank is. I did worry that he was going to clash with our landlord/lady, who was down there somewhere with yet another team of woodland experts, deciding what their plans are for our fields in a year's time, but all went smoothly.

January 13th

I had thirty-two goes at writing the next Flindt on Friday, and failed every time. I had a long walk, chatted with neighbours Darren and Debbie, met someone who used to be chemistry assistant at Churcher's College, ate flapjack - all failed to inspire.

Hazel had a more productive day, doing the pheasant feeders in Pig, and a late evening shop at Tesco. And that was about it for the day.

January 14th

It's a curious thing, this columnist lark. I spent the whole of yesterday struggling to come up with something, and then, in the small hours, decided to change topic altogether. Instead of another long whine about the misuse of the word 'nature' – which was repeatedly tuning into yet another anti- wokefarming rant – I thought the bald bit of barley in White Hill would make a better 600-word column.

It was on *Farmers Weekly's* desk by ten – and would have been earlier if the phone hadn't been suddenly busy. Neighbour Robert Junior wanted to come up and buy some of our fantastic hay, and then Hazel wanted a hand getting the big flail mower on her tractor to bash down some of the maize shooting strips. But when 600 finely crafted words did reach FW, they liked it. A picture of the bald patches was needed, I thought. But what should have been a quick trip out to White Hill turned into a lengthy discussion about Middle Eastern politics. I stopped for a chat with a couple having a picnic on the fallen beech tree near the Springshot gate, and spotted quite quickly that he was obviously not of this parish. "No, I'm from Iraq," he said. An hour later, we'd covered the plight of Christians in the Middle East, the Druze, the Alawites, the artificial nature of borders out there, the pros and cons of toppling despots who, for all their sins, managed to keep tribes at peace and treat Christians (like him) with respect, and the heartbreak of monasteries being sacked. We also somehow got on to shooting, and he was a proud owner of a 1960s Baikal DT O/U, and he wouldn't swap it for the world. I told him to go and buy *The Field* and read the motoring column.

Once the photo of the patch in the barley reached FW, they slotted it into the article, and sent me the proof just as it got dark, having come up with a brilliant headline and standfirst. And I'd spent all of yesterday fretting. Funny old game, this writing lark.

January 15th and 16th

Two almost indistinguishable days. Stunning sun rises and sunsets, cold and frosty all day. Hazel went picking-up with Bella and Tim (his first day out) on the Saturday, and went training with Tim at Mullenscote on the Sunday.

I walked the other dogs, watched too much television (*Shrek 3* isn't that bad, really) and snoozed.

Highlight of the whole weekend was Tim, out shooting for the first time, running round ninety-nine to the dozen, absolutely flat out and full of enthusiasm, taking his cue from his mother, Bella. Not a bloody clue what he was actually supposed to do, but had a fantastic time doing it.

It's very frustrating having all this lovely drilling weather. For the last two years, we've spent January desperately longing for two dry days to catch up with the backlog of winter wheat; this year we're drilled up, but no spring barley seed has arrived yet. I've had a couple of confusing emails from the new supplier, demanding lots of details to open a new account, but there's no sign of any result yet.

The calm and lazy weekend was brought to a sudden halt just before midnight, when I was woken by a noisy engine going past the house, down the hill a bit, and then stopping. There were voices, cracks of an airgun, and, sure enough, as I peeked out of the window, spotlights lighting up the trees. The 'poachers' were back, and judging by the fluttering and shouting from the hen pheasants above them, they were having a lot of success in their endeavours.

It's a dilemma. Go back to bed? Ring 999? Ring 101? Actually, that last idea is absurd. I texted Policeman Ian to ask if he was on duty, and then gathered my dressing gown, my attack dog and my wellies, and drove quietly down the hill – lights off – to see if I could move them on. At the bottom of the hill was a big white Transit (what a shock) which drove away smartly as   I came round the corner, by now with my lights on. I followed it – heart in mouth – as it turned off to Kilmeston. The two vehicles trundled in convoy along the sunken lane until we reached White Hill, at which point the Transit shot off, belching clouds of diesel that suggested it hadn't seen an MOT test for some time. What a shock. Again.

I headed home for bed, relieved that there had been no face-to-face confrontation.

January 17th

Not surprisingly, I didn't sleep well after all that. But once I was up and about, I started texting our two local Countrywatch PCs. I – quite rightly – got a bit of an earful for not ringing the poachers in at the time. Trouble is, last time I did, I got a condescending operator who made it quite clear I was wasting her time ringing in poachers.

Policeman Ian – once he'd stopped scolding me for not reporting the poachers at the time– was quite cheerful. They've had some great anti-poaching/hare-coursing results recently, and that's before the new legislation comes into effect. He, too, said that the big change is that he's getting more help and feedback from the general public, who seem to be more aware of what's going on than ever before. Very good news – as is the extra member of his team that's imminent.

Not such good news was the noisy Mitsubishi Doublecab that arrived just outside the bedroom window at ten o'clock in the evening, shouting and firing air rifles; I had to go through the whole 'see them off' procedure again. I hope this isn't going to be a nightly routine.

January 18th

Once Hazel had set off for Barrow Hill with Bella and Tim, it was a busy day for the kettle. The National Trust agent came round for a chat about the Big Plan, the first of what will probably be a long series of meetings to sort out the ten thousand unexpected consequences of what's been decided.

First on today's agenda, for instance, was the electricity supply down at the grain stores. There was a time when we cleaned and dried all our corn on site, and for two or three months of the summer there was a deafening array of fans, diesel burners, elevators and conveyors – many of them using three- phase supply – and we'd have electricity bills to match.

I've forgotten the last time I fired up one of those huge three-phase beasts, listening for the star-delta routine to kick in. I do remember, after one expensive winter service, how one of the electric motors on the Alvan Blanch grain drier would switch over too quickly. I pointed this out to the electrical engineers who had done the service, suggesting to them that it wasn't safe; it hadn't reached proper speed when the switchover point came, and would overload. I was told it was fine.

Some months later, it blew up on switch over; there were flames everywhere, with the hideous and unique smell of an electrical fire. Thanks goodness we had working fire extinguishers down there, and after a frantic shutdown of everything I could think of, I managed to put the fire out. I think I was also blessed that it wasn't a full-on harvest day – I was catching up with the backlog. I rang the electrical company to say the motor had blown up, and might they like to quote for a rewire/ replacement – expecting a 'terribly sorry – you were right, we'll do it for nothing'. Next thing I knew, they'd been out without telling me, done a rebuild and sent a bill for the thick end of a grand. Back then, I wasn't very good at kicking up a fuss, of course, so the bastards got away with a nice little earner. I didn't use them again.

Twenty-five years on, and the only electricity we use down there is for occasionally turning the lights on, or a few days a year pressure-washing the combine, both of which only need a piddly single-phase supply. Somehow, though, we've ended up with the same monthly bill. 'Somehow' implies it's some sort of mystery, when we all know it's down to the Swedish Doom Goblin and her green policies.

Hazel is bravely taking on Scottish and Southern Energy to point out that £300/ month is a bit silly, and it is proving an absolute nightmare to sort out. Hours (literally) on hold, being passed around from department to department, no one really interested in helping; why would they, if they're raking in that much cash every month?

The simple solution is to ring them up and ask to be disconnected. After all, I'll be trading in the combine after this harvest, and the scrupulous back- to-front clean will be nice, but not essential. I reckon we can do without power down there. But can the Trust, when they take the little yard over in September? Their agent said it might be useful in the future, so why didn't we ask for power (and bills) to stop, but leave the infrastructure there so the Trust can get it reconnected in the future? I'll put it Hazel, who I'm sure would love to have another three hours trying to speak to yet another department.

There were other trivial queries to be discussed, but apart from them, it was a nice positive meeting, with much satisfaction that everyone seems happy with what's been agreed.

The next long chat was with a planning expert, who had been recommended to us as someone who would take one look at the range of woefully underused farm buildings we've got (and will continue to have when we've done the Big Plan) and tell us what we should do with each one.

He sounded very enthusiastic as we looked at the old stable, the tractor ban, the old calf pens and the shoot shed. All of them are ripe for development and becoming our income source for the rest of our career here. Over a cup of tea I had to pull him up for talking jargon as if I was also an expert in these matters. I pointed out that we have never owned any property anywhere, and so have never had any dealings with planning – the new back barn put up for Hazel's thriving suckler herd (pre-BSE, of course) doesn't count, being a new build. The rest of the chat was somewhat less technical, but still scary. I was left worrying that we could easily plunge all our savings into these buildings without any guarantee of a profitable return in the next ten years. I think we might see what we can do with them with the bare minimum of conversion.

By the time I rang Robert for a Pots trip, I had drunk so much tea that I was slightly dizzy and deaf in one ear. Mind you, it made no difference to the standard of chat in the Pots. I was tempted to use the new Land Rover Defender Commercial that their Press Office sent out today, but with the police on poacher stand-by, the last thing I needed was to be spotted driving clumsily through the lanes in a strange vehicle.

January 19th

I felt ill enough this morning to dig out the box of lateral flow tests. Much ghastly poking up the nose and shaking of vials later, I was 'negative'. Quite a relief. Mind you, most of the swab was blood. Even so, I really did not want to have to ring Robert and say I was off-colour in the pub last night because of Kung Flu. And I definitely did not want to have to cancel tomorrow's shoot. Would I have been brave enough to keep it quiet if it had been positive? Probably not.

Shoot preparation continued. Hazel cooked stuff, and I went to APM in some cold and unforecast rain for batteries for shoot radios – and to give the Defender a good-ish run. It's a beast. Quite scary on narrow lanes. Should be lots to write about, though.

It was pretty busy with lots of farmers ordering up their spring cultivations stuff. Those of us who turned up without wearing masks were given a bit of a scolding – Boris's mask-free announcement doesn't take effect for a few days yet. I have a feeling that he's going to come out of the 'partygate' shitstorm smelling of roses. Again.

January 20th

Probably the coldest day of the winter so far, but with sparkling sunshine for our last shoot of the season. Yesterday's rain had frozen, leaving things quite slippery. It took ages to de-ice Tigger for its food-laden run down to the grain store, ready for our mid-shoot sugar frenzy.

I was waiting for Hazel to come down in the Scout to pick me up when I spotted a lady with a loose dog in Rick and Clump. I jogged over to catch up with her (nearly going arse over tit on the ice at New Pond), and the traditional exchange took place as she hurriedly put the blighter back on its lead. No, she said, she's not lost, she didn't realise this was private farmland, and she doesn't like the road, and doesn't this all belong to the National Trust anyway? I kept as polite as I could, and we parted as friends, but an end-of-January shoot will not be helped by a dog rampaging through what's left of the covers.

It really was an end-of-January shoot. We staggered to double figures – although better marksmanship might have meant a better bag. We marked the end of the season in the warm-ish sun at the grain store with cocktails. I wasn't convinced. I can hear Dad saying, "There's a time and a place for everything." Pink goo with an umbrella in the muddy yard proves his point.

It was slightly melancholy – and not just because it was the last day of the season. We walked up to Stanmore and did the three drives up there – and that's the last time walking over 'my' fields. Next time we get up there to shoot – and the existing shoot lease has three years to go over the whole estate – it will be back in the hands of the Trust, and goodness knows what will be going on up there. Still, this morning's exchange with the dog walker is all that's needed to remind me that the Big Plan is a good thing.

Shoot lunch went on far too long. I pointed out to the team that we'd overdone the willy jokes a fortnight ago (according to one guest's wife), and so we were all under strict instructions to jolly well grow up a bit. That lasted for all of ten minutes, when discussions on the Trust's plans for the farm once we're done with it started. 'Beavers' was one suggestion. It all went downhill from there.

January 21st

A bit of a cattle day – once the sore heads had cleared after yesterday's shoot. Hazel has decided on a plan for her herd of heifers. They've been unsettled for a week or two, and the time has come to get them onto some bagged grub to supplement their hay (which, oddly, they don't seem keen on; very unusual for our hay) and the grass in the Back Meadow – which occasionally tempts them out of the barn but never for very long.

She placed an order with Mole Valley for a bulk load of nuts, and went into their Winnall store to get a few bags to be going on with. That meant an afternoon digging troughs out of the brambles and hanging them on the gates. A good way to clear the head, but a job that has to be done with caution these days to avoid twanging something in the lower back – and I've got my first 'awayday' shoot for some time tomorrow.

Jonathan caught a train down from London for the weekend, and I picked him up quite late from Winchester. It'll be nice to catch up with him – if only for a couple of days. I miss school holidays, when we had them all home for weeks at a time; we're lucky to get them home for more than a weekend at a time now they're all doing proper jobs. Even Christmas was horribly short.

January 22nd

Beaters' day at Murph's – and I was shooting as 'Hazel', who has, after all, picked-up there most of the season. It was my first 'away' shoot for ages, and in a way it was nice not having to do all the shoot morning admin and logistics. All I had to do was pick up my kit and go, but I was still nervous as heck.

It was two teams of eight, 'beat one, shoot one', with BYO sandwiches and soup in the snug shed up at Brockwood after four drives. I missed my first three birds and then went downhill from there, and ended the day in a minor strop, promising myself more clay shooting, more lessons, or perhaps a new gun; that's always the way to sort out lack of talent. Hey, it works with my keyboards.

I don't think I've seen Hazel working two flatcoats at what they're supposed to do – i.e. stand behind the guns and retrieve. When she's out with them on our little shoot, they're flushing and beating all day, with the odd retrieve thrown in. Doing their real job was pretty impressive and very well received on a shoot with towering birds and several runners. Bella's retrieve through a sheep fence, gently pawing a dead bird towards her and then slowly pulling it through the netting, was a joy to behold

The final bag was somewhere in the mid-forties, and we all stayed dry, and, thanks to the manic stick-waving we all did every other drive, warm and well exercised. If Jonathan had come down from London hoping for a long meaningful chat with his parents, he was disappointed. There was a mass outbreak of sleep by eight o'clock.

January 23rd

We'd all woken up a bit by the time we had a proper Sunday lunch to mark Jonathan's twenty-second birthday – a day early. His twenty-first was ruined by the lockdown. It's the youngsters who have been hit hardest by what is rapidly collapsing into a complete shambles – and a shocking con.

I spent most of the morning battling a complete article block; FW should have had it on Thursday, but in the end I came up with something a bit lame and sent it off. Not sure if it's the lack of farming going on, or the Big Plan, but I'm short of inspiration at the moment.

We had a super bit of beef and then STP, and then, to no one's surprise, all fell asleep again. As I dropped Jonathan back at the station in the early evening, I apologised for him not having a nice lively weekend, but he said he was fine with it. All he needed was a day or two of cats and dogs and fields, and it had been perfect. Good lad.

January 24th

There was a funny 'let's get farming' feeling in the air, and the phone calls reflected it. Tod decided he'd come out and have a walk round, and then put all the band kit back together; it was all piled into Shed 3b in the small hours of New Year's Day. We were planning a full rehearsal tonight.

The company supplying the barley seed were true to their word, and rang to say they'd like to deliver tomorrow. In fact, they were so efficient that the transport company rang too, to say they'd like to deliver tomorrow. And then the driver himself rang to check – using Google Streetview – exactly where he should turn up, and was it alright if he got here at seven in the morning. I told him – misquoting *Casablanca* – that I'd be in my tractor seat at eight. But there was no chance of an article moaning about seed deliveries turning up unannounced.

The Land Rover team turned up to take the Defender away, and I was sad to see it go. Reduced to a 'commercial' spec, it's a very attractive farm vehicle: practical and surprisingly no-nonsense. But, my word, it's big. I found myself dropping out of the driver's door to the ground. I'll hack into the main design computer at JLR and reduce all dimensions by 20%. That'll sort it.

And just in case the seed lorry really does arrive in the dark tomorrow, I switched the Massey over from front grab to big bag lifter, and put the pack of weights on the back. It was the most 'farmy' day we've had in ages. And a very loud band rehearsal in the evening really did make it seem as though things are returning to normal.

January 25th

I suppose that at some stage the days will get longer. It was still pitch dark when I finished my porridge and headed out to get the tractor parked up and ready for unloading the lorry. I'd given the driver directions yesterday which ended with "and you'll see a red tractor parked outside the barn. That's where we unload." It would be foolish if he got lost in his hunt for a tractor that wasn't yet parked where I said it would be.

As I was unlocking the gates, he arrived. I was able to flag him down in his headlights and get him to stop out of the way until I'd got the tractor in the right place. And then it was a very significant moment: the last load of seed to be lifted off and put in the tractor barn. All done in semi-darkness, and all done remarkably smoothly. So it bloody should be after all these years of unloading seed. First with a Ford 6610, then a Sanderson 6.22, then a Deutz 4.57, then a Fendt 309, then a Massey 5455, and now with a Massey 5713. Blimey, what a lot of tractors. What a lot of seed. What a lot of years. I reckon thirty-five.

I was on the verge of getting quite tearful when Tod rang to say he'd left his computer in Shed 3b last night and would be flying in to retrieve it. That put a stop to any lachrymose nostalgia.

The lorry driver was very grateful for the early unload, and set off back down the hill just before eight o'clock. And it was just about getting light.

Hazel set off with two brown dogs for another day picking-up at Barrow Hill, and I settled down for a bit of an office/tea drinking day. Policeman Ian dropped in for yet more tea, and to once again talk us through the run of good results they've had with the hare-coursing fraternity. His only frustration was the lack of commitment from the CPS when it comes to taking matters to court. Still, we agreed that Hampshire getting a 'bad' reputation for helicopters, sizeable police numbers and seizing of dogs can only be a good thing.

January 26th

It seems like a thousand years ago now, but just before the pandemic hit, Hazel resigned as Trade Stand Secretary for the Alresford Show. She'd been doing it for ages, sorting out countless traders, large and small, cheerful and grumpy and generally spending the second half of the summer getting into a well-controlled panic about the upcoming Show. A new secretary was found to replace her, and the first meetings were just getting under way to brief the new girl when the virus struck.

The Show was cancelled in 2020, of course, and again in 2021 – which seemed a bit pessimistic at the time, but there we go. It's 'full speed ahead' for this year, though – except Hazel's replacement has resigned. A couple of pleading messages later, Hazel agreed to step back into the role. That's why she spent most of the morning with Val, the Show Secretary, getting up to speed with this year's plans. I think she was quietly quite pleased to be doing it again. It's hard work, but a fantastically social thing to do.

At the shoot on Saturday, I found myself wedged in the gun bus next to a bigwig from Trinity Grain. He's not a very big fellow, so I was more 'on top of' him rather than 'next to' him. Anyway, we got chatting about Trinity, and I mentioned our 'downsize' and the fact that as from September, we would no longer need our thousand tons of grain storage. I asked him what we should do with our virtual barn. He ran me through the options in a bit of a hurry – the next drive was imminent. We could keep it and lease it out to other farmers, or sell it. If we sold it cheaply, of course, it would go quickly; if we held out for the official rate, it might take longer. He mentioned a 'quick sale' figure which was a lot more than I'd expected. No wonder I didn't hit anything for the rest of the day.

We agreed he'd come out for a proper chat, and he said it would be handy if we could find all the relevant paperwork to go with our piece-by-piece purchases over the years. That meant only one thing: everyone up to the attic. After an hour's intensive rummaging in assorted boxes, there was nothing.

Actually, that's not quite true; there were hundreds of fascinating bits of paper and uncovered memories – but none of them anything to do with our membership of Hampshire/Trinity Grain. It was beginning to get dark when Hazel remembered that half a dozen boxes of stuff were still downstairs in the old playroom. And, sure enough, there was the original 'Hampshire Grain' file. Still, we'd had a lovely time in the attic.

All day, we had an ear open for a lorry, due to deliver a pallet of cattle grub. A couple of late afternoon phone calls established that there had been a bit of a mix-up, and it wasn't coming today. We were promised delivery tomorrow morning.

Better news was the dozen drums of Roundup that finally got delivered. It should have come with an armed guard and helicopter escort at that price, but it means that the next job – killing off some stubbles ready for spring barley – can be added to the long list of stuff to procrastinate about.

Sasha and I had a lovely walk in the dry calm evening. It wouldn't take much to be persuaded to get in the tractor and do some farming. That was my cue to ring Hunt's and get the 100-hour service organised on the nearly new Deere 6155M. They said they'd be out first thing Friday. Perfect.

January 27th

It was an interesting session with the Trinity Grain bigwig. Over the course of a dozen years, we've bought a thousand tonnes of storage space. We will not need it any more after September, so what are the options? We went through them all again;, we could keep it, and rent it out in years when there are farmers looking for a temporary bit of extra space. All well and good if those farmers are out there, but in poor years, we will end up paying fees for not using our space.

We could put our space on the market; if we want a quick sale, we could sell it cheap – but still more than we paid for it over those dozen years. If we were happy to hang on for bit, we could well get a better price – although he suggested that we won't be the only farmers getting out of arable production the next few years, so people looking to buy our space might be fewer and farther between. We decided we'd have a good long think about it – but we'll probably sell quickly and add it to the pension fund.

The rest of the 'meeting' involved gossip about mutual friends and reminiscence about a little pre-prep school that almost every farmer's son went to in the 1960s – Eastacre in Winchester. I set up a Facebook page for it a few years ago, as it seems to have escaped the attentions of the internet completely. The man from Trinity promised he'd dig out his huge archive of photos. My favourite comment of the morning was when one mutual friend came up. Whatever happened to her? "Oh, she married a German. It didn't work out." That earns lots of points on your '60-somethings talking about life' scorecard.

The cattle feed finally arrived. "Where were you yesterday – we were expecting you," I asked.

"Can't have been me, mate. I was in South Wales yesterday." Hardly worth getting in a fuss about. Hazel was just relieved that she wasn't going to have to drive into Winchester and buy a few more bags to tide her over.

I thought it would be wise to unhitch the tractor from the sprayer for its 100-hour service tomorrow, but there was a problem. The battery was as flat as a pancake. True, it hasn't moved for over two months, but there must be a trickle draining somewhere. I should disconnect every control box before leaving it that long. After several false starts with extension cables and battery chargers, I left it to charge overnight.

After a late afternoon haircut – ready for the imminent arrival of spring – Robert and I adjourned for a rare Thursday evening in the Flowerpots. It was heaving. Rammed solid. We managed to find a table in the public bar, but the noise was terrible – fantastic for the pub, of course, but not good for two grumpy farmers with iffy hearing. Later in the evening, the other bar emptied, and we moved in there, only for a very jolly crowd of yoof to pile in and be noisier still. Again, fantastic news for 'our' pub, but we decided that sticking to Tuesdays might be a more sensible decision. We might be repeating everything we said the week before, but you don't know if you can't hear it. You might actually miss something original.

January 28th

A very cold and frosty start. First job: get the Deere in the barn for its 100- hour service. The lights on the battery charger were glowing very brightly at 0630 (yes, really) and suggested that the overnight charge had been successful, but it was still a relief when the tractor fired up nicely. I hitched the sprayer off by floodlight and then drove the tractor round to the barn for the service. The best oil changes are done with the oil warm and having run down into the sump for an hour. I hope the man from Hunt's appreciated my efforts.

The maintenance theme continued with a call from Oliver's who supplied our brand-new combine last summer. Could they come out on Monday and start checking the Tucano over for its winter service? Of course, I said.

It meant a trip down to the Drier Yard to see if the combine is OK – but not until Hazel had done the bloody awkward job of getting the graunchy old roller shutter door open. She was in the barn scooping out wheat for the post-season pheasants. Another post-Big Plan thought struck me; we're going to have to buy wheat from next year.

The Claas started fine, but after a minute or two started bleating about the hydraulic oil being too cold, so I didn't leave it going for too long. I didn't want any damage done. By the time Hazel and Sasha got back from doing all the feeders, the two of them looked pretty chilly, too. This run of cold calm weather is all very entertaining (keep checking the Gridwatch web pages to see how useless wind and solar power are proving when we need it most) but a warm day or two would be nice.

Phil the Claas tractor dealer happened to call in, wanting a copy of Book Two. He'd had the very first copy of Book One in August 2019, and I took great pleasure in flogging him Copy No 1,000 of Book Two. I told him about the Big Plan, and he was yet another one to respond positively – especially when I told him that there would be a lightly used two-harvest combine up for sale. Trouble is, we're not officially on his books, but he did promise to pass the message on.

January 29th

As if we'd ordered it, a slightly warmer day came along – and a windy one, too, and a bit of rain overnight, although that last bit wasn't very welcome. Hazel set off for her last picking-up day of what has been a tremendous season for her, over at Murph's again. Despite mastering handling two dogs for the first time, she decided to only take Evie this time, to give her a proper run out. I enjoyed some Saturday trash TV, but was interrupted by Mac, who had finally come up with some sort of bill for a summer's baling and carting of hay and straw.

It turned into a two-hour gossip, and another book sale, and another fellow farmer pondering our Big Plan news for a moment or two and announcing that it seems eminently sensible.

By evening, the skies had cleared, and another hard frost seemed imminent. Hazel (and Evie) were asleep on the sofa by nine o'clock. Now the season's over, I might get some company.

January 30th

So much for the 'get some company' theory; Hazel was off again, in the dark, for another day's training up at Mullenscote. Tim went along for the day's experience.

Once I'd scraped the hard frost off Tigger, I went to get the papers from Cheriton shop. A senior (i.e. pre-White Settler) Kilmeston resident was there at the same time. "Sorry to hear your news," he said, with a solemn face.

"Why – has someone died?" I asked.

"No – I hear you're giving up farming," he explained, giving the impression of being the first person I've met who hasn't been entirely positive about the Big Plan. But after five minutes of me setting out some of the whys and wherefores, he had a compete change of attitude. "Well done. You two certainly deserve it."

A lazy afternoon on the sofa was rudely interrupted by a fantastic game of rugby between Sale Sharks and Leicester Tigers. There were loads of points, several sessions of handbag swinging, and – unless I imagined it – Dan Cole didn't come out on top of every scrum. Nah, I must have been hallucinating. I took the three remaining dogs out for a loop round Clump in the stunning sunshine. I think I'm going to have to get the newly serviced tractor up and running soon. I can't go on ignoring weather like this for ever.

Hazel and Tim were back late afternoon, having had another good day. Tim, apparently, struts round the training ground, meeting and greeting clients, making friends with all the other dogs, and generally behaving as if he owns the place. But that was Hazel's mission; he was a lockdown pup (born February 2020) and he missed out on socialisation in his first few months. Mission accomplished. Mind you, they were both sound asleep on the sofa by nine o'clock. Again.

January 31st

First job: open up the barn down at the Drier Yard so that Olivers can give the new combine its first winter service. Quite a historic moment – our first non-New

Holland combine service since 1995, and first not done by Luke the Combine Wizard in about twenty years. I dug out the list of niggles from last harvest (always worth jotting down somewhere), printed it out on a nice clean sheet of A4 and taped it to the door glass.

The northeast wind picked up, which was perfect for one of our occasional bonfires out next to the new cattle barn. Unfortunately, the pile of gardening waste and cuttings that Anthony had piled up over his summer down here hadn't dried much, and we only managed to get rid of about half of it. It would have been a lovely afternoon, leaning on a prong to watch the heat, occasionally adding segments of hay to help the fire along.

It took me back to one of my first winters here – I think it might have been '85 or '86. Ernie and I were doing the annual cleaning up down at the grain store, in blisteringly cold conditions. Back then, the right-hand lean-to was still used as a hay store, and he and I would take turns to fetch a small bale and have a brief but blazing fire and a couple of much-needed cigarettes, sheltering from the wind around the back of the barn. And all the time listening out for Dad's Land Rover, just in case we had to scuttle back into the barn and look busy.

God, it was cold back then. I can remember the dress code: T-shirt, shirt, Guernsey jumper (supplied regularly by Mum after yet another holiday to Jersey), SCATS wax jacket (a bit of Barbour knock-off, but usually £19.99 – so you could use it to lie on during oil changes), motorcycle gauntlets (from the Army and Navy surplus store in Alton) with wicket-keeping inners underneath, two pairs of socks under the rough-and-ready black Argyll wellies. The tops of the legs were coldest, and made me long for the DPM padded trousers I'd somehow swiped – and lost – after CCF at school.

Was it colder back then? We seemed to have snow more often, but meteorological memories are notoriously fallible. We were certainly out in the cold more often, but that's a sign of our change in working practices. We were doing the eight-till-five back then, come what may. These days, with no staff, I'm quite content to sit indoors and do other stuff rather than sweep barns in minus five degrees.

The one thing Ernie and I didn't have to put up with back then was a row of heifers blaring at you from twenty yards away. Hazel's girls have decided that that's what you do all day. Not sure why; one or two of them are bulling, and the rest think they should have another bag of nuts because reasons. We need some warmth to get them out on the grass again. Noisy buggers.

February 1st

First of the month; deadline for *The Field's* motoring column. I spent the morning putting several hundred words together and got them sent off. There was lots to be said about the Defender Commercial, so it wasn't a hard write-up.

The ammonium sulphate was delivered – it's a 'water conditioner', supposed to combat the water hardness that reduces glyphosate's efficiency. And with glyphosate being the price it is at the moment, it needs all the help it can get. But now I really had run out of excuses not to go spraying, so I hitched the sprayer back on, and parked it up next to the tank. Both were empty, and with our dismal water pressure on top of the hill, I'd need a long filling session before I could get going. I put the pipe in the sprayer and left it running for the afternoon.

The Pots was back to normal in the evening – nice 'n' empty, with only the clear plastic screens still hanging above the bar giving any clue that we've had a pandemic. Neighbour Robert and I had a jolly evening, and I even remembered to switch off the hose pipe from the sprayer to the water tank once I got back home.

February 2nd

The man from 'Catchment Sensitive Farming' looked awfully familiar. "Of course I am," he explained. "I used to sell combines and tractors all round here!" That made sense. It was also good news. Hazel had asked him to drop in for a chat and to give us some ideas and pointers for the Big Retirement Plan. It soon became apparent that he knew exactly and instinctively what we're thinking of, and had some great ideas and suggestions. We'd timed our Big Plan decision perfectly, too (he said). Land like ours is exactly what the authorities are looking for: land coming out of arable production, in a national park, and sited near important rivers. He left us with pages of maps and schemes – and plenty to ponder.

I spent the rest of the day putting 2.5l/ha glyphosate (and 1l/ha of vital water conditioner) on the stubbles. I did Roe Hill, Rick/Clump and Big Field in two long tanks. The fantastic sunshine and warmth meant that the footpaths were heaving, and I had to do a lot of diplomatic stopping near the headlands. Nice to be out doing some proper 'chemical' farming, though, despite this morning's meeting.

Slightly scary that it's Candlemas Day, and 'if Candlemas Day be fine and clear, we shall have two winters that year'. The BBC did an evening feature on Groundhog Day, seemingly unaware that it's just an Americanism of the Candlemas Day predictions, and featuring a commentator who seemed unaware that 'Groundhog Day – the weather concept' pre-dates 'Groundhog Day – the movie'. For such brilliant awareness and insights we are forced to pay a Telly Tax.

February 3rd

The man delivering the Alfa Giulia rang early, just checking how to get here. I'd only just looked up in the diary when this latest test car was due, so managed to not sound too surprised. I asked if he had a wingman to take him away; he said that he didn't, and could he please have a lift to Winchester station. It's a bit of a nuisance, bearing in mind I wanted to keep on spraying, but very good news that normality is returning to the world. Not long ago, I was lucky to get test cars at all, and if I did, they were delivered by someone in surgical kit who would hop from sterile car to sterile car with panic in his eyes. Hazel very kindly offered to take the driver to the station, which meant that spraying plans weren't disrupted. You don't turn down such perfect spraying weather and conditions at this time of year.

I did most of Blackhouse Road before lunch, but my post-lunch tank was delayed somewhat by a quick farmyard tour for a three-year-old. I saw him and his slightly fraught young mother at the kissing gate out of the top of Englands, and he was in a state of high excitement at seeing a tractor. There's only one thing to be done in these situations: stop doing what you're doing, and usher them into the yard for a bit. Ten minutes of utter joy followed, and not just for him. He could barely contain himself as he spotted new bits of kit, and shrieked with delight. And when we got him up into the tractor cab – well, I thought he was going to explode. In fact, he sat on the edge of the seat, gripping the steering wheel for all he was worth, and lapsed into joyful silence. We've all been there. Fantastic.

When I finally got going again, I finished Blackhouse Road, popped in and out of BML's, and did the long drive to Godwin's Park. I was undisturbed by walkers all day, which made a nice change, and even had enough left over to do the south and west shooting strips in Chalks. Just to finish the job properly, I had a bit spare to respray the brome-filled patch in the middle. A quick in-field rinse out, and that was all the spring stubbles done, cleanly, without making a mess, and most of it in fantastic February sunshine. A wonderful couple of busy days. Why am I giving up this job?

February 4th

Yesterday's encounter with the exuberant three-year-old was perfect material for the next Flindt on Friday – which was already a day late. Funny how stuff falls into your lap when things get up and running. I sent it off and they seemed to like it.

I foolishly did one of my occasional checks of my Twitter account, and found that my column in today's *Farmers Weekly* had already upset all the usual suspects. All I'd said was that I was still pleased at the result of the Brexit vote (one of my fellow columnists had said a few weeks ago that we Brexiteers surely all realised we'd 'been had'). Sure enough, there was something called a 'Twitterstorm' going on, and the comments were, as is traditional, rather unpleasant. Mind you, I'd predicted exactly that in the article. I decided to not bother with Twitter for a bit.

An early sliver of rain blew through, and it turned fine and very cold, with the strong wind still blowing. Sasha and I had to cut short our walk round Hurst Down. I'd gone up to see if it might be dry enough to start on a bit of fertiliser, and the tractor would have travelled fine. The liquid fertiliser, however, would have blown across the valley to Murph's.

It dawned on me that some work was needed on the fertiliser tank – or, more specifically, the intake pipe – before I could start drawing any stuff out of it. I'd cut off the banjo coupling last year when taking a bit of fertiliser out and then putting it back into the tank (all part of the winter antifreeze routine), and put the coupling safely somewhere. Inevitably, it had gone missing, so on a recent trip to APM I got another one.

Ten minutes with a Thermos of boiling water and a jug proved that the one I'd bought was too big; there's always confusion about 2" versus 50mm, and I'd bought the former to fit the latter. Bother. A random trip round the tractor barn revealed a spare 50mm coupling which fitted perfectly after a bit of hot water treatment. I bet it was the 'lost' one after all.

I couldn't resist a trip into the Conder bins. They consist of ten 50-tonne capacity square bins bolted together with a roof fixed over the top, with elevators and conveyors to move grain around. There's a cleaner and a huge Typhoon fan, and an intake pit designed for trailers of the 1970s – when it was built. Dad had one spectacularly good grass seed year (before his son, c/w hay fever, came along and put a stop to grass seed growing) and put the new wonder barn up with the proceeds.

It was a self-contained cleaning/drying/storage unit, and in its heyday could bash out thirty tons an hour from its unloading spout into a waiting lorry. By the end of the 1990s, it was getting a bit tired; the ventilated floors were peeling off their timbers, the elevators and conveyors were on their last legs – and we'd joined Hampshire Grain. We never found an alternative use for it, so it has sat down there, doing nothing. I still have nightmares about the battles against the rats, and the floors exploding, and grain all over the place after elevators stop unexpectedly. I climbed up the terrifying 80° ladder one last time, and carefully walked the length of the catwalk, hoping that the wooden floor was still sound.

Disappointingly, all the bins were empty; what fun it would have been to find a forgotten fifty tons up there – especially at today's absurd prices. Mind you, I suspect it would have been pretty mouldy after twenty years. I pocketed a few metal rat traps and made my way gingerly back down the ladder. There was a time when I could half run down that ladder, face first. With age comes, oddly, vertigo – and I was very relieved to get to the bottom. I know it would break Dad's heart to see his bins being scrapped, but I don't think I'll shed a tear. I did today, though, as I slid the doors shut for what I hope will be the last time. Mind you, I got a faceful of dirt and rust at the same time.

A long-overdue pub trip with ex-neighbour Rufus had been organised on

Facebook a day or two ago, and I confess that I was slightly nervous. For many years, he and I have getting together and agreeing very loudly on all things political, but he's had a very nasty bout of Kung Flu – several days in intensive care and everything – and that can do funny things to a man. (See Boris.) Rufus was unchanged: large, loud, and opinionated. As a result, we had a wonderful evening.

I had also been worried about the Thomas Lord, which in recent years has veered from chi-chi pretentiousness to ghastly boorishness, but now seems to have found a wonderful middle ground. It was full but fun, relaxed and easy – and apart from a well-worn sign on the floor asking us to keep our distance (which no one does anymore) you wouldn't think there was a pandemic on. In theory, anyway. You might ask if, after almost exactly two years, things are really back to normal.

February 5th

A quiet Saturday. Or that was the plan, anyway, now that the shooting season is over. Unfortunately, four hyper-fit dogs don't do calendars. Somehow they knew it was Saturday and spent the whole day bouncing off the walls demanding to go and find something to pick up. Especially as the wind and rain would have been perfect for a day's shooting. I think Hazel was quite glad to miss the rain for once.

It made my afternoon snoozing on the sofa rather unsuccessful – as did the rugby, which was very exciting, even if the last five minutes of the Scotland vs England match featured a remarkable change in the scrum rules which meant England consistently failed to win a much-deserved penalty.

I had enough trouble getting to sleep after a lazy day without a noisy car going past the house and sounding its horn just before it got to the bottom of the hill. First thought: it's just a car going through and sounding its horn – perhaps a badger was in the road. Second thought: that's exactly where the poachers have been doing their recent catapulting, and where I've chased them away. Are they coming through and just being bloody-minded? I got out of bed and watched from the window for ten minutes. The car went down the road towards Springshot, and I could have sworn I saw a flash of lights as if they'd turned up Dark Lane towards Drier Field. But then nothing. There was a howling gale, too, so straining my ears to listen for roaring and revving was in vain. I went back to bed for some unsettled sleep.

February 6th

Hazel was back to doing dog work, setting off in the wind and rain to Mullenscote for more training. She left Tim behind this time – he has a bit of gash on a pad, and a quiet day or two for him is needed. I saw her off and went straight back to bed to catch up a bit. Cain – who was already on the bad – thought this was the best news EVAH, and moved from on top of the duvet, to next to my neck, to down under the duvet, where he purred so loudly and enthusiastically that I feared for his oxygen supply, especially when I did a vintage morning fart. He was still alive when I finally decided to get up and make porridge. Thanks goodness.

The paper run revealed no sign of poachers' tracks or tyre marks, which was also a relief. I had another quiet day – and with Hazel away, all four dogs go into silent hibernation. Lots of tea, lots of property porn (could we really move away after the Big Plan happens? Really?) and then another thrilling rugby match.

Hazel was back late afternoon, looking somewhat shotblasted, and then had to take all the dogs for a long walk. I would have offered, but it wouldn't have been the same if I'd done it. And anyway, the French were just getting going.

February 7th

Another grim night with poachers. Just after midnight, an engine could be heard just outside my window, along with the tell-tale cracks of air rifles and much shouting and laughing. I crept over to the window to look. Sure enough, a merry gang were methodically working their way down the hill, shooting roosting pheasants out of the trees.

For the first time in my life, I decided to ignore them. I watched for a bit, but didn't grab a dressing gown and a dog, jump in Tigger and go and chase them away. I just couldn't sum up the enthusiasm. It looked like it would be four against one – if they decided not to be chased. I've got a lot of drilling to do, and I did not need a broken leg, or my head caved in, or a ball bearing in my face – or my dog's.

I also didn't ring 999 and give the codeword, only to have to answer a questionnaire on my pronouns, and then have a BMW hurtling through the village in three hours' time, and then ring on my mobile when I'd finally got to sleep – which wasn't until three o'clock. It was a moment of great shame.

It meant that I was still very asleep when Hazel set off for an early dog walk, and tired and grumpy for most of the morning. The *Farmers Weekly* and I got the next column polished up to everyone's satisfaction, and then it was fertiliser time. I got two tanks on the winter barley. I did most of White Hill – about twenty acres has vanished to slugs and wet weather – and Drier Field. It seems a tad early, but the fields are dry and it'll be nice not to have those to do when the weather turns to spring.

Band rehearsal was a bit flat. Ian the Drummer had tested positive again, and one potential punter, coming along to see if we were good enough for her event in the summer, couldn't make it.

February 8th

Dontcha just love it when you buy something online, and make a great song and dance about insisting the delivery driver ring you to give an hour's notice – just in case you're out at the other end of the farm – and then you get a phone call from a delivery driver, and you ask where he is, and he says he's 'outside the gates'? Well, that's what happened today, as I was indoors polishing up the speech for tonight – which was lucky.

A few days ago, I ordered a new transport box from Agri Linc. I bought a Fleming one ages ago, and found very quickly that it didn't actually fit on any of our tractors; it was designed for the little smallholder machines. It has consistently failed to find a buyer at a couple of Crap Sales (the farm auction at the West Meon Hut crossroads), so it'll have to be eBay soon. The new one – by Proforge – looks a bit chunkier, and some measuring with a handy twig suggested that it will fit nicely on the Deere or the Massey – perfect for the log cart we're planning. The farm is littered with fallen trees, and we need to have a concerted effort to clear them and get the lean-to stacked before we wave goodbye to those fields.

After a quick lunch and a session packing all the pills and lotions that go with a day away (more medicine than clothes, these days), I set off in the Giulia for Stamford. It was lovely drive, and the 'one hour to Oxford' benchmark I used forty years ago in the Alfasud still applied. I paused for some sandwiches and a bottle of Coke after the short stretch of the M40, and cracked on. Up the A43 and under the M1, round the south side of Northampton, and on through the countryside (being systematically wrecked by housebuilding) past Kettering and on to Stamford.

The George in Stamford – sorry, the George at Stamford, as it insists it should be called – is something else. If Harry Potter did hotels, this would be it. Creaky staircases, wonky floors, assorted ancient stonework popping up apparently at random in rooms and corridors. I climbed several sets of stairs to get to my very smart room, only to find a lawn outside the window. All very odd. I had time for a snooze and shower, and then made my way down to the bar to join the couple of dozen farmers who were already getting well warmed up for the dinner.

They seemed to like my speech, although some of the jokes are now getting a bit old for a farming discussion group whose average age seemed to be about forty. The committee took it upon themselves to market my books among the members – which is what I ask for in lieu of any fee – and by the time everyone staggered home, thirty-one copies had been sold. Not bad at all for an attendance of twenty-one. A nice boost for sales, which have not unexpectedly died down a lot recently.

I got to bed well after midnight, slightly pissed and very pleased with the evening's work.

February 9th

Not a brilliant night's sleep. The hotel bed was one of those 'memory foam' ones, which I've never been fond of. And there was no duvet – just a sheet and a thin blanket under a massive bed cover. I'd turned the heating down as soon as I arrived, and really should have got up to turn it back up, but I was too busy chasing sleep.

The George did a splendid breakfast, after which I had a walk round Stamford, checking out the ancient alleys and narrow streets, remarkably free from Big

Chain Boo Hiss shops and stores. And how many enormous churches does one town need? It looked stunning in the February sunshine. I said my farewells to the wonderful chatty staff, and set off home, but did a detour into the mysterious Northamptonshire countryside for a welcome cup of tea with Tim, once my mentor at *Farmers Weekly*. He was very interested in the Big Plan and said lots of kind things about what might happen after I've stopped driving a tractor. He might be right – we'll see.

The drive on home was fantastic, and I really warmed to the Giulia. I also drained the fuel tank horribly quickly, and had to stop near Brackley to put twenty quid in. And if you've stopped once, you might as well stop for a second time, and that might as well be at the Winchester services for a McDonald's. They were out of strawberry milkshake, which I was cross about. I must get out more. No, really, I should. If all goes to plan after the Big Plan, and I get a proper job, I might have to grow out of swooping into McDonald's as if it's a rare treat.

The Growmore Quiz restarted today. They're doing a truncated version, with fewer rounds, so that the final can be at the proper time of year. It's all part of everything getting back to normal, and let's give Boris credit; he is at the helm of the movement. He took a punt on defying the lockdown zealots just before Christmas, and it seems that it was a good call. I think it will be enough to save him from the Remainer-inspired 'partygate' crisis, and he really will come up smelling of roses.

We 'won' the quiz – although the unique way the Growmore is run means that there's no actual winning involved; we just scored more points than the oppo, and those points go into the table. It was another long social evening, with the little bar in the West Meon pavilion doing good business. Everyone seems determined to get out and have a good time, even if it is on a dark and cold February night. There's a lot of lost time to make up. And a bloody good thing, too.

February 10th

Not surprisingly, it was a bit of a quiet 'catch up' day. We had a delivery of cattle feed, complete with a nice phone call giving us an hour's warning; that's how it should be done. Hazel continued her self-imposed 'body MOT' with a visit to the ear testing centre in Alresford. To no one's surprise, her hearing was perfect – a bit like her eyes, which were so good at her recent test that even the independent eye specialists couldn't do their notorious 'we'd now like to sell you these £500 glasses' routine.

I continued to spoil my post-shooting season health routine (see recent dinners and completely unnecessary burgers) by enjoying another evening in the Pots with neighbour Robert. It was much quieter than the last time we went on a Thursday, which was lucky: Robert was desperate to know how the trip to Lincolnshire had gone.

Hazel was on the phone when I got in at about ten fifteen, which seemed odd.

She had a serious voice and face, too, and was desperately trying to silence the dogs who, as usual, were in full voice to greet me. It turned out she'd had a text from Nationwide, asking if she'd really used her debit card to buy 'minutes' on her O2 account. No, she hadn't, not least because she doesn't have an O2 account. She rang the number in the text (after Googling it first to check it wasn't dodgy) and got through to the Nationwide card team.

Someone, somehow, had used Hazel's card – numbers off the front <u>and</u> back, one assumes - to buy a £30 'top up' from O2. That payment had gone through, but obviously set off some bloody clever alarm bells at Nationwide. Another attempt, this time for only £10, was blocked – and messages were sent to Hazel. By the time she'd had an efficient and friendly chat with the fraud team, the card had been 'stopped', and a refund for the £30 was on its way. Full marks to them for their system – but we still spent an hour trying to work out how those crucial numbers had been obtained.

That nice Mr Google said that because the 'security' number on the back is only three digits, and getting hold of the 16-digit number and the name on the front of the card isn't too difficult, it's not that much work to keep trying, using an automated system, until the fraudsters get lucky with the one on the back. At worst it'll take 999 tries. He also said that the £30 sum is typical of a 'tester' transaction, to see what the response is. For there, it can go two ways – lots more small transactions while trying to keep under the radar, or go for one huge one and hope the security systems haven't spotted the 'tester'. Either way, we – or rather, Nationwide, who would have to refund any losses (although being a building society, that would end up being us as members) – were lucky.

February 11th

The next Flindt on Friday should have gone in yesterday, and I'm very fortunate that they seem relaxed about it being consistently a day late. The dinner in Lincolnshire was perfect material – how all those young-ish farmers are positive and upbeat about the future.

They're promising a breakdown in the weather next week, so I thought I ought to get up to the heavy land at Stanmore with some fertiliser. It would only take a couple of tanks, but now travelling up there through the woods is impossible, it's a bit of long old haul round the road from the Drier Yard (where the tank is). There was a time, when tractors were smaller and the trees weren't so large, when popping up through the woods from the road to Blackhouse Farm wasn't a problem. It was routine. Mind you, there weren't locked gates and ten thousand National Trust Visitors in the rides back then.

Harvest is always the biggest problem. It's relatively easy with low-yielding break crops or dismal wheat that has half-rotted away in the autumn rain (as in harvest '21). Once or twice in recent years we have had good yields up there, and just about managed to cope, but that was with the old combine. The new Claas is far higher capacity. If the wheat up there turns out to be a long-overdue good crop, we might find ourselves committing the ultimate harvest sin: stopping the combine. We might have a lopping session down the route of the old pipeline and into Drier Field, which will have been harvested well before we get up to Stanmore.

It was sticky, but travelable. Pipeline looked the weakest field, while Long and Broom were much more encouraging. Everything looked a bit spindly and hungry (second wheats always do) so 135l/ha of N35S should spice it up a bit. It isn't often you get the chance to drive all over that clay land in the middle of February – so that's a bit of a bonus.

February 12th

There's big rain coming this weekend, so I contemplated getting some fertiliser on the Hurst Down/JA/DC wheats, which would mean all the second cereals would have had a good first dose. But the wind got up too strongly for that – the dense drops of liquid fertiliser can cope with higher winds than the fine drops of spray coming out of a flat fan 110-degree nozzle, but they still need to land somewhere near where you want them.

Tim and I did the Clump walk and came back frozen. He thought the conditions were fantastic and did vast solo zoomies in the dry stubbles. He's just turned two, and is a beast of a dog, with phenomenal speed. It was a joy to watch him, even if the dry ground made me feel I should really be doing some sort of farming.

The Six Nations took priority, and it was worth the effort. ('Effort' means putting the heater on in the sitting room, fetching the spare duvet down from the bedroom – once I'd tipped the cats off – and eating far too much flapjack.) The rugby also meant that Hazel had to volunteer to pick up Anthony from Bentley, where he was doing a day's gardening and then coming down for bit of a lie-in and recharge. Only a short visit, but good to see him anyway.

February 13th

Hazel was off early for another dog-training day at Mullenscote, grasping as much wet weather gear as she could find; the forecast is grim for lunchtime onwards. I managed to get three dogs out for a dry walk (Bella stood pathetically on the edge of the grass, waving a paw as if injured. The radar suggested that there was no time to argue with her, so I let her back in and whizzed round the Clump loop with the others).

The radar was right; it went dark very suddenly, and we had wind and rain for most of the afternoon. It meant I could watch England beat Italy with a clear conscience. That was why I couldn't possibly take Anthony back to the station, and Hazel had to volunteer to do it.

February 14th

Only a couple of days ago, I was yomping round the farm, amazed at the general dryness, and making plans to be out drilling. Well, yesterday's deluge squashed that sense of enthusiasm. Everything was drenched. I drove down to New Pond, anticipating a big puddle and a blocked ditch, but found the pond was full, the road was full, and the water was running into Blackhouse Road field. No drilling today.

I was cheered up when I found that *The Times* printed my letter suggesting that their 'nature correspondent' (woodcuts, hoppity bunny wabbits, etc.) should stop moaning about gas bangers noisily scaring pigeons off the crops, and volunteer to run round the fields herself from dawn to dusk, waving flags. Mind you, she did have a point; some of the gas guns do end up far too near houses.

No band rehearsal tonight; Ian the drummer couldn't possibly make it on Valentine's Day, which was sweet. Bless. He got a lot of stick on the texts for it, though. Drummer gets stick. How apt.

February 15th

A very sad email came through today. I've been chasing up the next set of press cars, trying to get them all booked before things get busy, and had a brutal reply from Skoda. Cutbacks and the new car crisis mean that little magazines like *The Field* don't merit getting a press car anymore. Ouch. The fact that *Field* readers own half of Scotland and love Skodas was irrelevant, apparently. Not to mention the numerous sales I've made on Skoda's behalf. Or the two Octavias we've had as family cars for decades. It's the way of the world at the moment.

Band rehearsal was much more productive. A full house, and a bit of a 'back to basics' decision with the PA. Everyone could hear everyone, the volume stayed low, and we bashed our way through most of the set. We even decided to dig a couple of old favourites out of the mental archives (*Dance the Night Away, Hush*) – although that leaves us with the dilemma of what song we drop to make room. I'm all for dropping *Crossroads*, which would free up half an hour. And avoid the sight of an audience all thinking it's a terrible dirge.

February 16th

After yesterday's news about press cars, I thought I should make a concerted effort to chase up come other makes – and hope that the VAG decision doesn't apply across the whole industry. I'd hate to be the man who ends the *Field's* motoring column after all these years. It's bad enough that I'm doing it to farming at Hinton Ampner. I sent out a clutch of emails to assorted contacts, and quickly had a reply from Honda, offering a Civic. Phew – that's another month sorted.

The Men from APECS (a local farm building company) came out late morning to look at the cattle barn. It sits halfway down the farm hill and is somewhat neglected. It was erected in the late sixties – I think – when Mr Dutton (the owner of the village at the time) was unhappy about Dad outwintering store cattle in the pastures around Hinton Ampner House. "If you can build me somewhere to put them," said Dad, "I'll put them indoors." A site was chosen, mainly by one of the estate workers (Arthur Howe, if I remember correctly), waving a handkerchief on a long stick until it could not be seen from the House. This was decades before mobile phones, of course, and one of Mr Dutton's minions shuttled back and forth from the top of the hill with reports on the new barn's site. Finally, Mr Dutton was happy, and the diggers could get to work.

The finished product was huge, cutting well back into the chalky hillside, and it had a yard, fenced with sleepers and some very chunky wire, which stretched out to the south of the barn. Some of the chalk was used to build a ramp, halfway up one side of the barn. The plan was to use the back quarter of the barn as a silage clamp (tipping the cut grass off the ramp), and then feed the cattle over the winter directly from the silage face.

It didn't last. Eighty or so big store cattle very quickly turned it into a quagmire, and the self-feeding concept didn't work, either. Within a couple of years, the cattle were back out in the open all winter, and the barn ended up being used for hay and straw storage. Outdoor cattle are always better, anyway.

It made a good barn for Hazel's sucklers in the early 1990s, once I'd wired up some strip lights and bought a generator for those night-time calvings. March 21st 1996 put paid to that, and the barn has done little more than store big bales of forage since then.

It'll still be ours after the Big Plan, and we thought it was time to give it some TLC. The men from APECS did a lot of tooth-sucking, and gave their verdict: we could repair the numerous holes in the roof, or replace the whole roof, or flatten the whole barn and start again. It all depends on what we're planning to do with it. A new barn could be a fantastic diversification opportunity, with its easy access. I asked them to do a range of quotes and get back to me.

I had an 'unknown' phone call after lunch, and it turned out to be Hampshire Police firearms department. Did I know that my shotgun licence runs out on Monday? Eeek – I didn't. I had an inkling but was relying on the reminder letter that the Police have traditionally sent out to give us fair warning of imminent expiry. I'd had no such letter.

The nice lady didn't seem to want to talk about the sending or otherwise of letters, but ran through the list of stuff that I was going to have to do a bit sharpish. First, fill in the application form online. Because I will not have time to get a doctor's certificate sorted out (not had to do that before) I should make a blank PDF and submit that. Curiously, it sounded like well-used advice, which suggests that I am not the first gun owner to have been caught on the hop by not having the reminder letter.

I will then have to print off the form for the doctor to fill in and drop that at the surgery. Meanwhile, because my guns will be unlicenced, I'll have to find a certificate holder with space in their gun cabinet who is happy to look after them for however long it takes for the new licence to be sorted. And then notify all the relevant authorities blah blah blah. All very frustrating. I do wish they'd sent the letter – as their website still says they will. I feel an angry letter of my own coming on; but I might wait until it's all done and dusted.

February 17th

First job was to drive up to the doctor's in Medstead and hand in my form to be filled in. They're open early, and it was all very cheerful, even if masks were still the order of the day. They didn't look at it as if I was mad, and suggested that it would take a week to ten days to get sorted. They said they'd give me a shout when it was ready to be picked up, and that would be when I would have to pay for the privilege of the doctor saying I'm not a nutter.

Much of the rest of the day was spent getting ready for the arrival of Storm Eunice, which is due to be the worst storm EVAH. It's curious to note that lockdown is being advised for tomorrow, which seems awfully familiar to what was going on two years ago.

Still, it's better to be prepared, I suppose, so I charged up the electric chainsaw and gave the venerable Stihl a going over, sharpening its blade and finally getting the two-stroke started. And I managed it without damaging my shoulder, which is actually an achievement.

Curiously, when I set off to the pub for an evening with neighbour Robert and the ex-Editor, it was spookily calm. It even felt slightly frosty. What Granny Flindt would have called a 'weathermaker'.

February 18th

Storm Eunice duly arrived, but not before I'd got the next Flindt on Friday done and sent off. One must begrudgingly give credit to the weather muppets who predicted Eunice's arrival before it had formed out in the Atlantic. And yes, it was bloody scary, but not a patch on October 1987 or January 1990. We spent most of the day indoors, with the lights flickering on and off; you never know whether to shut the computer down to avoid damage – but then you'd miss the latest updates on the rainfall radar and the official observations updated hourly from RAF Odiham.

By late afternoon, the rain had stopped and bright sunshine came out. I took three dogs for an exhilarating walk, which was quite scary at times. On the top of Clump, I was leaning forward into the wind at a scary angle, and Tim the puppy kept coming to heel, looking slightly worried about the roar coming from the distant trees and the gusts which were still knocking us back a few paces as we walked into it.

There was a very interesting email from *Farmers Weekly* when I got in; yes, they liked the latest column, and how did I fancy doing a spoken version that they could add to a podcast as part of World Book Day. No one likes the sound of their own voice like I do, so, of course, I accepted. Could be a bit of a laugh.

Things had calmed down enough by evening to head down to the ex- Editor's clutching some beer take-outs from the Pots (which had been closed all day). We were originally planning to head down their garden into their shed/den, but a warm fire and a scrap with couple of feisty Sealyhams was far more tempting, and we headed indoors to their sitting room. It's a relic of the last two years of lunacy that we still felt uneasy as we entered.

February 19th

A day for damage checking/reporting. Or it would have been if I hadn't left Tigger's door not shut properly a couple of days ago, after it had been left wide open for a bit to dry out in the wind and sun. The battery was flat. Hazel and Nessa went off for a long dog walk and reported back: trees down here and there, a couple of paths blocked, but nothing too dramatic.

There was a distinct lack of sport on television – only lengthy outdoor reports from news organisations saying that this was the worst storm EVAH and we mustn't go outdoors. I took their advice and did some internet searching for a decent USB microphone for this new 'voiceover' project. Impossible to avoid buying from China, of course, so it will probably break down after 366 days. Or give my computer a virus.

February 20th

Very windy again. I'd forgotten to cancel my membership of Amazon Prime after using it for… well, not sure actually. I suspect it was sport of some sort. Autumn rugby internationals? I think it's only £7/month, so it's easy to ignore on the credit card bill. It did mean that yesterday's order of a smart new microphone arrived late morning. No Sundays off for the poor folk delivering in their beaten-up Transits. Hard to believe that not many years ago, such an idea would have been impossible.

A mate in Bramdean had offered to look after my two shotguns in his capacious and secure gunroom (as one has) while my licence gets renewed, and even better, volunteered to come up and pick them up. He brought two very noisy children who crashed their way round the house, pursued amicably by all the dogs. Sasha is particularly fond of small children and considers it her job to monitor and supervise these odd beasts that occasionally arrive in the farmhouse. They certainly need protecting from idiotic flatcoats.

I had a fun afternoon playing with my new microphone. As usual, it's always a gamble whether another internet-sourced bit of Chinese tat will actually work, but it did. It was a challenge getting software to talk to hardware, but eventually everything worked. I did a couple of 'test' reads of the latest FonF and dabbled with editing and boosting treble levels (although that's probably just my ears at fault) and ended up with a four-minute hi-definition reading. There was the slight issue of it being far too big a file to send to anyone, so I'll have to make some enquiries as to how I get it to *Farmers Weekly*. It's a good start, though. My quest to find a new job that is about as far away as is possible from sitting in a tractor might have finally succeeded – although the material being read out is about sitting in a tractor. Funny old world.

February 21st

Yet another worst storm EVAH came through in the night. Mind you, it was grim. I had to sleep with the windows all shut and Classic FM on loud. Good thing we're one of the lucky ones with power still on. Hazel's early walk revealed a chestnut tree toppled over onto the gates at the bottom of the hill – but somehow missing the hanging post.

My attempts to complete my first ever spoken version of Flindt on Friday weren't going very well. I'd had a play with Audacity and Windows Voice Recorder, and got some fairly chunky files ready to send to *Farmers Weekly*, but the files were too big to send. Email couldn't handle them, and my Dropbox account kept on deciding (after a few minutes of uploading) that it didn't want them either.

Only one man to ask in these situations: Matt Hopper, DJ, radio producer and the man who asked me to do some voiceover work many years ago. I sent him a long and complicated description of the issue. Within half a minute, I got a three-word reply (he's a very busy man, obviously): "We use WeTransfer." Half an hour later, my 25MB file had arrived successfully on FW's desk.

We had another long session with Chris the Land Agent to run through all our options as the Big Plan looms closer and closer. We had hoped that we'd slowly eliminate all the different possibilities until one obvious one emerged – but there was no chance of that. We talked through all the environmental schemes (the more lucrative, the more work needed, of course), possible ways to dispose of our entitlements (lease/sell), the pros and cons of taking the new 'retirement' lump sum and the pros and cons of keeping them and making the most of the decoupling payments thingy.

As usual, my brain fogged over after a bit, but even I picked up that if we were happy filling in forms and letting the men with clipboards roam all over the farm, there are ways of raising remarkable sums by sowing the right mixtures of stuff out in the fields. I couldn't help thinking that we would still be farming – which sort of defeats the purpose. In an ideal world, our financial position would mean we can do what we want and not have to tell anyone. Nice idea, but is it practical in the long term? Blimey – a lot to think about.

The farmhouse attic has had more attention in the last few months that it has had in years – today we were up there cutting a piece of plywood to cover the hole left where a pane of glass blew out sometime over the last few days. Ah, the joys of being a National Trust tenant, with windows falling to pieces as we watch.

I took Sasha and Evie for a big loop from the Drier Yard up to Pipeline and Long Field, and back through White Hill, the Folly and Drier Field. Over two miles (according to that clever Mr Google), but worth more in muddy wellies. Although the mud isn't as bad as I'd thought up there. I think some tractor work might beckon soon.

Policeman Ian rang at teatime to discuss shotgun certificates. I'd sent him a half-serious text about how cross I was with Hants Constabulary Firearms Department for failing to post out a reminder about my certificate. Ian being Ian, he took it very seriously, and said he'd make some enquiries. I told him not to make too much of a fuss, otherwise my application might mysteriously end up at the bottom of the heap.

February 22nd

It's all very well having a farm littered with fallen trees, but our extensive range of chainsaws is in need of some serious TLC before we venture out gathering winter foo-ooo-eeeell. The diminutive and venerable Stihl MS180C, bought, if I remember rightly, after a huge gale ages ago (it was the last one on the shelf) is beginning to show its age. The throttle control is a bit iffy, the guide bar really needs replacement and the chain doesn't stop as suddenly as it should when 'throttle off'. I love it, though, with its easy-start system and tool-free chain tensioning system. Oh, and it doesn't weigh a ton. I gave it a thorough clean-up and a resharpen.

Then there's the Oregon CS300, a cordless saw with a 36V battery. I bought this a couple of winters ago when a shoulder was knackered (is it ever not knackered?) and it does very well for a bit of firewood processing in the lean- to. By the time the battery dies, you need a break, too. The handle's gone a bit wobbly after some over-zealous farm sawing, so that needed some tightening up. It needed topping up with oil, too, which sort of flies in the face of the eco idea. It's also a part of maintenance that's easy to forget when you're feeling smug for using no fossil fuels. The chain self-sharpens on a built-in stone (no danger from sparks as there's no petrol) which means one less chore.

The Makita EM2600L is a short chainsaw on a long pole. They always work better in the brochure than they do in the field, but they're handy for low hanging branches in gateways. It also now has a strimmer head and a hedgetrimmer attachment, but all of these aren't much use when the base unit won't run properly. I cleaned out filters and sparkplugs, but soon decided it was a carburettor problem, and I'm not good with carburettors. I Googled in vain for a replacement (I got one for the Honda mower for £15, all the way from China) and decided that was a job for another day.

It got dark and cold horribly early. Luckily, we had enough wood in stock to light a fire. And the Pots was even warmer for my evening with neighbour Robert.

February 23rd

A calm, cold and frosty start. It was enough to make me jump in Hazel's tractor and drive down to Joan's Acre to move the anti-poacher telegraph pole. I was all set up for another day's fertiliser, just in time for the long spell of fine weather which would mean that all the spring barley sowing would then take priority.

But no sooner had I got home and had a cuppa than another gale got up, everything clouded over, and it turned into another admin day. While Hazel went off to Alresford to give blood ("Have you had sex recently with anyone HIV positive?" they asked) I sat down and endured my own little blood- letting ordeal: I needed to order more farm diesel. I could probably wait for a day or two, but something tells me that things in Ukraine are not going to drive prices down. I went through the usual procedure, ringing round my usual range of suppliers, and managed to get one quote just under 80p/litre, which I jumped at. It's a heck of a price hike from the last order, which was 50p/litre, but there's not exactly anything one can do about it. They promised delivery on Monday, so I must remember to get the main tank clear before then.

Paul the NT Ranger called in for a chat and more tea – we've very keen to keep talking to as many relevant parties as possible as the Big Plan gets nearer, although Paul made it clear that he's not fully informed as to what the Trust's plans are. Wheels move very slowly at the Trust. I suspect that there will be a whole lot of nothing happening out there on our old fields for some time. I doubt it will be pretty, but, hey, that won't be our problem anymore.

I stayed indoors after that and did office stuff.

February 24th

The 'light rain' that was promised for this morning arrived just after six, with some terrifying gusts and a ten-minute deluge. My plans to get back in the tractor seem to get pushed back further and further every day.

Not to worry – there's an article to be written for *Farmers Weekly*, and just for a change, it was one that had been brewing for a few days in my head. It needed careful phrasing – being about the project to rediscover all those lost footpaths – but I had it done by lunchtime.

By then, snow showers were piling in, and my session down at the grain store with a torch and a tyre lever, trying to mend the bottom of the roller shutter doors where they had been blown out of their vertical guide rails, was not fun.

Of course, all of this was eclipsed by events in Ukraine. It's an ill wind (as they say) as wheat shot up £20/t to add to the £12/t boost that was caused by rumours of the Russian invasion. I didn't dare look at the diesel price, but I was still pleased I'd ordered just in time.

On Tuesday, in the pub, neighbour Robert and I hatched a plan to go back down there tonight and gatecrash the NFU social event that was taking place.

Or, if they won't let us in, pull faces/moon at the window. This plan was going swimmingly well until I checked the copy of the NFU's invite that someone had sent me, to ask if I'd be going. (He didn't know I'd resigned from the NFU.) The event was March 24th, not February 24th. I rang Robert with the news, but we decided we'd head down anyway. I'd already had a shower and wasn't going to waste all that soapy hard work.

February 25th

My column in *Farmers Weekly* had a new banner across the top of it; "Go online to FWi and listen to Charlie read this column!" it said. Blimey, it didn't take them long to approve the idea. I thought I'd strike while the iron's hot, and get the next column recorded. It didn't take long, and my post-pub voice was particularly sexy (though I say it myself). I'm even starting to get the hang of the editing features in Audacity – it was tempting to add reverb and some autotune, but I stuck with chopping out the cock-ups and the pauses that were too long. Five minutes on WeTransfer, and it was done and dusted. What a funny new world.

Old school farming beckoned in the afternoon. Hazel's bouncy and incredibly shouty cattle are due TB tests next week, which meant we had to assemble the handling kit. We dragged half a dozen metal hurdles and the crush out the brambles and got them all set up on the concrete next to the back barn. It didn't take long – those metal hurdles were the best buy we made all those years ago when Hazel was starting the suckler herd. God, it seems a million years ago – pre-children, pre-BSE, back in the days when you could keep cattle (including a bull, FFS) on your pastures…

Having ordered more red diesel, I thought I ought to make sure there's room for it in the main tank. I filled Hazel's tractor to the brim, did the same with mine, and then played 'diesel barn Tetris' to get the bowser near enough to the main tank to fill it. Quite hard work moving the bowser, the sheep trailer, Pig and the Deere ride-on mower over a muddy barn floor. In the end, only about 300 litres needed draining out to leave the tank ready for the spring fill.

And to finish off an enthusiastic Friday, I sat down with a bit of paper and a calculator and did my Trinity Grain harvest commitments. Only four crops this year, of course – no break crops – and some creative button pushing resulted in nearly a thousand tonnes both 'off the combine' at harvest, and in the long pool to be sold from September onwards. All very encouraging, although the manic spike in prices after the Ukraine invasion seems to have dropped almost as much as it went up. Profit taking by the funds, I assume.

February 26th

The world did seem to be drying out enough to maybe provoke a bit of farm work, but after a walk across Hurst Down with three dogs (and a thousand hares and two dozen deer) I decided that it was still too sticky – and the wind (still cold, still strong) would have wrecked the application of liquid fertiliser. The rugby was fantastic. France were magnificent against Scotland, and England beat Wales once they'd woken up from their first half snooze.

February 27th

Hazel was off by seven with Tim for her dog-training day, I did a walk with three other dogs, and then settled down for a hugely disappointing Ireland vs Italy game. I got myself fired up for the rugby by challenging a walker in the middle of Chalks. He'd been there for some time by the time I caught up with him, and he had an out-of-control mongrel swinging round on a very long line. I did my normal "you look lost!" line – very topical, as that's the next *Farmers Weekly* column – and had the usual run of fantastic excuses. "But I live in Bramdean." (I won't say the real address he gave). "It's a rescue dog!" No, really. Bend me over and call me Susan, what a surprise. "It's too dangerous to take it on the footpath!" Suddenly, fencing off Dead Dog Farm (as I'm keen to call the bit of farm we're keeping) seems more attractive an idea than ever.

You can bet half the farm on Italy losing, but there was an early sending off of a hooker, then his replacement got injured, scrums were then uncontested – and Italy had to play on with only 13 men. Something to do with a rule change after a game when a lot of dodgy injuries were claimed in a front row. All very confusing.

Towards the end, they had another man yellow-carded, and ended the game with twelve. As a prop, I never understood the laws of rugby – and today's events proved that nothing has changed. Ireland should really have got into three figures. A slightly flat way to end a weekend of rugby. I should have got the drill up and running and bashed in some spring barley on the light ground. Ho hum.

February 28th

Finally, a proper farming day. Sarah the vet was on the doorstep at eight thirty (I'm sure we'd agreed nine when she rang yesterday, but somehow her schedule had crept on by half an hour) and we all got togged up for the first half of the TB test on Hazel's dopey moos. Well, Sarah did anyway: waterproof overalls, plastic gloves, lots of sterile scrubbing and sloshing. Hazel and I just put wellies on.

The cattle were, of course, angelic, slotting quietly into the crush with hardly a murmur for the 'shave, measure and jab' routine. It was all very calm, and we gossiped all the way through. Sarah is another one of the local vets that we've known for too many years to count. It was all over in an hour, and Sarah disrobed and sped off, politely declining the offer of a cuppa on the quite sensible grounds that she was just back from a skiing holiday, and there's no better breeding ground for nasty viruses of any sort than the fuselage of a holiday jet. Very wise.

I had a cuppa anyway, and having checked the domestic oil level in our tank and found it precariously low, ordered another batch. Once again, the phones were chaotic – some unanswered, some cut me off at random – and the prices were terrifying. But we need it, and there's nothing you can do but breathe in and place the order.

Tractor work beckoned, at last, and I set off to do a first dose of liquid fert on the late drilled Skyscraper in Hurst Down and JA/DC. It was dry as a bone after the weekend's high and dry wind, and I hardly made a mark. Mind you, I could hardly see my mark in places, and managed to miss the second land work tramline, probably by counting eight turns of the drill as if it had been sown with the CO3 rather than with the ST4. Oh well. If I can't find a tramline after all these years, I really should be retiring.

Joan's Acre and Dell Close are probably the weakest crops on the farm at the moment, but I'm not ordering any more seed now. Some rain and a bit of warmth to stimulate what plants there are there (along with the 135l/ha of N35(S) I was applying) is what they need.

The rain came in just as I was finishing and went on hard into the night. There goes all the weekend's drying. Bother.

March 1st

My computer had a funny turn. I switched it on before making my porridge, as usual, and by the time I got back to it, something didn't look right. The screensaver had changed, and all the hundreds of 'icons' had gone. It decided that I should use 'Bing' as my thingy engine, and, worst of all, I couldn't find anything in the 'documents' folder – and that includes all the writing stuff and decades' worth of photos. After a great deal of swearing and all-round panic, Hazel stepped in (ex-programmer), did some tweaks, and did a 'restart'. Everything was cured. The wonderful *IT Crowd* springs to mind.

As a result, I had time to get the review of the Alfa Giulia done and sent off before out National Trust agent arrived for a cuppa and chat about the Big Plan. She was waving paperwork for the last half-year of the tenancy on Godwin's (it's on a rolling FBT) and the tenancy for the new down-sized shoot that will start in three years' time. But it all seemed very positive, and everyone still seems very happy with the deal. I tried to get the message across – again – that they will need to put fences or ditches around the fields they're taking back if they have no immediate plans for them. Hare coursing is a nuisance, but it is nothing compared to waking up one morning to find ten lorries' worth of asbestos has been dumped overnight.

She'd only just gone when the ex-Editor arrived (Tuesday morning? The joys of retirement) – more tea, more gossip, and a totally missed chance to get him to witness/sign all the documents we'd just been given. Not to worry – far better to just sit and gossip.

The red diesel arrived safely, which should set us up nicely for the next few months – if the sun ever comes out again. Last night's rain kept going all day, although it was slightly warmer, thank goodness; the lack of heating oil meant we'd turned off the central heating to prioritise the Aga.

Tomorrow I'm off to Liverpool to tell my joke to another roomful of drunk farmers, which meant the Octavia needed a check over. The tyres were all good, although the spare (a full size one, bought off eBay shortly after we bought the car) needed a couple of psi. The oil was a bit low, but I had half a litre of whizzy super synthetic in the garage, so put that in. I miss the days when you could raid the farm drum of 'universal'. A quick top-up of windscreen washer fluid and she was ready for the 500-mile road trip.

March 2nd

Tod was round early for a catch-up and a crop walk-round. Well, he walked round, I didn't. We also checked out the spray store; in an ideal world, I will do my last ever tank of spray in a few months' time and come back to an empty spray store. It'll take some skill and judgement to achieve that, I think. We also discussed the philosophy of this season's spraying: in theory, we'll apply pesticides to avoid yield loss, but not for weed control for future years. I did ask the Trust during the Big Plan discussions if they wanted us to farm with the next farmer (whoever that might be) in mind, but they seemed happy that we think of all that arable land being 'wound up'. With every passing day, events in Ukraine suggest that it's a lunatic policy, but we've signed the agreement, so it's no skin off our noses.

I had an early lunch and set off for Lancashire at about twelve thirty. The roads are busy again, and I treated myself to a couple of leisurely comfort breaks. As a result, I reached the smart new house where I was staying around five thirty. It was still daylight, which always makes finding a venue slightly easier. My hosts were ex-dairy farmers who had undergone a major life change – selling up and moving out – over the last few years. The smart modern house was warm and cosy and filled with all the paraphernalia of a farmhouse: upright piano, barometer, grandfather clock, and, of course, a couple of lively jack russells. The kitchen table was magnificent; a bit of old farm machinery had been shotblasted and painted, and then a thick piece of glass was attached to it somehow.

After a quick cuppa and a shower, we set off to the hotel for the dinner. There were about seventy attending – all men, which I soon discovered was a bit of an issue up there at that time – and it was back to the more traditional post-dinner (rather than pre-) routine for the speech. I think it went down well. Everyone chuckled at the right places, and I made a point of explaining to the youngsters there what 'land girls' and 'Wrens' were. I'd been caught out with blank faces when I'd made references to them in a room full of forty-somethings in Lincolnshire the other day, and wasn't making that mistake again.

Best of all, they bought books – lots of them. I took what I thought was an optimistic seventy-two copies (two boxes of Book One, and two boxes of Book Two) and sold nearly fifty. I don't charge a fee to speak, so coming away with a roll of notes is perfect. Everyone seemed very grateful, and the whole evening had a sense of camaraderie. It was lovely overhearing some people greeting each other after two years apart.

I was out for the count almost as soon as my head hit the pillow. And I'd only drunk one pint.

March 3rd

No sign of 'strange bed' syndrome – I slept really well. I had a very strange dream about Granny Flindt, which was probably brought on by all those references to Wrens last night.

My hosts had rung round a few chums and invited them over for breakfast bacon butties, which turned into a continuation of lasts night's dinner. I sold more books, got more friendly insults, and had to text Hazel for a string of answers to a string of questions about our cattle. I could manage "they're black" and that's about it. There was also a young writer from *Farmers Weekly*'s deadly rival, *Farmers Guardian* – the farming magazine that is probably more at home up there in the north-west. She was local, in her twenties, tiny, flame red-haired, and (please note I use this word only in extreme circumstances) passionate about her 'salt marsh beef'. A bit like the Lincolnshire farmers at the last dinner – if she's the future of farming, we can all relax. As breakfast finished, Hazel texted to say her cattle had passed the TB test.

I had a quick walk with my hostess along some lanes and paths, and I think even she would admit that the flat sodden black earth of the south Lancashire plain on a wet drizzly March morning was unlikely to feature in an English countryside calendar. I took a picture of it anyway.

My plan to save fuel by offloading books was scuppered by a free bag of potatoes which somehow made it into the back of the Skoda, but the onboard computer suggested I should make it home without refilling. The motorway fuel price was already over £1.70/litre.

There was a bizarre run of calls to my mobile (left safely on the passenger seat, please note). It is hard to tell how many were 'live' calls, and how many were 'voicemails', but the annoying ringtone (still set at 'in the tractor' volume) went on for about an hour. I showed great restraint in not answering them or throwing the phone out of the car window into the interminable M6 roadworks.

A comfort break beckoned on the M6 Toll service. (God, how we love the M6 Toll – quiet, fast, smooth, if a tad expensive.) I could finally sort out the phone calls. I'd missed three: one from the NFU pensions team wanting to know if the accounts were back yet. Another was from the organiser of next week's dinner, asking if I was still OK for it, and the third was a more serious one. It was from one the tenants in the cottages, experiencing a rat 'swarm' in his little semi. We had one of these a couple of years ago in the yard. It was terrifying out there in the open, so God knows what it's like to have one in a tiny house. He said that that they are digging and chewing their way in through every hole possible – and he's got young children in the house. I rang him back and said I'd get our rat control man sorted as soon as I could. As I swung back onto the motorway, I decided I'm not going to miss being a 'landlord'.

The McDonald's magnet worked its magic again, and that, combined with the 500-mile round trip in mostly rain, and the enormous dinner, meant that I wasn't that disappointed when neighbour Robert rang to cry off the scheduled pub trip. Mrs Robert has tested positive, and he thought it wise and responsible to stay at home. It suited me fine, and an early night beckoned. But not before I'd rung the organiser of the next dinner to say that yes, I was on – and asked about logistics. Numbers, microphone, dress code – all that sort of stuff. It all seemed under control except that there was a mumble of disapproval when I said I didn't have a suit that fitted me at the moment. That was my cue to get onto the internet and order a cheap 'n' cheerful suit from M&S. I'd been meaning to get one for ages, as the shoot flapjacks have been so reluctant to shift. I miss the post-hip op days, when I got down to fourteen-and-a-bit stone. I'm now back over seventeen.

Hazel had very kindly changed all the sheets while I was away, and a bed without Cain's (and Abel's, now he is turning into a house cat) grit and hairballs is very welcome.

March 4th

So much for sleeping the sleep of a thousand nights; at some stage in the early hours, something moved into my head armed with a 4lb club hammer, and spent the next few hours banging against my skull from the inside. It was probably a reaction to dehydration (I never drink enough water on those trips) or a lack of caffeine (my tea intake drops from a dozen cups to a couple). Or the McDonald's.

In a way, it was a good thing; I needed to get up and write the next column with a certain amount of urgency, but it meant that I was on the paracetamol a bit early, and on an empty stomach, which isn't a good thing. They worked, though, and 600 words on the frustration of the computer having a funny turn reached FW's desk nice and early.

The rest of the day was quiet. Everything was still soaked from the rain, and I didn't fancy doing the tractor shuffle that will be needed before I can get any drilling done. Our rat control man arrived (Hazel had summoned him after the panic phone call from one of our tenants) and headed off to the little semi. I wished him luck.

Feed wheat touched £300/tonne. Scary.

March 5th

A freezing north wind set in, good for drying, not much good for persuading us that spring is here. There was no rugby on the telly, not even a couple of Saturday films. I took Sasha on the Drier loop (grateful that I'd donned hat, gloves and scarf) and snoozed on the sofa anyway. Hazel popped into Petersfield to pick up the suit I'd ordered. I'd chosen the biggest possible trousers, which fitted fine. I'd ordered the biggest possible jacket, which also fitted fine. On a whim, I'd ordered a waistcoat, in the biggest possible size. There was room for three fat farmers in it. It might have to go back.

There were flakes of sleet in the air for much of the day, too – but the forecast suggests that some dry weather is coming. Mind you, they said just that about the week just gone. That's another thing I'm not going to miss; being let down by the weather muppets.

March 6th

Hazel was off dog training again – it being Sunday – and I thought I really ought to get ready for some drilling, what with all the fine weather on the way. First job, unhitch the sprayer from the Deere. All its pipes are full of liquid fertiliser, so there no worry about frost damage if the frosts do return as promised. Then down to the Drier Yard to hitch onto the ST4 and pull it out of the left-hand lean-to, where it has been living, nice and dry, since the end of autumn drilling. There was a lot of dry mud to be shed as it rolled out of the barn, and it was quite a challenge to find the air valves for the rear tyres. Many of them were flat, which was a bit worrying; I hope it's just after the long layoff rather than permanent punctures. I hitched the drill back off and drove home. I swapped the Deere for the Massey, and loaded up the old bale trailer – rustier than ever – with nine bags of Planet spring barley and headed back down to the Drier Yard. After reversing the trailer into the now vacant left-hand lean-to, I took one bag off and put it in the ST4.

Then home again, to swap tractors (again), and find all my calibrating kit: three buckets and the wonderful but temperamental digital scales. Back down to the Drier for a calibrate. There was much confusion as I thought the batch number ('38') was the thousand grain weight, which suggested a seed/sq. m. rate of well over 500. In the end, I divided the delivered tonnage by the area to be sown, and came up with an entirely plausible 200kg/ha, and stuck with that.

I drove carefully along the lane from the Drier to New Pond, and then up the track and into BOMS. I even marked it out, ready to make a start tomorrow, and parked up behind the trees – safely, I hope. Hazel, now home from dog training, had driven Tigger down to the Drier Yard and walked the dogs home, so all I had to do was walk over to the Drier from BOMS and head home for tea and buns. Much deserved, I reckon. I was bloomin' knackered. There's a lot of inter-tine yoga that goes on when calibrating, and I'm not as flexible as I was. I blame shoot flapjacks.

March 7th

The headline of the next *Farmers Weekly* column didn't feel right, and over breakfast a better version came to mind. They liked it, too, and changed it – and a couple of other minor things. I did a voice recording of it for them, even though they'd said they didn't really need it, and sent it over via WeTransfer.

Then – fanfare – farming. Once Hazel had fed the bellowing cattle (I think they're outstaying their welcome a bit) I grabbed the loader and set off. BOMS went like a dream, even though it has a lot of short work, no matter which way you sow it.

I had a little moment when I finished the last turn of headland. Another field sown for the last time, after centuries of arable farming. I consoled myself by making plans for the new 100-acre shoot that we'll be left with in a couple of years.

The question was then where to go next. It's tempting to crack on with the light stuff, and head over to BML's, but that's on the cusp of being ripped up for the installation of the new oil pipeline. The trench itself will take up a good portion of the field, and will probably cut off the far side of it. There's an imminent meeting with the pipeline team; I think I'll wait until I hear their plans before sowing that field.

Instead, I made a start on Rick/Clump. Rick, being another chalky one, was fine

– Clumps, slightly less fine. But I got through it and cracked on. A good roll after a day or two of this freezing wind will sort it out. By sunset, I'd done a respectable (for this farm) 38 acres.

The evening job was to get the Skoda down to North's garage for a service. It had started bonging at us about an oil change when I was on the way to Lancashire the other day. It's a mighty fine beast, so we want to keep it in tip-top condition.

It's nice to be proper busy again.

March 8th

A slightly frustrating drilling day. I had a bit of a session pumping up the Horsch's rear tyres (again – I knew I should have done a winter overhaul) so I didn't quite get Rick and Clump done before lunch. I then had a meeting with the National Trust and the team doing the new pipeline through the east end of the farm. The meeting was brief, and I managed to get all the information I needed – when's it starting (soon), will we have access points to get to 'cut off' bits of fields (yes) and when will it be finished (before harvest) – and could head off back to my tractor.

I finished Rick and Clump and after marking out what feels like several miles of headland around Big Field, made a start on the land work. I was once again interrupted, this time by an aged blue Defender 90 which arrived in the bottom gateway. It was, of course, neighbour Robert, out on patrol. It was just like the old days, when Dad would arrive in the field, and once the tractor/combine/sprayer had finally shut down, would say "Mustn't stop those who would work!"

Robert's still suffering from the Covid, so I stood well upwind and we shouted at each other from a distance. A bit like a typical evening in the Pots. He said he's feeling croaky and has a bit of a sore throat, but, thankfully, there's nothing else. "Thank God I've had all the jabs!" he said. It was tempting to shout back "Fat lot of good all those jabs did!" – but I didn't.

Diesel was running short on the new Deere sooner than expected – the ground is pretty tough in places, and I suspect it's not properly run in yet. I had a reasonably early finish. Hazel had done a long afternoon with the rollers, and the first bits of spring '22 drilling looked an absolute treat in the early March evening. Why are we giving up? Especially when wheat settled down a bit at £310/ton.

March 9th

The service on the Skoda was a reasonable £200, but the paperwork suggested a couple of issues when the MOT comes round in a month or so. There's a whine from the rear propshaft and some iffy rear brake disks. Still, it is well past 70,000 miles, so you can't be too surprised. While I was down at North's garage, I popped into the next-door barn, where the White Hunter cricket club captain has his hedge and tree business HQ.

He wasn't there, but up at the far end of the barn, almost hidden under mountains of ready-to-lay hedges was a figure, well wrapped up in hats, scarves and coats. She was going about her business unaware that I was standing in the huge doorway. It wasn't until I started doing John Travolta moves to the Abba track that was blasting out from one of those unbelievably small music machines that she noticed me.

Rather than scolding me for getting my musical genres mixed up, she asked if she could help. I said I was looking for Richard, because I need a whole bunch of planting done. She pointed out that she could help. I explained our situation – the Big Plan, and the project to fill Dead Dog Farm with new spinneys and copses for the downsized shoot. She said she knew exactly what I needed, and had had a lot of shooting people making the same sort of enquiry. Her only worry was that the planting season has only a couple of months left to run. I pointed out that we wouldn't be doing anything until after harvest – we agreed that we had plenty of time to come up with a plan or two. And, no, supplies weren't running short. And she never mentioned my Travolta routine.

I got another couple of bags of seed barley in the ground before lunch, and almost the same again after lunch, but got distracted by a vehicle that had driven into the Drier Yard. Its owner could be seen from the top of Big Field wandering about down there. I was already on the cusp of giving up early for the day, and drove the tractor all the way back to BOMS to see if I could catch it. It was, of course, the ex-Editor on pigeon patrol, although he'd headed off by the time I'd shut the tractor down and started to walk over for a chat. That was my cue to go home.

It's Growmore Quiz night, you see – and today we were away to Lymington Grockles. And when I say 'away', I mean 'away'. Down the M3 from Winchester, west along the M27, then off at Cadnam, south through Lyndhurst and Brockenhurst, and left into the depths of the Forest's curious semi-rural fringe to a tiny village called Boldre. We – four of us in neighbour John's BMW X3 – met up with the other two members of our team at a frightfully smart new memorial hall, but there was no sign of any oppo. One of the two rooms in the hall contained what looked like a bridge tournament, and the other sports hall section was still in darkness. One thing conspicuous by its absence was anything like a bar. Tod went looking for one, and reported back with a face like a wet weekend.

A second 'away' team then arrived, as baffled as we were to find no 'home' team, nothing set up, and, of course, no bar. Just as the worried phone calls were starting, a man in a hi-viz arrived and said "Petersfield Wey?" That's us. "Follow me!" So we did, down the lovely little high street to a well-worn pub, where chairs were set out for two teams, two scorers and, of course, the question master. And, it had a bar. D'oh.

A few hours later, we had lost again, had had a couple of very jolly beers with the oppo, and, in my case, been presented with an honorary hippo. You see, some months ago I told the story (in FW) of the young lad who arrived in the farmyard, overcome with excitement at a machinery tour. As he was going, he shrieked "gotta hippo?" out of nowhere. (His Mum said he just loved hippos.) I foolishly promised I'd have one when he came back to see the combine at harvest. I finished the article with a plea for a hippo, otherwise my new young best friend would never forgive me. I then forgot all about it. The good folk of Lymington Grockles, however, had taken this very seriously. They had borrowed a vast bronze hippo from someone's garden, put it in the back of a truck, then onto a trolley, and into the pub. They wrapped it in a Hippobag (of course), and wheeled it out at the end of the quiz. There was a surreal moment as the three-foot-high hippo was presented to me and then wheeled away again. We'd had a few beers already, so it all made perfect sense. I got to keep the multiple packets of HobNobs that were in its mouth, though. Not that I need them at all.

On the long drive back, talk turned to filming Book Two, and who would play whom. Kenneth Branagh for me, of course, and Rene Russo for Hazel, but the most challenging ones were Mr and Mrs Literary Agent in their gorgeous Arts and Craft house up the Joan's Acre valley. We settled on Bill Nighy and Catherine Deneuve. And we agreed we'd tell no one about the discussion. Oh bother.

March 10th

A good writing morning. I got the next FonF done, and the next test car – a Honda Civic – was safely and efficiently delivered. The driver was not of these parts, so I asked him where he was from. It turned out he was Polish, and a short but depressing chat ensued about the state of his homeland. Hazel very kindly took him to the station so he could get back to base, and I headed back into the office.

By lunchtime, I had done all I could do to the speech for tomorrow, and thought I'd do some more drilling. I loaded up the trailer with nine bags of barley seed, took them down to the left-hand lean-to and then carefully brought one bag over to where the drill was parked. I put it in the drill, drove over to Big Field and finished the land work. It was all short work, above and below the trees. You just have to go into a drilling 'trance' and put up with the fact that you spend as much time turning as you actually do drilling. It was nice to get it done as the forecast has got much worse for tomorrow. Heavy rain is imminent.

I brought the tractor and drill back to New Pond, hitched off the drill and drove the tractor home. Hazel had finished her afternoon's bookkeeping at the stables by now and I gave her a lift out in Tigger to pick up the loader tractor. We got everything safely home and parked in the yard ready for the long weekend.

March 11th

What you want for a long drive up to Norfolk is a nice dry day and lots of free-flowing roads. What I got was a deluge and lots of Friday traffic jams – the traffic has reached pre-pandemic proportions. The little Honda was lovely though, and made the drive much more interesting

The heavy traffic started at Oxford and kept going pretty well all the way up into East Anglia. The satnav took me off the main roads at March and out into the Fens. It was bad enough keeping going in a straight line while open-mouthed at the surrounding countryside (the like of which I'd never seen before) without the state of the roads themselves. Yes, they were straight, but they were rough as hell, with dips and bumps that suggested the ground underneath wasn't that stable. I found myself driving much too fast and in danger of being thrown off into one of the deep ditches, or rivers, or whatever they're called. I managed to bottom the Honda a couple of times.

The strong wind had blown over a 'road closed' sign at one stage and I ended up, after merrily driving up the road, having to do a very awkward U-turn when I reached the roadworks, and head back on myself. You might have thought the hard-working chaps in the diggers, and the ten hi-viz-clad supervisors, all watching the hole, might have wondered why so many cars were failing to stop coming up that bit of road, but obviously not.

The satnav then took me through even more remote countryside, which featured some irrational bends and corners, and I finally arrived at the hotel a good hour later than I thought I would do.

I still had time for a bit of a snooze and a good shower once I'd checked in and my host Tim picked me up on the dot of 6.15. We headed into Downham Market where 70 or 80 farmers were gathering in the Town Hall. They were very hospitable and determined to have a good time after the last couple of years. First job: judge the photography competition, which was a first for me. I think my speech went down well, especially now I've inserted a paragraph explaining to the young people what landgirls and Wrens are, although the average age of the audience suggested that no explanation was needed. I sold nearly forty books – which effectively pays my 'fee' – and they raised £600 in the raffle for the air ambulance. I'm hoping a cheque will wing its way to RABI as well. It was nearly midnight when we climbed into Tim's double cab pickup, slightly tiddly, and headed back to the hotel, and with much thanks and cheerful waves we went our separate ways

The hotel was in complete darkness. The front doors were all locked and unlit. I had a slightly scary moment: how on earth will I get in? Where the hell was I going to sleep? I didn't have a phone – I'd left it in my bag – and as far as I could tell I was stuck outside for the night. I had my room key/card and I looked in vain for some sort of slot to put it in to open the hotel's main door. I had the Honda keys and at one stage thought that using the Honda was going to be my only option, either to sleep in or to drive home in the dead of night; all the roads were empty, so it should only take three hours. It was a bit of a panic moment.

"This is stupid," I thought. "No hotel stays completely locked all night and it's only about midnight – not three in the morning!" I worked my way around the outside of the hotel checking all the doors, half expecting alarms to go off at any stage. Finally, I came across a well-lit door which opened automatically as I approached it. It was quite a relief, even though I was still in a strange part of the hotel, and it took me ten minutes to find my room. I felt a complete idiot. Just as the adrenaline of the evening – and the door-based idiocy – was wearing off, I had a text message from a local farmer who had called in at Hinton Ampner last summer while on holiday. They called in for a cuppa and a farm walk, and it turned into a long evening in the Flowerpots with neighbour Robert. He'd heard somehow that I was in the parish – one of their friends had 'Whatsapped' a picture of me flogging books – and insisted that I called in tomorrow on the way home. I decided to reply in the morning when I felt a bit more human.

March 12th

I didn't sleep brilliantly; the mattress was a bit squishy and at some stage in the night there was a twang from the bottom of my back. Always a worrying sign when there's another 180-mile journey to be done. Maybe the Honda seats weren't as good as I thought they were. I texted Mick, the local farmer, to say I'd be delighted to call in, and got a postcode off him. He was about 20 minutes away, which would be perfect if an early comfort break was needed

Porridge and a full English breakfast beckoned, not that I needed it after last night's dinner, and after I had re-packed I had a stroll through the village, alongside the huge river-type thing. 'Well Creek', I think it was called, which sounded a bit like my lower back felt. I walked as far as a magnificent church, and spent half an hour staring up at its towers in genuine awe – and that was enough to take my mind off back pain. I felt much better on the walk back to the hotel. The Miracle of Outwell they'll be calling it in years to come.

I warned the girl doing my checkout that CCTV might show a nutter trying all the doors late last night, and that that nutter was me. I think they understood my story, although they probably put me down as some weird bloke from down South. I was on the road by about nine fifteen.

Mick had a lovely new farmhouse just west of March, easily found with just a postcode. I had a warm welcome and an equally welcome cup of tea. There was a brief farm tour although the type of farming they do up there is completely wasted on me: potatoes, mustard and sugar beet. We exchanged words with the three lads putting Stocks dual wheels on a new Fendt and I couldn't help having laugh at the idea of taking such a monster machine down one of Hampshire's sunken lanes. At least there would be room for a car to drive underneath it.

I wanted to be home in time for the rugby, so I cracked on. I had thought the roads would be a bit emptier, it being Saturday. But, of course, the world turns out in its thousands to visit shopping centres on Saturdays, and the queues were fifteen or twenty minutes long every time a ring road met a 'retail park'. By the time I reached the hideous construction mess just south-west of Northampton where the A45 and the M1 meet, I was beginning to get a bit fed up. Even the multiple roundabouts on the way down to the M40 seemed pleasant after that.

The Honda seemed to gobble fuel – either that or the fuel tank was very small – and I had to stop and put £25 worth in at one stage. It didn't fill the fuel tank very much, what with the price being £1.78 per litre but it did mean I was at least going to get home. The Winchester services McDonald's magnet pulled me off the road again, which is fast becoming a tradition.

All seemed well at home. Hazel had had the ex-Editor in for a long coffee at some stage, discussing plans for the shoot on Dead Dog Farm, and Bev, one of our nannies that we employed all those years ago and are still in touch with, called in for a long catch-up. Hazel mentioned to her our plans, and the fact that we might be converting barns for diversification. Bev seemed very interested. She does bespoke jewellery and silverwork, and said she would be keen on a little workshop. We might fill our barns more easily than we thought we would.

The Scotland vs Italy game was over by the time I'd made a cup of tea and settled down on the sofa, And I slept through the first ten minutes of England versus Ireland, which meant I missed the crucial sending off of an England player after only 80 seconds. It was still a thriller though, even if England did understandably run out of steam with ten minutes to go. Mind you, I did, too, well before ten o'clock. A fantastically busy couple of days.

March 13th

Not a great night sleep. Lots of wind, lots of rain, a completely unnecessary burger and a back that was still a bit stiff. I managed to get up in time to see Hazel off on another day's dog training at Mullenscote. She left without a dog of her own this time, as Tim is feeling a bit sorry for himself. A couple of days ago, all the dogs charged into the brambles outside the tractor barn, chasing something, and she thinks Tim ran into a bit of machinery. He's got a sore head and can't pick anything up – which isn't much good if you're a retriever. Poor chap – he was mortified to be left behind.

I had a quiet morning. I got the Sunday papers and read them cover to cover. They don't make very good reading at the moment – unless you're a farmer trying to sell wheat and not in the market to buy fertiliser for next year, of course. I took Sasha out on the Hurst Down loop and was amazed to see how the wheat has moved on. I couldn't quite tell if it had taken up the fertiliser I put on a few days ago. The untreated triangles around telegraph poles didn't seem to be a lighter shade of green, anyway.

The Bottom of Hurst Down is looking as good as I've seen it in many years, although much of the wheat out there is probably volunteers from last year's crop. We haven't grown second wheat for ages, so it's a pleasant surprise seeing it look so good. It won't 'hide a hare in March', but it's certainly not in the realms of 'shall we rip it up?' It looks quite encouraging at £300 a tonne.

We have tried to avoid watching Crufts in recent years. It has become an infantile doggy version of Blue Peter, but there seems to have been a change in attitude. It seems much more grown-up these days. We also had to watch it because there was a flatcoat retriever involved. It had won the gundog class and was putting on a master display of loveability in the 'Best in Show' section. It was a bittersweet moment when he won – a joy to see a flatcoat retriever winning, but sad that it will now become a trendy breed. I told Hazel to get on and breed with Evie. The winning flatcoat did a fabulous victory lap with the rosette in its mouth, and the commentators even mentioned 'gun dogs' and 'shooting'. Best of all, the dog didn't go charging off into the crowd and bang his head on anything.

March 14th

All that driving around the country finally caught up with me, and I decided I'd have an indoor morning. I did a recording of the *Farmers Weekly* article once I'd agreed their proof, and gave the thumbs up to *The Field* for the proof of the Giulia review. The world was still sodden after the weekend's rain but I hitched the tractor onto the sprayer anyway, just in case tomorrow is dry enough for another batch of fertiliser before I start drilling again.

Some fencing was needed. Murph's sheep are arriving imminently, and Hazel's boundary walkabout found that the kissing gate near the church was knackered. No surprise, really – the foot traffic through it is huge. We loaded up Pig with fencing kit and squelched our way across the top of Englands. It was quite a relief that Pig started – the rats have developed a taste for the length of blue foam that we put across a sharp edge to protect the dogs when jumping in and out, and they've moved on to assorted pipes and wiring.

Once we'd made the kissing gate safe by banging in a couple of extra posts and repairing a couple of rails, we parked Pig in the calf pens, hoping it'll be a bit safer there. I had a rummage in the stable for the rat traps that I brought back from the Conder bins a few weeks ago, found Hazel's rat trap mix in the tub in the kitchen, and set four traps in Pig's barn. Well, you've got to do something.

The next livestock job was selling the cattle. You might think that this would be a long drawn-out process with endless negotiations and multiple buyers, but Phil the Farmer – who's been buying our cattle for some years – popped out in the afternoon, and the whole deal was done in minutes in the barn. It was the post-deal coffee that took the time. There was an awful lot to catch up on the state of farming, the price of this, the price of that, young people, old people, the ten thousand things that are going on in our industry. It was a well spent couple of hours putting the world to rights. And how many times has that happened in our kitchen in the last 500 years?

There's a tour coming up for the band, which meant that some rehearsals are desperately needed. We had a full house, Tod managed to get the in-ear monitors sorted out for the first time (which kept volumes level low), and we had an excellent rehearsal. You know a rehearsal is good when you glance at your phone and it's 9:50. You don't realise you've been playing for nearly two hours. Despite the extra sound insulation I've put into Shed 3b, I still like to knock off before ten, so we called it a night. A very satisfactory evening.

March 15th

There's big rain on the way tomorrow apparently – although you wouldn't believe it from the fabulous sunrise which had me leaning out of the bedroom window taking photographs. It was a sort of morning that Granny Flindt would have called a 'weathermaker'.

The ground was dry enough to keep going with some fertiliser, so I did the first wheats, which haven't had any yet. Only about 50 kg per hectare but that should look after them for a bit. The Folly looked a bit pale, but the Godwin's block looked as green as anything; it's different soil altogether. I had a very strange series of WhatsApp messages from a complete stranger, all about caravans and those who live in them. Apparently there was a green Subaru causing havoc somewhere in the country. I messaged back saying "I think you've got the wrong number, but I also think I know exactly what's going on; good luck!" Whoever it was replied, appreciative and apologetic.

The accountant came up for a brainstorming session after lunch. We fed him as much information as we could about what the next eighteen months hold, and he jotted down copious notes. We threw a few ideas backwards and forwards across the kitchen table, but, as usual, as soon as the word 'tax' was mentioned I clouded over completely and just nodded as if I knew what I was on about. The good news was that my decision to buy a new tractor and a new combine in the last year have actually paid off. Quite remarkably, I've managed to make a good tax decision with them.

I realised that the fertiliser tank was probably getting empty after the last couple of weeks and did some sums in the tractor cab which suggested that I had room for another lorry-load. I found the Yara number, my account number, and took my life in my hands and gave them a ring. I was half expecting much tooth-sucking and "Oh no, we haven't got any for another month", but it was all business as usual. "Would delivery by Friday be OK?" the chap on the phone asked. I said that would be fine. And that was that. We won't mention the price though.

Neighbour Robert rang sounding utterly fed up with doing bloody Covid tests and demanding that we go to the pub anyway. We headed down to the Flowerpots for a short-ish evening. He looked pale and had obviously lost a lot of weight with the virus, and only managed three pints – so he must have been ill. Hazel was very surprised to see me back well before 10 o'clock.

March 16th

Vast flocks of pigeons have found the spring barley seedbeds. I'm not sure they're doing any damage at this stage – they're probably cleaning stuff off the surface. But there was no sign of the ex-Editor whom I'd texted the other day, and I thought it was time to move them on somehow. I grabbed Sasha and a box of rope bangers, and we had a yomp across the surprisingly dry mud. We put two ropes out and were just heading back to New Pond when we saw a senior looking fellow with two dogs just starting up the track. I called Sasha in, and of course the first thing she wants to know is why she's being called in. It was that much harder to get her out of attack mode and into the truck as a result.

The senior looking fellow was in fact Graeme the ex-vet out for his morning constitutional. We had a good ten-minute chat – he's fascinated to know what our plans are and what's happening, but we had to move on because the drizzle was getting heavier. The sky was getting pinker, just as the forecasters had said it would, as a cloud of Sahara sand was headed over us, and the rain hitting the windscreen was a pink-brown. It was quite bizarre. By late morning it was coming on very hard – we won't be drilling for a day or two.

The ex-Editor did turn up in the end, but didn't do any pigeon shooting. On went the kettle, and a lengthy planning session for the small shoot on Dead Dog Farm ensued. It was agreed that he would try and pull some strings in the Game Conservancy and get a free set of advice as to what we should do with our 120 acres. He was confident that we could get some wise words out of one consultant in particular for nothing more than a good pub lunch.

The Honda is due to go back tomorrow, so I thought I'd put a few more miles on it – not least get rid of the petrol I put in it the other day. I drove to Alresford to pick up another huge batch of pills and creams. The chemists were unbelievably cheerful – no masks to be seen, and there was much laughter when I couldn't immediately come up with my first name. "I've come for my dementia pills," I claimed afterwards. Political correctness hasn't reached Alresford yet, so we could all still have a chuckle at my stunning wit. I pointed out that I'm on a prepaid card now that I get so many prescriptions every month. She pointed out that I'm now over 60, and I wouldn't be paying anyway. How depressing.

March 17th

Something tells me I'm going to get an awful lot of dreams like the one I had last night. It was a crystal-clear re-enactment of shutting down all the machinery in the grain store at the end of harvest. Every single button, every single motor, all the sequences, all the noises – as if it was yesterday, not over two decades ago. It even had the traditional grain store nightmare of checking the bins and finding that I've been putting one crop on top of another by mistake. It could be a long battle before I've got those issues out of my head.

On a more cheerful note, the sun shone and it felt like spring. I put more bangers out on the spring barley as huge flocks of pigeons wheeled round above me, and then I settled down and did the next *Farmers Weekly* column. Last week's comedy episode of being locked out of the hotel was too good a chance to miss. Its link to farming was tenuous – but worth writing up anyway.

Spring seems to be taking a long time to reach the Stanmore block. Sasha, Evie and I did a big loop from the Drier Yard up to Pipeline, Long field, Broom Field, White Hill and Folly. Up on the heavy land, the wheat looks better, but still 'winter weary'. But if the weather forecast is right, it should crack on this week.

It was while I was walking across the winter barley I suddenly remembered that Tod had sent through a spraying prescription for it some days ago. I'd forgotten all about it. It'll only be a couple of tanks, but I ought to get it done before switching back to sowing spring barley. I filled up the sprayer with clean water over the evening and then left the hose pipe to trickle into the main tank overnight.

March 18th

My enthusiasm-filled plan to rush out in the morning and get one tank of spray on before lunch was foiled, but in a really good way. I got back from the rope banger run to find Hazel loading up another load of straw for a buyer. This inevitably means a guided tour of the cattle, a chat in the yard, followed by an even longer chat in the kitchen over a cup of tea. A far more productive way to spend the morning.

Our guest left moments before Tod arrived for an agronomy chat, which involved the bare minimum of agronomy and an awful lot of discussion on band matters. The gigs are pouring in nicely for the summer. Well, at least two.

I had an early lunch once Tod had gone. Two long tanks of post-emergence grass weed killer on White Hill (what's left of it), Cheyney (what's left of it) and Drier Field, which – unlike the other two – doesn't have any bare patches in at all, and looks a treat.

The fertiliser lorry didn't turn up. They rang mid-afternoon to apologise and say it would be here on Monday or Tuesday. I told him not to worry – if I got the urge to rush out with some fertiliser over the weekend there's enough for a couple of loads in the big tank. Anthony is due down from London for the weekend, so if I'm not watching rugby I might be doing log cart anyway.

The cattle went off to their new home, as calmly and faithfully as ever. The back barn was suddenly horribly empty.

March 19th

The tree that fell on top of the gates at the bottom of the hill needed clearing. We had all the kit charged up, fuelled up and sharpened – and we had the muscle home for a day or two. As usual, the job turned out to be a lot bigger than we thought.

After an hour or two sawing and cutting we'd just about cleared enough space to get through the right-hand gate into Roe Hill. But many of the main branches and trunks were way too big for our DIY kit.

It didn't help that I managed to get the petrol chainsaw jammed in a limb, and attempts to free it resulted in the body of the tree crunching a little bit lower and jamming it tighter. We ended up fetching the tractor and pallet forks, and gingerly lifting the weight off the blade so we could pull it out. We might have to lean on the National Trust professionals to finish the job off.

But the morning's efforts did mean I could sit down and watch the rugby with a clear conscience. Italy vs Wales was fantastic, especially as it showed up the folly of awarding 'man of the match' with over five minutes to go. It was lovely to see the Welsh 'man of the match' handing over his medal to the brilliant Italian winger who scored the winning try in the last minute. I slept through Scotland vs Ireland although I was awake for a golden moment as Stuart Hogg, presented with a three-on-one certain try scoring opportunity, decided he'd do it himself and was bundled unceremoniously into touch.

We treated ourselves to a monster fish and chips from the chippy in Alresford, but were once again defeated by the size of the portions. I polished off my plateful as best as I could and then adjourned back to the sofa for England vs France. It went as expected but was still hugely entertaining. France were deserved winners. It's a sad moment when the Six Nations ends, but it should mean spring is coming. We can but hope.

March 20th

A typical Sunday: Hazel went dog training, I got the papers and Anthony had a bit of a lie-in. The fantastic forecast suggested that I really ought to get back in the tractor and do some farm work, so I put the first dose of fertiliser on BOMS and Rick/Clump. I don't think I've ever seen so many rooks and pigeons out there – I hope they're not actually damaging the crop rather than just working their way through surface stuff. One thing they are doing is making a mess of the pre-emergence marks left by the drill. Once or twice I lost my line altogether, and had to pace out 29 paces (usually comes to 24m) to find it. I don't think it's just us suffering with pigeons and rooks at the moment – the dawn till dusk fusillade of gas bangers suggests that the oilseed rape growers are having a similar problem.

Anthony did some work in the garden and then Hazel gave him a lift back to Petersfield station to catch the train back to London. He seems very content with his gardening work up there – it seems to suit him very well not being in an office and with hours that means he can have a social life.

My new shotgun certificate arrived safely last week, which is quicker than I thought it would be. The neighbour who had kindly hosted my guns for a few days while they had been out of my cabinet dropped them off in the afternoon. I spent much of the evening filling in the forms to say that they'd returned from their lodgings, and everything was now where it should be. You then must scan them into the computer and email them to the Hampshire Constabulary. Still – shouldn't complain; I'm armed and legal again. I might have to go and shoot a few rooks.

March 21st

Sometimes I amaze myself. I was wide awake and ready to go at five thirty. God knows why – the dogs hadn't barked, and the birds aren't going mental yet (or my hearing is now so bad that I can't hear them). I had just slept extremely well. I shall have to have a can of ginger beer and a mountain of peanuts every evening. Hold on – I already do.

It did mean I caught the dogs on the hop, and they were still a bit dopey when I let them out onto the frosty lawn. A beautiful start to spring. Or was that yesterday? I can never work it out. It was also Diana's 26th birthday. I hope she's cheery enough to enjoy it – she's having a bit of a nightmare with her accommodation in Cambridge. One of her flatmates has handed in her notice, and, quite bizarrely, that means they've all got to get out – within a matter of weeks. I think she was intending to move soon anyway, but it seems fairly brutal. The landlord has already put it on the market with a much higher rent, which explains everything. I texted her 'happy birthday' as early as seemed reasonable.

The next *Farmers Weekly* article didn't need many changes, and they seemed happy with my trivial suggestions. Hazel finally surfaced much later than normal, also having enjoyed a good lie-in, and I sent her off in the tractor to move the telegraph pole into Cheyney. That meant I could nip out and give it 140 litres/hectare of fertiliser to finally finish the first round of nitrogen. I got back to the yard and hitched off the sprayer, topped up the Adblue and the diesel in the tractor, and was ready to start drilling again.

Nick the pensions man arrived exactly on the dot of ten o'clock, and we spent a couple of hours running through all sorts of pension possibilities in light of what the next eighteen months appear to hold. I say 'appear' because I still can't quite believe it's all going to happen. We promised we'd all keep in touch so that we can keep on top of all our options.

After lunch it was a great relief to get down to the drill, still parked behind New Pond, and find it hadn't seized up after a week's soggy weather. Sometimes moisture gets in, stuff starts to grow and you have to empty all the seed onto the barn floor before you can do anything else. Not in this case though – I was off to Big Field to do five and a half turns of headland in fantastic sunshine. I did a half turn of headland because I popped across the track into BML's and had that drilled in a couple of hours.

Not terribly well though. One marker arm disintegrated just as I started the land work. And rather than have the arm's stalk resting on the soil, I did the uphill stretch by eye, and the downhill stretch using the one remaining working marker arm. Tomorrow's job will be to steal a disc off the CO3 and fit it. Good thing I haven't sold that yet, and it's still in the yard, ready to be cannibalised.

Two more fields that I will never sow again: Big Field and Behind My Love's. When the conditions are this good and the job goes this well, it's a slightly melancholy feeling to be towing the drill out of the field. BML's is unique; Dad ripped out the hedge up through the middle and ploughed up the turf in the mid-eighties, when Miss Ursula Dutton, who lived in Joan's Acre (Please note, National Trust), gave up that field. So we Flindts have been responsible for probably its only four decades of arable cultivation. And in a couple of weeks, the pipeline gang are on their way to rip it all up again anyway. Not quite sure why I sowed it.

I did the last half headland of Big Field, and headed to New Pond to park the drill up. Much as I love my new Deere 155M, it seems terribly thirsty, having gone through a third of a tank today. And it has to be said it's not quite as comfortable as my old 6630P. Either that or I'm getting older and everything starts to hurt earlier in the day. I had a lovely walk across Rick and Big Field up to the loader tractor, and brought it home ready for a fresh trailer- load of seed.

Arthur from the shoot cover company rang mid-afternoon, keen to come out and have a chat about next year's shooting strips. I told him to set aside a long afternoon because we were about to set up the small shoot, and I needed lots of advice on how to make the most of 120 acres. The real reason he was ringing was that he needed a speaker for a gamekeepers' conference and my name came up. It would be a great chance to sell a few more books, but I might have to rewrite the speech. I can't see my twenty minutes of farming stuff being remotely interesting to a bunch of keepers. I might dig out a lifetime's worth of shooting-related nonsense instead.

There was a late evening phone call from the fertiliser delivery driver, wisely checking his directions to get to the tank tomorrow. You can never be absolutely sure that he's listening to your directions; sometimes it's obvious that they're just going "yes, yes" to your carefully worded instructions, and then they turn up in the yard completely lost anyway. They need to be careful; with the price of fertiliser at the moment it won't be long before they start being held up at gunpoint on the road.

There was a curious flurry of book orders – five in half an hour. I did some Googling and found that an agricultural accountancy society had reviewed it very positively. To be accurate, the first half of the first page was positive; the rest was hidden behind a paywall. Book Two had as a result climbed to the top of the 'bestsellers' list in agricultural machinery again. Take that, Clarkson.

Hazel had been out soil sampling all afternoon, getting ready to enter Dead Dog Farm into lots of environmental schemes. The first thing you have to do is establish some sort of baseline when it comes to soil quality. She was knackered, and the dogs could hardly move. The house was very peaceful.

March 22nd

A five-minute job. That's what repairing the drill marker arm would be. If I backed Hazel's tractor up to the old CO3 in the yard, lowered one of the arms and undid the locknuts, I'd be able to remove the shaft with the disk on it and whip it over to the ST4. Easy-peasy.

True, that bit was easy. It just all went downhill from there. I got down to New Pond where the ST4 was parked, warmed up my 19mm socket, and set about removing the old shaft. Something told me the locking bolts hadn't been moved in a long time – the first one sheared straight off. That was the end of that plan; I had no intention of spending the day fighting with a broken-off bolt. I headed home with the disk assembly.

Ten minutes on the phone to the Horsch dealer revealed that they had all the parts needed to overhaul it – bearings, shims, seals – and, even better, they were happy for me to drop it off up there and they'd prioritise the job. Excellent. The Hyundai i20 needed a run out, and some fuel, so I grabbed a couple of twenties and set off for the West Meon Hut, but promptly got held up in roadworks in Bramdean for five minutes. There goes the 'five-minute job'. A couple of twenties hardly made a mark on the fuel gauge, but there we go.

From the Hut I went north for a bit, then cut across to Bramdean Common via Wolfhangar, enjoying my now-compulsory near-miss – this time with a Sainsbury's van, which pulled off left, and then swung immediately right, across the road, obviously trying to start a three-point turn – he simply didn't realise that I was behind him. There was a certain amount of arm waving which proved much more effective than the weedy horn on the Hyundai.

At the Horsch dealers, the disk assembly was whisked away into the workshop; they suggested that they might be able to do it while I waited. Much as I would have loved to spend an hour watching a valeting team give the biggest combine you ever saw a spruce up, I said I'd head home; but they should give me a ring the very moment the job's done.

I couldn't help thinking that the damage was due to a lack of maintenance, so I refilled the grease gun and spent a lengthy session giving the Sprinter a good going-over. It's a lot easier after a few days drilling in dry conditions when all the soil has dried out and dropped off; you can actually get to all   the grease nipples. It seemed a waste not to do anything in these perfect conditions, so I folded up the drill, and once I'd shoved the telegraph pole out of the way in the entrance to Blackhouse Road, crept along the lane and in. I did the huge 'mark out' lap, once again getting slightly sad that this was another case of 'last time I do this', and then did an hour's drilling, starting in the peak corner nearest New Pond, and gradually getting the turns longer.

By half past four, I was beginning to wonder where my phone call about the repairs had got to. I rang them. "Oh, we were waiting for you to bring the arm up, so we could re-attach it." I pointed out that this was news to me; we'd agreed that they'd ring as soon as – oh, never mind. Muppets. This sort of nonsense I will not miss. I drove home, grabbed the Skoda and raced up to Micheldever. We had a very entertaining game of 'have we fitted all the right parts?' It seemed that they had, so once I persuaded them to give me a freebie couple of feet of glasspaper tape to clean up the shaft, I headed home. Not much point in heading back out at this hour, especially as it's Tuesday, and neighbour Robert was up for a beer. He was feeling much better, to the extent that he'd been given a tractor with a mounted spring tine harrow, and despatched to the pastures for a couple of long days tarting up the pastures in the glorious sunshine. It would be unkind to repeat his story of losing the lynchpin from the top link and not noticing for an acre or two, so I won't. One shouldn't take the piss out of respectable senior farmers.

Hazel's big task today was to tell the Rural Payments Agency that we had surrendered bits of land to the National Trust. You might think this is a simple task, another five-minute job. We tried online, but couldn't somehow complete the process. Land agent Chris was summoned for help by phone, and he said recent guidelines had been introduced which meant that tenants had to jump through a couple more hoops. But even he seemed a bit baffled. Hazel did the most sensible thing and picked up the phone to the RPA. She spoke to a friendly Scotsman, who agreed that the online advice was a bit of a shambles. "Yes… the wording could be made a bit clearer to make it easier to understand," was his comment. His advice was simple: download an RLE1 form, and fill it in as simply as possible, listing the fields, saying who we were, and saying who the National Trust were. And that, in the end, really was a five-minute job.

March 23rd

Once I'd got the new marker disc on the drill, I had a long day sowing spring barley in Blackhouse Road. The state of last year's stubble brought back memories of last harvest, and Blackhouse Road was the first field I did with the brand-new combine. It turned up too late to do the winter barley, and I had had to call in Robert Raimes to do that. By the time the spring barley was fit, we'd had a lot of rain and the ground was sodden. It wasn't a great first few days in the new combine, trying to get familiar with the strange machine on the sloping land, bulldozing very manky barley. Mind you, at least by then it was working properly; the chaff spreader disintegrated halfway round its first turn of headland. The salesman was on board and we had a mechanic out in about half an hour. Let's hope this harvest is a bit kinder.

I tuned into Rishi Sunak delivering his budget, but had to abandon as I couldn't stand his delivery, never mind what he was actually saying. I do wish modern politicians could make a speech without sounding like a robot. Funny to think that nearly thirty years ago, I was listening to Ken Clarke deliver his budget (was it two a year back then?), in Blackhouse Road, sowing spring barley, in a Ford 7810 towing a four metre Bamlett CD4 drill. In those days the ground would have been ploughed for the winter and then had a springtine run through it before drilling. Now I'm straight in with the Horsch into untouched sprayed off ground.

Mr Clarke, whisky close at hand on the despatch box, promised tax cuts on cigarettes and beer. I cheered him loudly from the tractor cab.

Today was also the second anniversary of the first lockdown. What a different message our politicians were bringing us on 23rd March 2020. Almost as miserable and joy-free as the present Chancellor.

Never mind all that – the stunning weather is making drilling a dream. Curious that in my last ever drilling season, Mother Nature is tapping me on the shoulder and saying "are you sure you want to give up farming?"

March 24th

Numerous attempts to finish the next FonF failed. It started well, but then stuttered into failure. I went and loaded up another trailer of seed, expecting inspiration. None came. I refuelled the tractor, hoping for the same. None came. I had a borderline good-natured row with the spray delivery man who claimed that if he hadn't had three jabs, he would have had far worse than being bed-bound with Covid for a fortnight. I said that it was odd that he'd been bed-ridden for a fortnight after having had three jabs. We agreed to differ. But still; no inspiration came. I emailed Emma at FW and begged another day. She said that was fine, bless her.

Hazel and I had a long day in Blackhouse Road – which sounds familiar, but it is a large field. We were interrupted by the man from the electricity board coming to shut off the supply to the drier buildings. We'd finally got it organised after the standing charges went through the roof, and all we ever use it for is a bit of post-harvest combine pressure washing. He consulted his notes and said we'd paid more in standing charges in a month than we've paid in actual electricity in fifteen years. There was a time, before we joined Hampshire Grain, when for several long harvest months, a multitude of three-phase motors would be going flat out for eighteen hours a day, driving elevators, conveyors, compressors and massive fans. I don't miss those days at all. God knows what the electricity bill would be like now.

When I knocked off, there were only four long turns of headland left. If neighbour Robert and I hadn't been planning to head down the Pots again and try to cause mischief at the NFU meeting (hoping we'd got the date right this time), I would have cracked on and finished that field in the lengthening daylight. But it's all about priorities, so I came home and showered.

But our plans to mischievously disrupt the meeting didn't quite work out. After a couple of pints at a very crowded bar we decided to sneak round to the Flowerpots' new function room, only to find it empty save for the organiser and the guest speaker – everyone else had gone. We managed to persuade the latter to join us for half, and that was it for the evening. Neighbour Robert looked shattered, having done several long days of tractor work, and I confess I was beginning to flag a bit. Still, it was good to see the Flowerpots busy.

March 25th

I managed to get the next Flindt on Friday done just before the arrival of George, the National Trust's building manager. The Trust has finally decided to sort out the windows in the farmhouse, which range from 'brand new' in the kitchen to literally (and I don't use that word often) 'falling out'. It's going to be a pricey job, bearing in mind that our tenancy agreement stipulates that we have to pay for a fair proportion of the work.

George had a guided tour of the inside of the house, having checked things out from the outside first, and there was much discussion of the history of the house, including Granny Flindt's probably nonsensical stories of the multitude of servants up in the attic.

That took most of the morning, so I had an early lunch and then headed out to Blackhouse Road. I got the last turns of headland done, did the big fold up, a bit of shimmying at New Pond, and then drove up over Rick and Clump and into Chalks in the top corner. After marking out the headland I chose a line that wasn't from last year or the year before – you could just make them both out – and had a good session, starting in the short work. Chalks, of course, went like a dream, and last year's thick mat of winter barley straw flowed through the drill effortlessly.

I should have cracked on but there was a pub trip in the diary with the ex-Editor and his wife. It was one of those pub trips that was on, then off, then off, then on, and finally on for a couple of hours early in the evening. The Pots was heaving – we were lucky to get a table, but we all agreed that that many bums on seats has got to be a good sign for the future of our local.

March 26th

There's talk of this astonishing run of dry and warm weather finally coming to an end next week, and with no decent sport on the television (no surprise there) it was back in the tractor for both of us. I had two long sessions drilling, and by this time my vision had started to go a bit squiffy. I was left with half a turn of Chalks headland to do, which will cleverly take me into Godwin's Park.

Hazel finished rolling Blackhouse Road, did a bit of Chalks, mowed the lawn and did a Tesco pick up. We were in bed ridiculously early, and it was nothing to do with preparation for the change in the clocks.

Mind you, I was wide awake at eleven o'clock, as the first of the summer parties had started – and it's not even the end of March. In the distance was the dump dump dump dump of a heavy disco beat. I turned on Classic FM to try and drown out the noise and eventually fell asleep, dreaming of marquees impregnated with custard powder solution. (A non-Newtonian fluid, you see – perfect for stopping any loud noise getting out.)

March 27th

I couldn't work out why Hazel arrived in my bedroom in the darkness of the morning waving a cat. It was, of course, just an early sign of 'clock change chaos'. She was off to Mullenscote for some dog training and because it was really six o'clock, it was only just light. And because Cain was sitting outside my door when she got there, she felt obliged to pick him up and bring him in. Cain was thrilled, and we had a little snuggle. (Me and Cain, not me and Hazel.)

Talk of rain next week is becoming more definite, so, rather than have a Sunday off, I pushed on with the drilling. The tractor needed refuelling, which meant the usual palaver with Tigger and the bowser; the daft thing is that the tractor was parked next to the old tennis court, only about a hundred yards away from the diesel tank as the crow flies. In an ideal world I would have just cut the fences and driven through. After I topped up the Adblue too, I was ready to go. I did the last half turn of headland, filled in the details in the drill book, and popped across the track into Godwin's Park.

It went well, but not brilliantly. I think it was the last field we combined at the end of last harvest, after quite a lot of rain, and we left a selection of ruts in the clay. I was going across them at an angle, and by evening I was feeling pretty sore. The mechanical cab suspension in the Deere 155M is definitely less kind that the one on my beloved 6630P. I decided Roe Hill could wait for another day. Hazel, meanwhile, got back from dog training in time to jump in her tractor, roll Chalks and make a start on Godwin's Park. What a team we are. We're going to miss working together on stuff like this.

We had a catch up with Diana in the evening via the internet. She was on top form – her house move is all sorted, and the many months spent on her work project are about to come to fruition. It was lovely to hear a youngster say that she had been under great stress, and quite enjoyed it. Very good news. We were all in bed by ten. Or was it nine? Or it might even have been eleven.

March 28th

Another wonderfully busy day. I loaded up the last ever bags of seed from the barn and had to have a bit of a pause at the significance of the moment. How many tons and tonnes have I moved in and out of that awkward bloody barn? It really didn't bear thinking about. And it has been an extraordinary pile of spring barley seed this year. When Tod and I rewrote the cropping plan to reflect the end of arable farming on this farm, we took a bit of punt on the spring barley; it was going to have to fill all the areas that were once scheduled for break crops. "Let's just hope for a kind spring," we said. As I set off round the outside of Roe Hill, remembering to leave more bare strips for new environmental scheme areas, I couldn't help chuckling that this had indeed been the kindest and most benign spring I can remember. Once I'm done with Roe

Hill, there will be enough seed left over for patching up White Hill where the winter barley vanished, and that will be that. Actually, best not to think about that too much. I don't need tears in my eyes while trying to make straight lines.

It didn't help that Hazel had organised a flatcoat training day with some picker-up friends, and they were doing whatever they do on a training day in the Bottom of Englands. There's an awful lot of standing around, interspersed with hand signals and the occasional dog going hell-for-leather from one place to another. I'm sure it all makes sense to them, but it's distracting while you're trying to keep the drill straight over rough ground.

Mac arrived to muck out the back barn, which took no time at all. And we had a band rehearsal with a new 'sound man' – someone who is very happy to walk among us and tweak knobs. Oo er missis. What he actually did was put a stop to certain band members turning themselves up a bit as the evening went on, which meant that the evening stayed consistently bearable noise- wise. And that hasn't happened often in fourteen years of rehearsals.

March 29th

Not a great night. I woke at four o'clock with a bunged-up nose, a swollen throat, and drenched in sweat. I tiptoed (to avoid waking all the flatcoats) to the bathroom for some paracetamol, and returned to bed to consider my imminent demise. Had I finally fallen victim to the virus? Was it something I'd eaten or picked up on my travels round the farm? I'd been setting a lot of rat traps recently, as well as scratching myself on gates and brambles. Was it the imminent rain finally clearing the air of the heavy high-pressure pollution levels, and dumping it all in my lungs? After a couple hours of fitful drowsing, accompanied by Classic FM, I was writing my own obituary.

It was eight o'clock before I finally felt OK to get out of bed, just as Hazel was setting off for a yomp with Mrs ex-Editor. But an indoor day beckoned, even though the rain that did arrive was light and patchy, and I could have cracked on with the last bit of drilling. The rest of the week looks fine and dry, if a bit cold.

Darren rang from New Pond, saying that there was an 'environmental vehicle' in the Drier Yard – at least, I think that was what he said; the signal down there is terrible. I rushed down in Tigger, fully expecting some hi-viz clad wonk from some agency inspecting my fertiliser tank out of the blue and declaring it illegal. What pulled out of the yard as I arrived was a poo lorry, seeking the New Pond communal cess pit. The poor driver was not from these parts, as they say, and he was struggling to find the pit – not least because the instructions were quite clear: 'in farmyard opposite New Pond Cottages'. What they should have said was 'in the old beaters yard next to Keeper's Cottage'. But there aren't many here now who remember the beaters assembling in that little yard every other week through the winter. And the Trust chiselled away the wall-mounted plaque of 'Keepers Cottage' in a fit of woke renovation some years ago.

By the time I'd done a very pleasing tour of the spring barley in Rick/Clump and Big, he was hard at work, but I realised I shouldn't be driving; I headed home for the

October 1st - Out with the old, in with the new

October 27th - Winter barley in drier field

November 11th - Remembrance Day drilling

November 29th – Snowy sunset

December 16th – Mince pies for the Head Keeper

January 25th – Last unload of seed

February 9th – Stamford

February 21st – Another tree down

March 4th – Lancashire drizzle

March 9th – Working round an old bale

March 12th – Outwell

April 5th – Pipeline pathfinders

April 9th – The Full English Breakfast

April 21st – England in April

April 26th – Working around the new pipeline

May 10th – Sprayer MOT day

May 11th – Swarm of bees in May, something something something.

May 19th – New Range Rover launch

May 31st - Sowing shooting strips

June 2nd – Setting up for a gig.

June 5th – Water cart with the full pack

June 22nd – Trainee vets

June 30th – Storms over West Meon

July 5th – The return of the stolen trailer

July 6th – Mowing hay

July 8th – Hedgetrimming round Cheyney bends

August 1st – Not the tidiest combine cab.

August 2nd – Idyllic harvest weather

August 10th – Balerman is in

August 25th – The last lorry ever

September 16th – Back in the plough

September 30th – contract grass sowing

sofa, still distinctly woozy. I even did a quick LFT, which came up negative, but failed to convince me that I wasn't entering my final days. A couple of hours under a duvet watching daytime drivel TV, and I felt bit more human – human enough to get the next FonF done nice and early. It seemed a shame to waste an indoor day. It was also a slightly controversial one, and I might need to come up with something else if they reject it. If I'm still alive by then, of course.

Neighbour Robert rang about our Tuesday beer, and we agreed that we'd shelve it tonight. He said he was feeling breathless and struggling to get about. We do need some wind and rain to clear the air.

March 30th

What will we need for what should be my last day sowing corn? Well, the last of the seed, of course. A couple of bags of metaldehyde slug pellets, for two reasons. First, this last bit of seed is going in White Hill where the slugs ate the winter barley, and some pellets mixed in with the seed would be a good insurance. Second, using metaldehyde will be illegal from the end of March, and we need to get rid of them. We will still have a few bags of ferric phosphate left over, but Tod will be able to shift them to another grower still needing slug pellets.

I felt a bit better, but still not 100%, so Hazel very kindly got all the supplies onto the blue trailer, and opened up all the poacher barriers between Chalks and White Hill. I had an early lunch, packed some paracetamol, and set off from the top corner of Chalks, out past the shattered gate onto the road at the bottom of the hill, into the Folly, out of the Folly, into White Hill, and then the long haul up to Barracuda, where Hazel had left the seed trailer.

Three hours later, the job was done. I had sown my last acre of corn – in years to come there may well be lots of sowing of shooting strips and environmental mixtures, but my days of unloading bags of barley, wheat and beans – basic food commodities – are over. Thirty-five years I've been doing it, probably averaging 700 acres a year. The total area doesn't bear thinking about, never mind the mileage driven.

The very last acre was in Rough Field, right next to the site of the Barracuda plane crash in the Second World War. I fully expected the traditional machinery breakdown, but the ghost of Sub-lieutenant Daley let me off this time. Perhaps he was aware of the significance of the day. I sat for a moment on a wheel at the back of the drill and pondered thirty-five years of drilling with the Bamlett CD4, the Amazon power harrow combination units (two of them – one good, one bad), the Horsch CO3, which was our saviour in 2012 when I realised no-till drilling was the only option for us on this farm, and then the Sprinter ST4, which moved everything up a gear. It seemed remarkably apt that I should find another horseshoe lying on the surface of the seedbed. A broken one too – very suitable on land that will never be cultivated again. It was quite an emotional couple of minutes.

Still, we've done the deal, and we must live with it. If we'd had an awful drilling season, the deal would have looked splendid; the fact that we've had a textbook drilling season, and the deal still feels right, is very significant. Hazel and I spent an hour or two getting everything home, putting up the poacher barriers again and generally shutting up shop for tonight's snow and rain. I took two more paracetamol and hit the sofa for a much-needed snooze.

March 31st

This cold/flu/virus/hay fever wasn't getting any better. I had a proper quiet day, snoozing and sneezing, and generally feeling very sorry for myself. Hazel rolled the last bits of drilling before the snow and gales arrive, which added the rollers to the growing list of things we could sell if we were so inclined.

Today's other vital job was to read all the electricity meters and get the readings logged with the thieving bastards at SSE. Their prices are due to go up tomorrow by about 50%, and the internet is buzzing with the idea of getting your 'cheap' units logged in so that they don't try and charge April prices for March usage. Not surprisingly, all possible ways of getting in touch with the electricity companies crashed under the weight of demand (or were simply disconnected, ahem ahem) but we think we got ours in by phone. I thought the world was going mad two years ago; these days are doing their best to 'out bizarre' them.

I spent a couple hours looking at wood-burning stoves that did hot water – the immersion heater is our one huge user of electricity, and the farm is littered with logs. I dread to think what hoops we'd have to jump through to install one. Some years ago we were pondering converting the Aga back to solid fuel to make the most of free wood, but I have distant memories of Dad doing the daily 'clear out and refill' routine. It was not a cheerful chore.

On my evening rounds checking the spring barley (just to get that little thrill when fresh corn emerges) I met Mark the Deerman out in his doublecab. He'd heard about the Big Plan and wanted to know more. He'd already been approached by the Trust for more work, which is a good sign. More deer control will only be needed if more trees need protecting, and more trees means less cropping, which means less food, which means more of a shortage, which is good for farming. I'll be well out of it by then, though. I'll have done my bit to help, however.

Hazel headed off to The Shoe in Exton for a night out with picker- ups Julie and Nessa, so she's obviously not suffering. Neighbour Robert was disappointed when I cried off another pub trip – but it wouldn't be right to be sneezing over him.

April 1st

Another wasted morning feeling very sorry for myself. It was freezing, with high winds, snow and sleet showers again. I just about managed a walk over to Big Field and back, which failed to make me feel any better. Perhaps a little retail therapy might work, but a trip to Gaskin's for some Velcro tape (to stick the T-Jet guidance system's receiver to the roof of the new tractor) failed too; they didn't have any. I cast my eye over one of the new compact Kubota tractors he's got in stock in his yard, and couldn't help thinking that when the dust settles and we're left with a hundred acres, that's just what we'll want: simple, about 100hp and with side windows. But I think I was getting ahead of myself a bit.

It was time to take more paracetamol and do more machinery changing. Off came the drill, and on went the sprayer for more fertiliser. My mood was not improved by realising that I was – in theory – already behind with fertiliser applications. That's the curse of being a one-man arable farm: you can't do every job on the same day.

Bedtime was very early.

April 2nd

The dogs started barking early, even though it was still pretty dark. I felt like death warmed up, but got up and let them out to shut them up. Three of them formed a line on the lawn and did huge dumps – which might explain the barking. I had breakfast, and as soon as Hazel appeared, went back to bed. Cain, of course, was thrilled, snuggling down under the duvet and purring for Britain. I think the sheets might need changing again soon.

Trouble is, the wind had died down, there were fields needing fertiliser and the ground was dry as a bone. I made an appointment with Mr Paracetamol and managed two tanks – covering the winter barley in Drier Field and the unslugged bit of White Hill. I could have done more if my head hadn't been thumping, but there's a gig tonight and I needed to get myself ready for that. First thing – the last lateral flow test in our box. Once again, it was negative, but it did still leave me with a sense of unease at heading out for the evening. Tod and John were by now up in Shed 3b, packing up all the kit; I made it plain that if they were unhappy with me playing, I'd go with their decision.

'Play' was the decision.

The hall we were playing – in a pretty village not far down the Meon valley – was huge, but it had about 130 people in it, enjoying a good meal and a get-together. It was a hunting 'do', and, like so many clubs and societies, they hadn't met up for a couple of years. We had to wait behind the curtain for what seemed like ages, while speeches were made, awards were handed out and raffles were drawn. It was well after ten o'clock when we launched into 'Mojo'.

They all got up and danced – for a good two hours. And nothing makes you play better than watching a hall full of people dancing, and then they dance better, and so on. And some of the young people in the hunting fraternity can dance very well in their ludicrously well-fitting kit. I did lose concentration once or twice while mentally slotting one of two of them into jodhpurs and boots. I blame spending my formative years at Pony Club Camp. Our new sound monitoring system – being run by our new full-time knob twiddler – was fantastic, and I had perfect in-ear sound for the whole evening – and that's a first in fourteen years. Or it might even be fifteen.

It was past one o'clock when we'd packed up, eaten all the cheese rolls that we'd found laid out for us in the huge room under the stage, and enjoyed that special post-gig euphoria. There were well-oiled punters coming to find us to assure us what a great evening they'd had – at least, I think that's what they said. And it was nearly two o'clock when we'd unloaded everything back into Shed 3b, said our farewells, and I climbed into bed. Something tells me I'll pay for it tomorrow, though.

April 3rd

Hazel went dog training – Tim passed his end-of-term test with a distinction – and I went to bed. All day.

April 4th

A really handy batch of rain came through just before dawn, with gusty winds shaking the windows. Just what everything needs to get on and grow a bit. I couldn't help noticing that I felt better – at last. Or it may have been that 'farmer's feeling' when an unexpected burst of good (in this case, wet) weather arrives. I still couldn't get my head around writing up the Honda Civic, and managed to beg a couple of extra days. But, by late morning, I was beginning to feel up for some farm work. So much so that I got in the tractor, put 200l/ ha of fertiliser on Stanmore Broom, Long and Pipeline fields, and another load on TBHD.

Lunchtime was interrupted by Tod, still on a high after Saturday's gig. When we finally stopped talking about it, we got round to farming, and, yes, all his recommendations for spray were still valid.

All this rushing around applying fertiliser meant that more was needed. I got on the phone to Yara and found that their call team had been infected with woke ways. It used to be so simple: give an account number, confirm I'm Mr Flindt, confirm tank site, confirm order details ("a lorry of N35(S), please") and say cheerio. Not today. Today I had some annoying young squirt who wouldn't proceed with the order until he had my first name, and then proceeded to use it. Utterly ghastly. I suspect he had worked as a dental receptionist in a previous career.

There was a very significant moment halfway across the Top of Hurst Down, as I was dosing the surprisingly good second wheat up there: I found a solid bogey, the first for a week. And, yes, it was delicious.

April 5th

The Civic review finally got itself together in my head, and I sent it off. Once again, I found myself browsing Autotrader as part of the pre-write-up procedure, and realised I was thinking of buying one. I had liked it that much. Silly idea, really – we've got a yard full of cars, in assorted states of repair. The last thing we need is another one.

Sasha and I went out to see if the pipeline team had made it through Murph's land and onto ours. Just as we pulled into BML's there was a New Holland tractor pulling a huge bale trailer loaded with stakes and rope. A large Scottish gentleman was pacing out alongside the trailer as it rolled slowly across my pristine spring barley, lifting and placing a stake at regular intervals. I waited until he wasn't counting paces, and had a chat. A second large Scottish gentleman got out of his tractor and the traditional earthy conversation, filled with insults and laughter, ensued. They seemed grateful to find a farmer who is totally relaxed about his fields being dug up. I told them to crack on while this lovely dry weather persists, and while we all need lovely fossil fuels to power our planes. After all, those Climate Change delegates have to get to their next Caribbean conference somehow.

Sasha, promoted to the front passenger seat because Tigger is still full of pianos and stools from the gig, huffed and puffed and grumbled, and then decided that they were allowed to be in her field, and it was all I could do to stop her climbing out over my lap to say hello.

The new head man at Trinity Grain came out for a chat and a cuppa, and a gentle mauling by a pack of dogs. He's another South African, and they seem to have a way with fierce attack dogs. Sasha was sitting quietly at his feet within moments, having her ears scratched. He was here to discuss the protocol for us selling our thousand-tonne membership of Trinity Grain. We won't be needing it after the selling of this year's harvest produce, and I was keen to hear if the stories they told us when we originally signed up all those years ago - 'You'll be able to sell it on easily at a vast profit! It'll be your pension fund!' - were true.

The answer? True-ish. Not many months ago, farmers were heading inexorably to green schemes, and grain storage was the last thing on their minds. Mr Putin has changed all that, of course, and Mr Trinity said that the market for storage was healthy, but there was a lengthy queue of other sellers to be satisfied first. If we're in no hurry, he said, we should put it on the 'for sale' list and sit and wait.

It was too windy for spraying, but about right for that last couple of loads of liquid fert. I finished TBHD, dodging hi-viz pipeline crews as they marked out for the imminent diggers. I stopped and told them what I was doing, so they need not get into a stew about nasty pesticides. They were grateful and polite – obviously a different set from this morning's crew, who were grateful and lairy.

The fertiliser tank ran out on cue. I finished JA/DC and came home with a few hundred litres in the sprayer. Almost enough for another small dose on Cheyney, but I was flagging a bit. I needed freshening up if I was pubbing tonight with Robert.

Which didn't happen. He rang at six, struggling for breath. He's been hit hard, too, by whatever is going round, and is in the middle of a weapons- grade course of antibiotics and a steroid inhaler. Poor fellow sounded very under the weather. We agreed to shelve it for a few days. It did mean I could exploit the lovely long evening and do a yomp with Sasha. The ground is now so hard that she kept hanging back at the field edges, suggesting that grass would be kinder to her paws. Christ, we're all getting old.

April 6th

As the world grinds to a halt again with Kung Flu, there's another version doing the rounds: bird flu. Once upon a time it would have been a matter of great importance, back when we were an agricultural economy. But, like F&M and TB, it seems to have faded into obscurity. Mind you, that shouldn't stop those of us with chickens from getting them under cover, as the law demands. Rumours abound of DEFRA inspectors arriving unannounced. We did mull that our half-a-dozen egg producers wouldn't worry the inspectors, but then decided that we'd look very silly if we were caught out. They've been living in the partridge pen in the old estate yard, very happily. Unfortunately, they've gone through the grass supply, which means the eggs aren't top notch anymore. Hazel and I spent an hour trying to work out how to move/extend the cage for fresh grass, but decided that it was more trouble than it was worth. We'd fling in some grass cuttings if we think they need a top-up. And it was cold and miserable – time to head back indoors.

A long office morning was nicely interrupted by the ex-Editor on pigeon patrol. In other words, he was on the doorstep demanding coffee and a gossip. I pointed out that I was just getting rid of man-flu, while Hazel seemed to be going down with the female equivalent – which is obviously more severe. He was unworried – he had too many tales of his shooting expedition to tell us, and a highly infectious bit of Kung Flu wasn't going to spoil that.

On our list of legal things that we should be doing was getting the loader tractor certified. This involves someone coming out and having a look at all the pipes and hoses, giving us (we hope) a pass, and then sending us a huge bill. Such is the modern world. I suspect that there are some old machines out there that warrant a good check over, so I shouldn't be snarky. The fact that I had to put 15 litres of back axle oil in this morning (prompted by talk of inspections) should stop me being smug about maintenance.

Another speech beckons, and a haircut is much needed for it. While in Alresford, I popped my head round the door of the posh bookshop to check on book stocks. The good news was that they needed more. Excellent.

April 7th

Both of us were decidedly under the weather – and if Hazel goes down with something, you know it's serious. We had a bit of an indoor day. It helped that the last of the heavy overnight rain was blown away by some cold gales (just checking it is April) so no fieldwork was possible. There were lots of spray deliveries, but no fertiliser. I rang Yara to check that the order was on its way and hadn't gone missing in the argument about whether my first name was needed to actually place an order. They promised it late tonight or tomorrow. I emailed the organiser of tomorrow's dinner, up in Essex, pointing out that I was on the cusp of crying off. He fully understood – there's a lot of it about, as they say. The trouble is they've got 140 guests and have booked me a hotel room and all that. And I need to flog a few more of my books. I agreed that I'd take another test in the morning and we'd decide then. Sasha and I did the loop out to Big Field to convince ourselves that I felt better. I didn't really, but it was nice to see the barley cracking on, even if we are still freezing our nuts off.

April 8th

Hazel had managed to source some LFTs from a nursing chum, and despite feeling slightly better, I thought I'd do one anyway. Quite a hideous process – all that nasal swabbing (with a bout of sneezing as a result; it would be just my luck to put my back out with a long drive planned). It was 'negative'. I took a picture of it next to today's *Times*, just in case anyone wants some easily falsified evidence, and rang the dinner team; I'm on.

Packing for these dinners is becoming quite a well-oiled process; lots of creams and pills (God knows how I'd organise my dream three-month round- New Zealand trip) as well as a change of clothes and the smart-ish new suit.

While I was packing, the phone rang. It was Yara again, apologising for the lack of liquid fertiliser. It was no great surprise to find that they have staff shortages like everybody else and the load I was enthusiastically promised would be here a couple of days ago would now not be delivered until Monday or Tuesday of next week. There's absolutely nothing one can do in these circumstances; have a bit of a huff and a puff to feel better, but then agree there's nothing to be done. Let's get it here when it can get here. I wasn't really worried too much, because I'm going to be away for a couple of days anyway. It did seem odd that last night they had suggested the load was imminent within hours. Ho hum.

My next job was a first for me. I had decided to head off to Essex via the south side of the M25, which is very brave for me. I have never driven that road before. I would need to pay the DART charge. Only a fiver for the return trip, but worth buying in advance so that you don't forget it afterwards. All easily done online, were it not for the fact that having rejected my credit card the computer then took the money anyway. By this time, I'd switched to my debit card and ended up paying twice. This of course meant a long phone call, although I was pleasantly surprised to get through quickly to a human being who was as helpful as possible. She promised the money would be refunded within a couple of days.

It was probably an omen of what was to come. I headed off just after lunch, choosing to go through Four Marks to get to the A3, and then to the M25. I thought it was all easy-peasy, apart from the hideous concrete road surface which does nothing for your car's stability and makes the whole vehicle hum and whine in resonance. The trenches between the concrete sections make   it sound as though your car is being slapped with a wet towel five times a second, but I was making good progress. My plan to be there within a couple of hours and then have a nice look round Essex was going well.

And then the traffic slowed, and then stopped. Fire engines came flying down the other carriage way – the clockwise one – and then reappeared on our left going up the hard shoulder, sirens screaming. They had obviously gone south to a roundabout and then headed north again. Several fire engines, then police vehicles, then ambulances, then accident response units, and finally a highway repair team. Something big had obviously happened.

Time to switch the engine off and just sit patiently. After half an hour, doors started opening, people started strolling round, some of them heading to the embankment for a much-needed comfort break. My digestive system is always cruel under these circumstances and can convince me in moments that I'm going to have to find a secluded bush. I banished those thoughts by logging onto the internet with my phone (a very rare event) and checking out the traffic reports. The AA website was the most informative, with grim reports of a four-car pile-up just south of the Dartford crossing, and breaking the bad news that we could all be there for a couple of hours. I confess I had a look around the car for bottles or containers that might be suitable comfort-break material.

Just as my fellow drivers looked to be getting restless, there was a tsunami of lit brake lights down the queue, followed by lights going out and cars rolling forward. Within only a mile or so we passed the site of what had obviously been one hell of a crash. I couldn't help appreciating the fact that some people do this drive every night.

By now it was nearly five o'clock on a Friday night, and the A12 out towards Colchester wasn't any less crowded. I think Highways England are in league with the tyre manufacturers, judging by the state of the A12. I couldn't believe the shocks that the bits of rubber were taking.

The satnav took me straight to the hotel, which was actually a lovely pub with half a dozen historic rooms – sloping floors, beams, all that stuff. The bar downstairs was heaving with lively lads having a Friday night pint. It did cross my mind that if their evening went on beyond midnight, I would probably be better driving home. The M25 might even be empty at that time of night. I checked in, had a welcome shower and headed out to the Golf Club where I was speaking. It turned out to be another great evening, with well over a hundred farming types all out for a good meal. The sound system worked well and luckily I had packed Tod's lectern on which I could put the pages of my speech. They seemed to like it, although I spent the second half of the speech desperate to blow my nose which could have ruined the whole evening. There were raffles, prizes, the odd speech from members and most importantly I managed to flog nearly forty books, which certainly pays my 'fee'.

I need not have worried about the noise at the pub. Everything was silent, and, better still, I managed to get in without a panic about being locked out. I'm getting the hang of these hotels. But it was a strange bed on a sloping floor, and the young lads of Essex were keen to show off their motors in the village high street, so it wasn't a brilliant night sleep. But it was more sensible than driving home.

April 9th

I had booked breakfast for 8.30, but dozed way past that deadline. I got down to the bar just before nine, apologising profusely. Had I missed my breakfast slot? Of course I hadn't. I was forgiven when I sat down at the out-of-tune grand piano and bashed out the first half of 'I Will Survive' with the landlady singing along. A slightly surreal and utterly unplanned moment, but at least I earned my full English breakfast. The landlord brought out a mountain of beans, sausages and so on, and breakfast turned out to be very chatty.

It's always a good idea to have a stroll after breakfast before heading off home, and I had passed yet another enormous East Anglian church on the way in yesterday, so I thought I'd go and investigate it further. It was another hugely impressive structure, and I narrowly avoided being forced to come in for a cup of tea with the good folk of the village who were gathering for a Friday morning get-together. If they were as hospitable as my hosts at the pub I'd be lucky to get away by teatime.

Mind you I should have left at teatime. After a good drive down the A12, I found the M25 solid again. What was annoying was that my satnav was trying to tell me for some miles to head off into the countryside. I'm always reluctant to follow its instructions; I'm still 'old school' and don't trust it 100%. I and about 200 other drivers ended up taking the same diversion, down through the villages of Ockendon and then rejoining the M25 just north of the Queen Elizabeth bridge. By the time we'd wheeled our way through the villages, who I suspect were getting a bit fed up with the crocodile of cars, the M25 was flowing again, so I'm not sure I saved any time at all.

The Queen Elizabeth bridge was stunning on a bright morning, and for about a mile I was delighted that I had chosen that route. Things got back to normal once we approached the M25, and there were more queues and first-gear crawling. it wasn't until we got to the junctions for Gatwick that we could all push on, and I was very grateful to get onto the A3 and head for Guildford and down to Petersfield. Even my McDonald's at the Petersfield roundabout was disappointing. The Coke was warm, the chips were cold, and the Quarter Pounder was flaccid. The music was too loud (even if they did play 'Everything Now' by Arcade Fire) and the place was heaving with half-term school children and fraught-looking parents. There was one other single man, and we exchanged raised eyebrows.

Still, it was just the sort of trip out you need to make you count your blessings. To no one's surprise, I hit the sofa once I finally got home, and the Grand National was a thriller, even if I did snooze through most of it. That did mean that I was sleeping lightly when the latest van full of poachers drove through the village and paused just below the house. They spent fifteen minutes shooting pheasants out of the trees with much laughter and slamming of doors, and then drove on through to Brockwood. I spent fifteen minutes watching from the bedroom window, feeling somewhat cowardly for not going out and challenging them. It's profoundly depressing to think that it's easier these days to let them get on with it. At least nobody ends up with a broken leg or twenty years' worth of smashed windows for having upset their 'honour'.

April 10th

A welcome change to the Sunday routine, in that, instead of a dog-training day at Mullenscote, Hazel went off to the New Forest for a flatcoat meet up. They had a tremendous day splashing about in one of the rivers down there with about twenty other flatcoats. In theory it was preparation for some sort of competition, but I think it was just a good excuse to get together. Hazel told a lovely story of one twelve-year-old flatcoat (and that age for a flattie is an achievement in itself) who was totally deaf and silver in the muzzle, and who spent the day wandering around greeting everyone with a joyous bark and a wagging tail completely unaware of who he was talking to. You've got to love flatcoats.

It was a perfect spraying day, but the farm was heaving with walkers and visitors, so rather than waste the day, I gave the sprayer a bit of an overhaul. I cleaned out all the nozzles and inline filters, and even emptied the main filter of maggots from the fertiliser tank. It was a good workout for the shoulders, and I left the hose pipe in the sprayer so that it would soon be ready for a big day spraying tomorrow.

April 11th

So much for that plan. A force five got up in the night and continued all day. No chance of spraying, and I couldn't even switch to applying fertiliser; the lorry-load of liquid gold I'd ordered last Monday still hasn't turned up. Very frustrating. I had a productive office day instead, getting eight months' worth of invoices for *The Field* organised and three months' worth for *Farmers Weekly*. By the time I'd typed them up, converted them to PDFs, annotated them with the right numbers and finally emailed them to the right email addresses, I was owed a nice four-figure sum.

I have very little confidence that I did every single one correctly as the man-flu had decided to return with a vengeance, and I was filling up handkerchiefs with blood-stained wallpaper paste with terrifying regularity.

George the Trust's buildings manager came round for a look at the barns in the yard. The Trust have promised to make them shipshape and ready to be let out within a year of the Big Plan happening. They will then be our main source of income. George took a long look at the stable (falling down) and the tractor barn (falling down) and went very quiet. He made his excuses and vanished.

Hazel quite wisely decided to get out of the house and hitched the red tractor onto my lean mean tillage machine (which is a set of Proforge 3 metre discs connected to a six leg Opico Varitilth – which takes some lifting and pulling but also takes no prisoners) and set off around the farm ripping up some shooting strips. The word on the gamekeepers' street is that the bird flu epidemic has wrecked the pheasant trade and there are no poults or layers to be had. We are already discussing with the ex-Editor what to do, and the plan at the moment is to concentrate on getting the best possible shooting strips (that's 'best' as in 'most hospitable'), and hope we can keep the many wild birds we've still got on the farm now. If we shoot seven days next season and get ten per day then so be it.

April 12th

Dacia's man delivered the next car – a Jogger – and, because he had no wingman, I had to give him a lift into Petersfield station. My lorry-load of fertiliser stubbornly refused to be delivered, and I got on the phones. The boys at Yara did the "but it was loaded yesterday" routine again, and I pointed out that they had said exactly that last week just before they rang again to say that it couldn't be delivered. I then rang my local rep and gave him a bit of an earful. Not grumpy but still with meaning. I couldn't help asking if I had been dropped to the back of the queue because I'd initially refused to play along with giving my first name, despite repeated requests.

A couple of hours later, just as I was packing for the next speech, the mobile rang. It was the lorry driver on his way with the fertiliser. Result. Even better, he was one who had been before and didn't need directions. I could set off in the Jogger and leave him to it.

Mind you, it didn't stop him ringing twice, which was enough to make me pull over and ring back. He was just checking that the tank was empty, which was odd, bearing in mind the valve was open at the bottom of the tank – but there we go.

Today's trip on the M25 was up the west side and round to the north, and then pulling off left just after junction 21. Left again into sudden countryside, where there were winding lanes, nicely lived-in farmhouses, and even a teeny tiny airstrip tucked away in a triangle of roads. I found my host's farmhouse without trouble, and we settled down for a cup of tea with the roar of the M25 only yards away. The farmyard sat in a valley which once upon a time would have been staggeringly beautiful. It was still lovely, but I will never complain about the A272 again. There were dogs – eight of them – aged cats, lambs that were in the bottom right oven of the Aga, just about surviving, and a frenzy of farm activity. It was 'home from home' in a way.

After freshening up, we set off inside the M25 to find more unexpected countryside, a set of farm buildings that had been converted into a venue, and forty or so farmers determined to have a good evening. There was the usual mix of beer, insults and appreciation, and having sold plenty of books again I set off home just before eleven, looking forward to an unhindered blast back round the M25.

What I hadn't anticipated was that an empty M25 is the signal for the maintenance gangs to arrive, and rather than enjoy a lovely dry drive at unfettered speeds, my fellow motorists and I were shepherded into one lane every couple of miles where we had to crawl along at 40 miles an hour. Mile after mile of 'workforce in road' signs, and absolutely no sign of any workforce. Worst of all, there's no McDonald's on that route home. I had to make do with an apple once I got in, and then staggered to bed. A great evening, nonetheless.

April 13th

I had a good lie-in, but the lure of the tractor pulled me out of bed. I checked with Tod that the pre-emergence weed killer recs for all the spring barleys were still valid, and he confirmed again that they were. I half hoped he'd say they weren't, because spraying bright yellow goo during a busy holiday week isn't the best fun. Throw in a southerly wind that picked up just a tad too much, and it was an awkward day spent watching out for walkers. I didn't help matters by setting fire to the last bit of a barley bale at the top of Big Field, which lit beautifully and proceeded to send a plume of smoke horizontally in a north-north-east direction. Anyone so inclined could have worked out the wind speed from the smoke. When I got back in, I texted the residents of New Pond to apologise for the hideous smell of the Defy, which seemed to go down well.

Tod had reminded me in this morning's conversation that the Growmore Club quiz was on tonight. It's the last round in a curiously truncated season to try and get everything back in step. I don't think there are any semi-finals or finals this year; just four rounds and the winners are the ones with the highest points. We had our bottoms kicked by Basingstoke Tangier, which is not an unusual occurrence, but I had to make an early exit when the beers started flowing. I was just too tired to stand up. I've got no stamina anymore. Mind you, it's been a hard few days.

April 14th

I half expected to start getting rude emails from *Farmers Weekly*, reminding me that there's a bank holiday on the way. Friday and Monday are crucial days in the weekly preparation cycle, but with Easter looming, the deadlines are that bit tighter. It had to be in today, reminder or no reminder. I even cancelled an important insurance review with the NFU – the first one for ages. With the changes in circumstances it seemed wise to see if we could bring down our monster premiums a bit – but that would have to wait for another day. The writing took precedence. I mulled some serious topics, and then decided that the story of the piano and the huge breakfast in the lovely hotel in Essex would be perfect. I dug out the photo of the mountain of food and sent that in to go with the article.

We had a long meeting late in the morning with a kitchen consultant. It all sounds very fancy, but it was a simple idea Hazel and I had had. After twenty-five years in this farmhouse, during which time we've done next to no renovations or decorations, we thought the time had come to blitz the kitchen. It's grey and cold with a hard cold floor, cold grey units and a knackered Aga. We couldn't help thinking that now is the time to show the kitchen some TLC, and pour a bit of well-deserved money into it. I found a kitchen restoration company online in East Grinstead and the lady who runs it arrived in the yard in a cloud of diesel from a very old Tiguan just before eleven o'clock.

It turned out that we had a lot in common before we got on to kitchens. She worked spaniels, had rescue racehorses, and a daughter who worked in farming. Inevitably she had read some of my columns. She was blown away by the kitchen, and got more and more enthusiastic as we laid out a few of our plans. Lose the false ceiling, rediscover the well, renovate the Aga; her suggestions included a heated floor and smarter units. She went away with a pile of notes and measurements. Who knows how much it will cost, or what the timescale will be, but it would be a lovely way to start our retirement while still living in the farmhouse.

While all this was going on, the man from Hunt's arrived to do the Lola test on the loader tractor – a very important legal requirement. I couldn't quite tell what he was actually up to. There didn't seem to be an awful lot of groping and inspecting, but three hours later we had a pile of paper and a thumbs-up, and a tractor that would be legal for anyone to use this harvest. I think it is now a legal requirement even for me and Hazel.

Finally, it was back to the spraying and for a day that I had been dreading it went extremely well. I got hideous bright yellow spray on Godwin's Park, Chalks, Roe Hill, the last bit of Big Field and BML's. Even negotiating the route of the pipeline in BML's wasn't too bad, and the area meter suggested we'd only lost a couple of acres. I had enough leftovers to do about 50 yards on the headland and then did a water rinse out in the field. All that spraying and upset no one - a definite result.

When I got in, Hazel had been to fetch Diana from the park 'n' ride in Winchester, where the coach from London had dropped her off. She'd decided to come down for Easter and had also just had a week in Jersey, armed with a bus pass. Jersey was the holiday destination of choice for my parents for decades – same room, same hotel, same car hire company, and for a few glorious years Dad would treat us to a few days over there. It was just heaven for small children. Diana decided that she'd go over and do some nostalgia. I wonder if she met the seagull that would hang around on the balcony of Room 361 at Hotel l'Horizon, waiting to be fed by Grandpa Flindt. It's probably still there, fifteen years on from his last trip.

Neighbour Robert was on the phone demanding a pub trip even though he was still under the weather. We managed a couple of pints each, but it was obvious he was flagging a bit. Still, it was worth the effort, just to catch up after far too many weeks without beer.

April 15th

Some bugger stole our precious four-ton Warwick monocoque trailer last year; they drove cheekily into the barn at the bottom of the hill, and took it away – complete with about three tons of bean tailings that were sitting in it, waiting to be added to the harvest heap. We asked around, did social media appeals, told all the right authorities, but it was gone.

I was deep into *Farmers Weekly*'s machinery pages when I spluttered my coffee out all over the table. There was our trailer, at a well-known machinery dealer. I checked it on their website, and the better pictures did nothing to change my mind. I rang them up and got someone – rather surprisingly on Good Friday. I used all my acting skills to pose as an interested buyer but couldn't get answers to the questions I asked that would have identified it as ours for sure. She did send me some better hi-res pictures, and, once again, comparing them to one I found of it on the computer, it made me even more certain. I texted Policeman Ian, but he was off work, and the NFU insurance man. He did answer, and said I should really tell them why I'm interested – the last thing they'd want was to be known for handling stolen goods. I made a plan to drive up to the dealers tomorrow, and sent them an email to explain why I was so keen to know about the trailer.

I did three more tanks of liquid fertiliser – two on Blackhouse Road, and one on the excellent-looking wheat in Middle Broom and Child's Broom. A bit hot and scorchy for liquid, but my fertiliser programme is in slight disarray, and some catching up is needed.

Also in disarray is Hazel's inconsistent mission not to be a farmer anymore; she went down to Murph's yard with Diana and came back with a batch of orphan lambs. Everyone's happy – especially Sasha, who adores lambs with a fierceness that can be scary. But she is a Belgian Shepherd, after all.

Sleep should have been easy, but the 'poachers' were through again just before eleven, cruising past the house, torches flashing. No shots were fired, and they drove on slowly up Roe Hill. It then got even weirder, as five minutes later a car recovery lorry sped back through the village, lit up like a Christmas tree. No car on board, though, but very odd on Good Friday night.

April 16th

If I'm going to be on the road shortly after nine o'clock on a Saturday morning, there had better be a bloody good reason for it. In this case there was: on the dot of nine o'clock, I rang the Wiltshire dealer who appeared to have my stolen trailer for sale and asked if he wouldn't mind if I called in and had a look. He said that was fine, and seemed as astonished as anybody at my tale of woe. He also agreed that, judging by the photographs I had sent, the trailer was indeed mine.

The drive was beautiful. The bank holiday traffic hadn't built up, and it was another fabulous spring morning. This run of astonishing weather has been going for a few days now, and the forecast suggests it's going to go on for a bit yet. I'm glad we put all our spring barley in without too much soil disturbance and, therefore, moisture loss. And if the drought goes on for too long, it will be another factor in the shortage of food. Hazel's barns still full of straw and hay might yet be popular.

I drove up over Cheesefoot Head, up the A34 to the A303, round the outskirts of Andover, through Ludgershall – which was once a thriving if not terribly beautiful army town, but is now just a bit of a wreck. I stopped for a pee on one of the tank crossings on Salisbury Plain, and by the time I reached Devizes a more serious comfort break was needed at Sainsbury's. Then it was through some tiny country lanes until I reached the heavy iron gate of the machinery dealer.

He opened it up for me and within moments I knew it was our trailer. I'd compiled a list of distinctive features that I'd be looking for, and made sure he had that in his hand before I started looking for them. I felt it would add to my case that the trailer is mine. I felt very sorry for him; he had bought the trailer from a dealer in the West Country in good faith, and it now appeared that it was stolen. "Hold on a minute," he said. "I've got the receipt." I thought he meant the receipt for the deal he had done, but it turned out to be the receipt for the deal the West Country dealer had done with a farmer who lived… I had better not say anymore at this stage. Let's just say that an awful lot of questions were answered. It was a shame that it's the Easter weekend, as I couldn't raise any of our Countrywatch police, who I'm sure would be delighted with the whole case.

I thanked him for his time and asked him to take the trailer off the market, which he agreed to do. I had been tasked with picking up the boys from Winchester station as they were coming down for the Easter weekend – or at least some of it. Jonathan is too busy to do more than 36 hours at home. I knew I wouldn't get to the station now, so rang Anthony and suggested he make his own way home; if he wanted to get a taxi we'd sub him with a Granny Grant. ('Granny Grants' are of course named after my mother's habit of sending £10 notes which definitely were not in any way intended to cover parking fines that were incurred at Newcastle.)

This set me up nicely for a slow drive back with all the bank holiday traffic, and a totally unplanned lunch at the Winchester Services McDonald's. I felt it was very important, after the disappointing one the other day in Petersfield, to try another Big Mac Meal, just to check that their standards have been resumed.

The boys had just got in when I got home. For some reason they decided to catch a bus despite the offer of a sub, and had strolled all the way down from the railway station to the bus station, pausing for a pint in the Royal Oak. Good on them. We had a bit of a catch-up, and then I set off in the tractor to do a token tank of fertiliser on Big Field, just to make me feel I'd actually done some farming today, rather than detective work.

Hazel spent a couple of hours at the vets in Alton with Tim. Some months ago, he went charging into the brambles up round the back of the barns and ran into something. At least, that's what we assume he did. There was a clunk, and he came out looking very sorry for himself. Since then, he's had a nasty lump above his left eye that comes and goes. This morning, his eye had closed completely, so Hazel booked an appointment with an expert. Inevitably, the result was inconclusive; he'd have to go back on Tuesday for a sedated X-ray. All flatcoat owners live in fear of the dreaded cancer – we've lost one dog far too early in this way, so we're hypersensitive to any lumps and bumps. He shows no sign of being ill, and is as daft as a brush. Still a worry, though.

April 17th

Easter Sunday, and the fabulous fine weather changed slightly: it got cooler and windier. Perfect for not doing anything with the sprayer. We had a full house and a very full fridge. The former made short work of the latter. And I snoozed on the sofa a lot, too. Jonathan had to get back to London, and Hazel gave him a lift to the station in the evening. It's a stage in life, I suppose. Full family gatherings are going to be short, sweet and relatively rare.

April 18th

A quiet Easter Monday. Anthony and Diana went back to London, Hazel mowed lots of grass, and I put a couple more tanks of fertiliser on, dodging walkers as I went. Not that quiet, then.

April 19th

I had quite a long list of stuff to do this morning, most of them telephone- based, and most of them not possible until office opening time. While Hazel took poor old Tim off to the vet to look at the lump above his eye, I managed to order yet another load of fertiliser (compete with traditional refusal to give my first name

– again). I proofed the next FonF by email, and then managed to get hold of the NFU insurance man; today's the day we get to work on the stolen trailer. He was in his car in Wales, in a poor reception area, so I suspect he was on holiday. Despite this, he was quite happy to talk through what he thought we should do. He said we should get hold of the main NFU insurance team as quickly as possible, fill them in, and then get in touch with the police. The former was easy; I found the paperwork from back in April last year, which had all the right numbers on it – including the phone number for an office in Bristol. I rang up and explained the situation, and they sounded quite excited. "Leave it with us!" was their message.

Trying to get hold of the police was slightly more challenging. Nobody was answering their phone – not our Countrywatch Officer, not his Sergeant, and as for 101, it's a completely useless concept. I did try, but after five – no, fifteen – minutes of menu options and crackly lines, I abandoned it. I sent lots of emails instead; even to the Inspector, but reply came there none. I assumed everyone is on holiday.

The team from Dacia arrived in a Duster and took the Jogger away. I had time to sit in the Jogger and make a few pages of all-important notes ready for the write-up. There's a Volvo coming in a few days which will leave me nicely overstocked with articles.

The tractor beckoned again, and I thought I'd get the fertiliser tank empty just in case they did deliver quickly. I had enough to do 200 litres per hectare on the wheat in the Folly, and the same in Chalks. I ran out the dregs on the bottom headland and washed out the nozzles with the clean water I'd put in earlier.

A last despairing attempt to get anyone to answer the phone was finally successful, as I managed to get hold of Policeman Ian. He had indeed been on holiday for a couple of weeks and only come back today. As a result, he was in the middle of a mountain of paperwork and emails, but listened to my story of the trailer with interest. It took a bit of time to get the triangle of ownership and dealers clear, and while he wasn't too optimistic of the positive result that we all dream of getting using the information we've now got, he did say it was worth pursuing. I should bloody well hope so. I even did the grumpy routine – "come on, I've helped you lot enough over the last twenty-five years; let's have some payback". Not sure he was impressed with it.

Tim came back from the vets looking very sorry for himself. They'd decided it was a huge abscess (did it make his farts go 'Honda'?) and had lanced it. He was now in the cone of shame, with a gaping wound over his right eye, left open to hasten the draining process. Of course, being Tim, he took the whole thing in his good-natured gentle stride.

It's MOT time for the Skoda, so we took it down to North's ready for its test tomorrow. That'll give us a week or two to put right anything that's needed. There's a whine coming from the rear prop shaft which I suspect will need sorting, and I dare say a tyre or two will need replacing. I blame Hazel's driving style of course, not mine. Just as we got back, the ex-Editor and his wife trundled into the yard in their blue Jimny, which meant yet more tea and a good gossip. As they left, I suggested the ex-Editor should join neighbour Robert and me in the Pots.

He did, which meant I could sit and enjoy my two pints in silence while the two of them prattled on about the joys of oysters and rustic French cooking. My sole intervention – that nothing beats the Winchester Services McDonald's – was wasted, so I lapsed into silence again.

April 20th

One of the terms of the deal that we've done with the National Trust is that they will get the barns up together and suitable for us to sublet. The old stable block, which has been used as nothing but a storage area since the day the horses left in 1959, is in dire need of some TLC. The Trust are sending some structural engineers to have a look at the fabric of the building, but before that they will need all Granny's shrubs stripped off the outside. Hazel and I made a start on cutting and pruning, only to be confronted by two birds' nests, full of cowering chicks. Work stopped at once. I tried ringing the Trust's building man, but couldn't get hold of him. The engineers will have to do the best they can.

Spraying Hurst Down presented a bit of challenge. The team working on the new pipeline are out there in earnest, measuring and marking out in their distinctive day-glo jackets. I managed to keep downwind of them with the mix, and even then stopped and had a reassuring chat with them when I was done. I think it is going to be a complicated year up there.

Policeman Ian was on the phone with an update on the stolen trailer. Farmer X (as we must call him), who lives not far from here and supplied it to the first dealer, also supplied a selection of other kit – it was all on the invoice for the lorry-load of machinery that set off from Farmer X's farm to the West Country. Ian was going to have a bit of a rummage through the list and see if anything else set off alarms. The perfect job for a Countrywatch officer. In my next life, that's exactly the sort of job I'd love.

The National Trust's farming expert was next at the kitchen table, to discuss her vision for our fields once we've handed them back. I confess I had to bite my tongue occasionally, but the Trust are now in full control of them, and they can do what they want. I was asked if I'd be interested in doing much of the tractor work for them, which was a pleasant surprise. I could end up as a bit of a caretaker – paid, of course – on land that was once mine. That's an interesting idea. I do hope I wouldn't have to wear a Trust-branded gilet. I'm sure we used to call them 'bodywarmers'.

There's another speech coming up, and I can't use my standard farming script – it's for some gamekeepers, and they'll need something different. That was my late afternoon job.

April 21st

There was an early phone call from the girl delivering the next test car – a Volvo SUV. She was giving it a wash at Winnall services and would be here in about half an hour. I said that would be perfect, and asked if she had a wingman to take her to her next destination. She replied that she'd be happy to walk down to the bus stop and wait for the next bus. By the time she got here, we'd done some research on timetables – we used to know them off by heart when children used them constantly, but not any more. We pointed out that she'd have a two hour wait – the buses out here are not good. Hazel was on her way to Alresford with Tim to visit the vet and offered her a lift. The buses are more frequent from there, and she could find somewhere to sit down and have a coffee while waiting. She was very grateful.

I did another bunch of speech preparation, trying to fine tune it to an audience that I knew nothing about. Eventually, I thought I could do no more, and went and did a tank of spray on White Hill and Cheyney. I shouldn't really have been spraying; it was pretty windy, and I'm not sure the many National Trust walkers approved of the spray drift which could probably be seen from the road. The trouble is, once you've made the decision to go spraying, it's not really practical to stop with over 3,000 litres of chemical all mixed up. I persevered anyway, and did a bit of a clean water rinse out in case I don't get back out again for a day or two.

After a quick shower, I checked out the traffic from here to Ardingly, and decided it would take two hours to do the sixty miles. The A272 is notorious for crawling speeds. My estimate was about right, although I may have lost a bit of time going around Billingshurst. I think last time I drove through, it was a charming market town. Now, a semi-circular ring road going north of the town encloses 10,000 new character-free matchboxes. It's a scene that's all too common these days, but it's the way of the world. I just happened to have come across them all for the first time in my long winter of travelling around the country. It still makes me laugh that we farmers get fingers pointed at us for damaging topsoil.

I got to the South of England Showground in time to unload some books, have a chat with the organisers and enjoy a beer. A familiar face came across the room to greet me, and I realised it was a schoolmate from over forty years ago. We vanished down a rabbit hole of nostalgia, interrupted only by the small matter of me making my speech. I came on after Mike Swann from the Game Conservancy who had delivered a fairly matter-of-fact twenty minutes about the 'correct' use of vermin traps. As a warmup act, he was hardly Peter Kay.

But I think my twenty minutes went okay – people seemed very appreciative, and I managed to flog twenty-one books which nicely filled my pocket. My diesel costs were, of course, covered by the Volvo. My school friend and I swapped mobile numbers and made all the right promises to catch up again. We probably won't, of course.

Rather than head home via the A272 I thought I'd try the alternative route –

up to the M25, clockwise for a bit, then down the A3(M). It was certainly easier, took only ninety minutes, and saved me from having to look at Billingshurst again, but it was slightly less charming. The fact that we were diverted onto the A31 at Guildford meant that my plan for a late-night burger at Petersfield McDonald's was scuppered. Maybe not a bad thing. I needed to sleep well to get some inspiration from somewhere for tomorrow's *Farmers Weekly* article which had failed to materialise. I was home just after eleven.

April 22nd

As it happened, inspiration did creep into my bed sometime in the night, and supply me with six hundred words about the lunacy of treating farmyard manure as if it was some sort of precision input. It helped that my neighbour, now a 'Farmer Focus' writer in *Farmers Weekly*, had been moaning that his slurry application was inaccurate, even with the biggest and most modern kit.

They seemed happy with it, and I could relax. What actually happened was that I collapsed in a bit of a heap on the sofa, relieved that it was far too windy to do any spraying and too scorchy to do any fertiliser. I was much in need of a quiet time. Sasha, Evie and I managed a walk out to Big Field, coming back via the Drier and the Folly, but it was slightly disconcerting to see everything so dry. If this weather goes on, it will surely add to the pressure that Mr Putin has put on food production. The forward prices on the AHDB website seem to agree, and I keep doing mental arithmetic on what this harvest might yield. But let's concentrate on getting it in first.

April 23rd

Another unpleasant windy day, not helped by the fact that there were fires at Ash Ranges, to the north-east of us, and smoke was drifting all the way down here on the wind. The Facebook pages were full of demands that something should be done. "Has anyone rung the police?" is the traditional cry. I've taken to using it when people ask why the buses are late.

As it happened, the police were rather busy – or Policeman Ian was. He came round to take a statement from me in relation to the stolen trailer. I've done this before, and it involves sitting and drinking tea while an officer types away for half an hour (they've moved on from hand-written), and then putting an electronic signature to a prime piece of ploddledegook which should resemble what you've told them. It often doesn't but, in this case, it did, and Ian wasn't too offended by my offer to vet the grammar. He was in no mood to mess about with this little affair and was off to visit Farmer X for a chat.

Annoyingly and somewhat inevitably, Farmer X stuck with his story that he'd bought my trailer off someone on Facebook, with cash, and he had no record of who the other bloke was. Well, cover me in brandy butter and call me a Christmas pudding; what a shock.

April 24th

When there's evidence that a shower has passed through in the night – a tiny puddle in the corner of the manhole cover outside the back door and some dregs in the plastic wheelbarrow – and it's a cause for minor celebration, you know it's a dry spell. All the crops would benefit from a good drink, not least to wash in some fertiliser applications. But you can't help thinking what a wonderful thing a drought would be: more reduced yields, more gradual realisation that food is going to be short. The only flip side is that the eco catastrophists would be in full cry, and all droughts these days, unlike all previous droughts through the millennia, must be the result of climate change. Therefore, we must give up cars, holidays and meat. Obvs.

Mind you, this is a drought-proof farm. If we get a dry spell at this time of year, the crop roots go a-hunting for moisture. Down they go, into the chalk aquifer below the clay, and they're sorted. This theory is, of course, Grandpa Flindt Farming Wisdom, so is probably nonsense. But it certainly held true in '83, when we couldn't believe the post-drought yields. And there was no 'climate change' back then.

I'll still need to look after the crops, so I headed out to Drier Field to spray the last bit of winter barley. The wind promptly got up, and I was contemplating only doing the one tank when my exit from the field was interrupted by a mud-covered Range Rover. Out jumped what was obviously a farmer, wanting to say hello. That was my cue to abandon Sunday spraying and head home, with him in tow, for a chat and long cuppa. (And a book sale.) Hazel just had time say 'nice to meet you' before she headed off to the New Forest with Bella (it should have been Tim, but he's still grounded) for a training day among the bogs and ditches. It was a beginners' class, so Bella aced it, but it was still good practice for her.

I decided the day would be better spent on the British Touring Car Championship, only to find that wokeness has hit that, too, and it's all about the 'hybrid'. I miss the days when you put petrol in a racing car and tried to drive as fast as you can.

April 25th

The weather forecasters were adamant: today would be the day that would see some decent rain. Well, heavy showers anyway. I made an early start on the fertiliser to capitalise on this good news. It meant I missed the visit of the structural engineer who had been sent by the National Trust to look at the old stable block. Hazel was at home, and could show him the worst points, and also guide him into the tractor barn, which (we've been told by our building team) we really shouldn't be going into. The west end of it is suffering from serious subsidence. He made lots of notes and went on his way.

I thought I'd start as far away as possible with the fertiliser and head slowly home. Pipeline Field was therefore first on my list, and then it was into Long Field and Broom Field. Broom Field looked as good as I've seen it in years, and the rest of that block didn't look too bad at all. It needs some rain, of   course. White Hill was next, now in two blocks, some of it winter barley, some of it spring barley. The winter barley only needed a light dose, which meant a high-speed run -– which was fairly uncomfortable in the new Deere.

By the time I had finished White Hill, I was ready to call it a day. Tod was on his way to get the band rehearsal room up together. We haven't rehearsed since our gig a few weeks ago and everything needs connecting and setting up. Somehow, and I can't quite workout how, we agreed he'd buy a McDonald's on his way. It was completely unnecessary but delicious. We sat at the kitchen table and ate lukewarm burgers and chips like a couple of ten-year-olds. Tod made the mistake of giving a chip to one dog, and then spent 20 minutes fighting off the other three.

Meanwhile, Hazel's new calves had arrived, and been carefully sorted into individual pens in the back barn. There was a great deal of mooing and bleating as they tried to get used to their new home.

We had just finished getting warmed up in Shed 3b when my mobile rang. It was Kate from just along the road, asking if we had baby calves. I said we had, and she said two of them were heading along the road towards the A272 in the dusk. I rushed indoors to find Hazel tucked up with a white wine in front of the telly, and by the time she had donned wellies and headed out, there were nine of us herding two slightly bewildered calves back along the road. Three of the calves were straight off the cow, and the pen that Hazel had assembled for them wasn't quite strong enough. They had been up and over, out of the barn and off into the wilderness without anybody noticing – until Kate spotted them. We were very lucky that she did; it was one of those slightly chilling moments when we considered that our next call may have been from the police down on the main road.

A slightly truncated rehearsal (once the dust had settled) was brilliant, with new soundman Lawrence keeping everything well balanced and slightly quieter. Plans to do an ABBA song for the ex-vet's 60th birthday party in July progressed nicely. It's funny how a bunch of amateur musicians who would never admit to finding ABBA anything but naff somehow know all the chords and all the words.

As for the famous rain showers, they swept in from East Anglia, south-west across London, set a course down the M3 and A3, and promptly vanished. Oh well. We get what we get.

April 26th

More fertiliser. I did Hurst Down, JA/DC and the Folly. It was nice to see my neighbours out doing fertiliser as well. If they – proper farmers – are still doing it, maybe I'm not as far behind as I thought. Tod was round again, having failed completely to do any agronomy yesterday, and I adjourned to the Pots with Robert for another quiet-ish evening. He's hoping to get some results from his chest X-ray soon, which should be the first step on him getting back up to speed – and the correct number of pints on an evening.

April 27th

Yet more fertiliser. My ambition today was to get the tank empty so the decision to switch to spraying would be made for me. And with Tod suggesting that something needed to be added to the existing tickets (meaning I couldn't go spraying until the new chemical was delivered) I had a quiet afternoon planned.

Just for once it all went to plan. I finished Drier and had just enough to give BML's a final dose. I gave the sprayer a rinse out from the clean water tank and travelled home. I treated myself to a few hours on the sofa to catch up on a bit of sleep.

Sasha, Evie and I did the Big Field loop and froze to death. I couldn't believe how cold it was in the north-east wind. No wonder the spring barleys are looking a bit sorry for themselves, desperately in need of a warm wet day or two. The prices for wheat and barley are still on the up, so it's an ill wind and all that - even if it is a freezing cold one.

Working on the assumption that in a week's time I'll be up together, I agreed to do another after-dinner speech in Norfolk, this time at the hotel where I was staying when I did the speech in Downham Market. I rang the organiser who had emailed me some time ago just to check that it wouldn't be a room full of people who had heard the speech before. He promised that only he and his wife were at the previous dinner, and he promised that they would not spoil the joke.

April 28th

Both phones rang – the landline and the mobile – within seconds of each other; it gave me quite a fright. It wasn't some sort of cyber-attack, but just an amazing coincidence. One call was from a spray delivery driver outside the silver gates in the yard trying to get in to drop off Tod's herbicide prescription. The other was from the fertiliser delivery driver, doing his one hour's notice phone call. The latter had been before so did not need directions, but, like a good lad, was obeying instructions to tell us he was on the way. I wished him luck getting through the crap parking at the bottom of Hinton Hill.

Once I got all this lot sorted out, I could sit down and write Flindt on Friday, which was based on an incident with a hare-coursing spaniel in Big Field the other day. Old and well-worn territory, I know, but still worth writing. Once that was done, I headed down to the Drier Yard to mend the roller shutter door into the drier building itself – again. The wind had blown it out of its runners ages ago and the door had become almost unusable. The fertiliser driver was already down there, having sneaked in silently, and we had a good chat about life, the universe and farming. It was so cold that I nearly suggested we open the roller shutter door, now mended, and take shelter from the north-east breeze in the barn.

This did mean I could have gone back to fertiliser, but decided to press on with spraying instead, and did a Tod megamix on the wheat in Stanmore and some of the Folly. I could have cracked on for a late tank, but I realised that the Volvo test car was on its way back tomorrow. I needed just a bit more of a drive to firm up my opinions on it. I did the Petersfield to Selborne to Chawton to West Meon Hut loop, and then sat in the cabin with my notebook jotting down two pages of thoughts, which usually suffice.

Hazel had had the vet out to check out the new calves. He seemed happy with them but suggested that we all keep an eye on the navel sucking which seems to be compulsory with male calves these days. She then vanished off for a dog-training session with picker-up Nessa for the best part of two hours on a stunning if cold April evening. What a life.

April 29th

Two more tanks of spray finished current tickets, leaving only some flag leaf stuff on the winter barley for later. This gave me time to have an afternoon shower and get cleaned up ready for a very important visit. The top team from *Farmers Weekly* were on their way to discuss life after retirement. They've already suggested that they're very keen for me to keep doing something, even though the whole concept of Flindt on Friday – i.e. grumpy farmer in his tractor cab – will no longer be valid.

They both made it down from London in quite good time despite the bank holiday traffic (another bloody bank holiday?) and we headed down to the Flowerpots for a quiet evening with neighbour Robert. They were delighted to find that not only did the Pots actually exist, Robert did too. It was the first time we've eaten down there since it was worked over during lockdown, and it was splendid. The menu was a bit pretentious – my ham, egg and chips should really have just been called 'ham, egg and chips', rather than ten thousand words of waffle. Robert, still struggling with his chest (but now on a course of weapons-grade antibiotics) managed a pint and a bowl of soup, but the rest of us had a bit more.

This was all very well, but we hadn't yet touched on the purpose of their visit, which was to discuss our retirement plans. It was soon clear that they were very keen to keep me in the pages somehow, and – even more gratifying – that they'd be keen for me to do a lot more audio work. All these discussions were done on the sofa, well after midnight, and with the complete menagerie (except Abel, who was obviously busy elsewhere) climbing all over our guests. Tim was soon asleep in the FW Editor's lap, and Cain – not usually a fan of strangers – settled down on top of Emma. Now *that's* how you work from home.

April 30th

Our two houseguests continued to prove the ideal temporary lodgers. He was up early – only just after me and Hazel – and immediately grabbed a bucket of freshly-made calf milk and headed out to the back barn with Hazel. By the time that job was done, she was up, too, and we had a very long and leisurely breakfast of poached eggs and bacon.

You could tell that they were proper journalists by the way the kitchen table vanished under a layer of newspapers and magazines. No formal and polite conversation needed – just a very satisfying munching and occasional comments.

Hazel's phone rang with news that immediately spoiled the mood. It was Kate from next door, and their shed had been broken into overnight. The buggers had also been into Godwin's Yard and taken stuff from there, and smashed their way into Robin the Beeman's barn. It wasn't long before Facebook started showing similar stories from Cheriton and Bramdean, with doorbell footage showing a large white van and a car, and several hooded lads, doing the rounds at around three in the morning. Bastards. It was quite a relief to start our farm tour in Shed 3b and find it intact.

We continued with the old estate workshop, and then jumped into Tigger for a drive round. There was a time when all the gates and tracks were open and accessible, and you could do a proper 'round the farm' tour.

Those days are gone. We drove out across the Godwin's track, pointing out the site of the Battle of Cheriton, and Robert's vineyards. Then on, along the ridge through the top of Chalks, Clump, Big Field and down to Joan's Acre. We crossed the road gingerly, went through the wheat, and paused at the Hurst Down dell. For those who have never come across a dell before it's quite a sight.

I dropped them off at the Neck, and Hazel led them down through the woods to enjoy the staggering display of bluebells. I retraced my steps in Tigger as far as the road, and drove round to the entrance to Blackhouse Farm to pick them up again. We thought we'd check out the pastures, mainly to show them Hinton House in the sunshine, but ended up chasing escaped lambs. Well, the FW Editor did; we stood and watched. He got them back in.

After another cuppa, they went on their way. It had been a very positive get-together, and their ideas for the future are certainly food for thought. Or would have been if I hadn't been on the sofa snoring within an hour.

A whole day not in the tractor. Blimey.

May 1ˢᵗ

Hazel was off ridiculously early again, but this time without Tim, and not off to Mullenscote. There was a Flatcoat Society 'Inter Area Working Test' down in the New Forest, and Bella was her weapon of choice. It took some time to persuade Bella that she really was being summoned off the dog bed for a day; it's funny how they get so used to routine. Hazel left me with a list of lamb- and calf-based feeding instructions and vanished.

The radar suggested showers were imminent, so I did a tank of fertiliser on Childs Broom and Middle Broom, and had to have the wipers on 'occasional', which was very satisfying. The FW Editor texted to say that he'd decided to bring his wife back to Hinton to do the proper NT walk, and could they drop in? The timing was perfect, as I'd finished one tank, refilled, and then paused for lunch.

Mrs FW Editor is another Ulster Girl, and in a way it was a shame that Hazel wasn't here to compare notes on growing up in the Province. But we drank too much tea and ate too many ginger biscuits anyway.

My second tank did Big Broom and finished some very sorry-looking spring barley in Godwin's Park. It really does need a day's hot rain, but there's no sign of that. I did wonder whether it was worth its second dose, but pushed on anyway.

Hazel was back and feeding calves by the time I finished, and was as pleased as punch; she and Bella and her teammates had come second, but only after a run-off after they had tied for first. Bella had excelled herself, and only dropped three points out of one hundred.

Policeman Ian rang in the evening, to say he'd done all he could do about the trailer. Farmer X is sticking to his story that he bought it from a stranger on Facebook, and that he had no records or paperwork of the deal. Ian said that it could go no further, and the next step would be for the NFU insurance mob to start whatever they have to do. Very frustrating. The two dealers involved in the daisy chain of transactions have – he said – come to an agreement on splitting the losses, so, if we get the trailer back, and repay the insurance money we got, then everyone will be as happy as can be expected. Especially fucking Farmer X, who has got away with it.

May 2ⁿᵈ

It was probably a bit ambitious to set off doing more fertiliser on a stunning Bank Holiday Monday, but I was desperate to get all the spring barley done before the much-promised rain. My starting point for the day was the top corner of Chalks, and I sat there for about twenty minutes waiting for a break in the crocodile of people setting off on the Dutton Memorial Walk for the bluebell woods. Even once I'd finished Chalks and made a start in Roe Hill, the road trip to the Drier Yard to refill was fairly challenging. The sunken lanes do not make for easy negotiations of walkers and cyclists. By the time I'd finished BOMS, I decided to call it a day, and joined the flatcoats for a snoozing afternoon.

May 3rd

The weather muppets are surer than ever that today we'll get a proper bunch of rain. However, the last of the fertiliser had to wait as I wrote up the Dacia Jogger and sent it in.

There was still no sign of rain by the time I got back in the tractor, and I did Rick/Clump, Big and half of Blackhouse Road, watching the sky. It got darker and darker, but there was still none.

Bizarrely, the radar suggested a huge storm was over the top of us just after tea, but I think it's the radar machine at Stockbridge giving false info again. The same happened at bedtime, although there were spots in the air. Somehow I doubt we'll wake to a drenched farm.

May 4th

I texted 'Happy Star Wars Day' to the children and, as usual these days, got no reply. It's a shame they're all grown up now.

Murph came round for a cuppa and a long chat about Trailergate; without giving too much away, it might affect his plans, although we all agreed that – all being well – it shouldn't. If that doesn't sound too cryptic.

The promised storms were brewing nicely as I set off to finish the fertiliser. One more tank on Blackhouse Road, and then the dregs working out perfectly on the redrilled bits of White Hill. All that's left is the late small dose on the wheats.

The storms brewed up fantastically, glowing red and white on the rainfall radar; not a single one reached us.

May 5th

About this time of year, every year, I end up writing a column about the difficulties of spraying – or, more specifically, the nightmare of getting chemicals out of their cans and into the sprayer itself. Usually, I write it, and abandon it, realising I did the same column last year. I thought I'd give it another go this year, because I had a great idea in the tractor the other day about a spoof game show, featuring product managers from chemical companies who are subjected to great pain and agony for as long as it takes us to get their chemicals out of their cans. I spun the idea out to six hundred words and sent it off. They seemed to like it, so it can be one last dig at the companies before we stop spraying forever.

While I was in keen spraying mode, I thought I'd give the sprayer a bit of TLC before doing the last two tanks on Tod's list. I unfolded it in the yard and cleaned all the filters. I'm a great fan of nozzle filters, but on a 24-metre sprayer there are 48 of them; it's not a five-minute job. It helped that it was warm and sunny – nozzle cleaning in November is a nightmare. While I had it unfolded in the yard, I also went round the grease nipples, which is always good for the conscience.

I had rather hoped that the farm would be underwater today, and I'd be able to jump in the car and drive up to Lamma meet a few farmers and sell a few books. Unfortunately, the rain missed us completely, and I felt obliged to get on with the spraying, not least because the winter barley is coming out in awns and the last straw shortener needs to be on soon. I did the two tanks after lunch and came home quite pleased with the state of the winter barley. If this drought goes on it'll be a good test for Grandpa's theory that this is a drought-proof farm – if we get the root growth at the right time of year. Five minutes of looking up forward prices on the AHDB website was quite scary, but in a good way. Feed wheat prices for what's in our store at Trinity Grain now are extraordinary, and the forward prices for next harvest are racing on as well; £330/tonne is unheard of in my lifetime.

May 6th

Time for the last speech of the season, and another long trip to Norfolk. I'm much more relaxed about them now; I've got 3,500 words which never fail to raise a chuckle, and enough miles under my belt to set off with confidence onto the nation's motorway network. Google said the journey would take three and a half hours, but despite this prediction, I was on the road at twelve thirty.

My self-assurance lasted about twenty minutes. After a bit of a wait on the Winnall roundabout, I was on the bit where the northbound road splits into the A33 and the A34. A huge container lorry came tanking up the lane destined for the A33, and then decided to veer left on the A34 section. It's common practice, but it's normally done by wankers in BMWs, and slightly earlier than at the very last minute. The lorry, which had a wanker-in-a- BMW-style 'personalised' plate, simply turned on an indicator and changed lane. I was left with no choice but to brake suddenly and take evasive action. I pressed the dashcam 'save this bit' button, if only to make me feel better. The drive went downhill from there. The A34 was shut at Oxford, so I did an M4 west turn and headed up the A338 to Wantage. A great road, but fairly busy with the traffic all doing the same thing. I rejoined the A34 at Oxford and headed on.

The Friday traffic was building, and the M40 wasn't much fun – once I'd got onto it. Northampton was the same, and it wasn't until I got out into north Cambridgeshire that things quietened down a bit. I managed to get lost among all the villages that end in 'well', which all have identical huge creeks running through, with roads on both sides and lovely houses. I drove around in a circle for some time before reaching the hotel. It had been a five-hour drive. My host had solemnly promised that he and his wife were the only two at the dinner who had been at the Downham Market dinner a few weeks ago; everyone else would never have heard the speech/joke before. I think he was being a tad economical with the truth; there were a lot of familiar faces there, and once the speech was done, book sales were poor enough to suggest that I was trying to flog them to people who had already bought copies. I must remember to tap him for diesel – otherwise I'll be out of pocket on the whole trip.

The speech itself seemed to go well, and if many of them had heard the joke, they were polite enough to laugh. It was the first speech I'd done when there was a hard core of farmers keen to push on into the evening. It was well past one o'clock when I staggered across the car park to my room. I'll be needing a nice leisurely drive back tomorrow.

May 7th

It took some time to get on the road home. There was a lot of beer to be processed, not to mention the small matter of another full English breakfast. But, brave little soldier that I am, I managed to be out on the road shortly after ten, heading for Diana's new house in St Ives. (No, not the one in Cornwall.) Her years of sharing a modern development in central Cambridge had ended abruptly when one of her flatmates had handed in her notice to the landlord. The landlord promptly gave all four tenants in the property a couple of weeks to get out – which he claimed he was entitled to do. Diana and her mates took some professional advice, which forced the landlord to change his tune slightly; they had a couple of months to leave, but leave they had to.

It turned out to be a blessing in disguise, provoking Diana to find a new place, and, for the first time in her life, somewhere on her own. She found a perfectly acceptable place in St Ives, which was a lot nicer in the flesh than on the internet. It is in a leafy suburb, full of trees and birds singing, and a stone's throw away from large green walking/jogging areas. I was very impressed. She seemed delighted to be there and was busy stocking it up with her own furniture.

I offered a trip to Homebase or B&Q to stock up further, but she was happy with a trip to an enormous branch of Morrison's where we did a bit of a food shop. I gave her a 'Granny grant' for that, and then topped it up with a few more notes, and set off on my way, really pleased to see her new situation. Last time I did that route home on a Saturday it was a nightmare, but this time – possibly because it was later in the day by now – the roundabouts and bypasses were a bit clearer. The A34 continued its form of being Hell on tarmac by being shut at Abingdon. There had been a huge crash shortly after midnight, and the clearance, including carriageway repairs, was taking forever. We were funnelled into one lane, and finally off at Abingdon – but we were all crawling for the best part of an hour.

The traffic was being herded left, into town; I chose right, and headed for Wantage again. Oh yes, that was a clever move that would outwit the flock – and give me another blast down the A338, my new favourite road. I had it to myself, and thoroughly enjoyed myself. The perfect pick-me-up after all that queuing.

It was rather odd, therefore, when I rejoined the A34 at Chieveley, to find myself overtaking traffic that I'd been passing in the long traffic jam. That meant the official diversion through Abington town had been quicker. Oh well; I had a lovely drive.

I thought my suffering had been so severe that I deserved another McDonald's

Big Mac, and I got home in a relatively cheerful state of mind. It had been another long drive. It was great to find Anthony at home, having come down for a couple of days of contract gardening, although whether draining the pool of a winter's water and strimming and mowing around it counts as 'contract gardening' I don't know. Still, nothing should break the drought like us putting up the pool. After another huge meal, which I really didn't need after the McDonald's, I was asleep very quickly.

May 8th

Not altogether surprisingly, a quiet day. Anthony did a bit more strimming, and Hazel dropped him off at Bentley for another gardening session at his housemate's parents' house. Hazel and I both agree that the new lifestyle is suiting him down to the ground. He's looking and sounding well; I just hope he's earning enough to afford living up in London.

The vicar dropped in for a surprise chat, in his work kit. I'm not a man who bothers God a lot, if at all, but I'm very fond of the vicar. He's funny, sharp, and perfectly at home with people who take the Lord's name in vain twice a minute. He was here to chat about the Blake's Trust with Hazel, but we ended up covering a vast range of topics – and when I half-seriously pointed out that, thanks to our retirement plans, we would no longer be after him to sort out the poor tortured soul in Rough Field, his eyes became very hard and intense. "Tell me more," he said. I re-told the sad tale of Sub-Lt Norman Daley, killed when his Fairey Barracuda plummeted to earth in Rough Field on the 13th November 1943, and ran through the long list of breakdowns and incidents that I've witnessed over the past forty years. "We must do something," the vicar announced. "We have a department for just these things." The rest of the conversation was quite scary – and he asked that it be kept confidential, which did little to lessen the slightly surreal nature of the discussion. But it would be lovely if our last act in Rough Field would be to let poor Norman find peace.

The first half of the top-level live rugby was so crushingly dull that I went down to the Drier Yard and got the combine out. We're due a minibus full of students from Sparsholt College in the morning. They're agricultural engineering students, and they need a combine to inspect. I somehow got volunteered to help out; I'm delighted to do so, of course, but I'm not entirely sure how I agreed.

I got back to find I'd missed forty-five minutes of scintillating rugby. Ho hum. I went to sleep on the sofa in a sulk.

May 9th

I was down at the Drier Yard nice and early, getting myself ready for an invasion of students. What would they be like? Would they resemble in any way me and my mates at Newcastle forty years ago? Mind you, I wanted to get down there nice and early just in case our white van friends had spotted a combine parked outside its barn and helped themselves to its diesel, or its wheels, or anything they fancied. A silver Defender drove slowly by, on its way down to Blackhouse Farm. It was my neighbour who lives down there – or will, once the multimillion-pound restoration project is done. I waved, of course. He's been trundling past for some years now, but we've never got past waving status.

Until today. With much gearbox whining, the Defender reversed its way back, and pulled into the yard. We had a very pleasant chat – and I think I may have persuaded him to book the band for the housewarming party, when it finally happens.

Just as he set off again, the Sparsholt College minibus arrived. Out jumped two lecturers and a squad of students. You never saw anything so keen. There seemed to be hundreds of 'em, swarming all over the Claas, poking, prodding, swinging off the superstructure, rolling around underneath, rolling suspicious cigarettes (no, not really) and all in the hunt for faults. There was an oil leak near the header accumulator and a slightly wobbly idler pulley for the straw chopper drive – both of them nicely hard to find. In the end, I left them to it, but not before I'd had a chat with the two lecturers and found that news of our imminent retirement had reached the hallowed halls of Sparsholt College. "You should come and work with us!" they said, and I don't think they were joking.

I got back home just in time to meet up with an Aga company who were keen to give the aged Aga a good going over. The sixty-something year old beast was given a good poking and prodding (like the combine), and we were promised a set of quotes for anything from a new lid and top, to a complete new model. We'll see. By the time we'd had lengthy chats and coffee with the engineers, the Sparsholt team had gone, and I was able to take the front off the combine and put it away again.

The sprayer MOT man rang mid-afternoon, suggesting that he popped out tomorrow to give the sprayer its annual once-over. "It'll be raining," he said. I laughed at his confidence but agreed that tomorrow would suit. I've still got nothing to do at the moment. If it does rain, I'll be cross that the last batch of fertiliser hasn't arrived.

Hazel did a run round the farm topping up pheasant feeders, and we had a splendid band rehearsal. The ABBA numbers were coming along nicely.

May 10th

Guy the MOT man was absolutely right; we woke to a damp farm. Not proper wet, but there had been a bit of rain overnight. What's more, it kept going for the morning, and he ended up doing the MOT in light rain. It's quite handy in a way – it means that water running across the yard doesn't look so out of place, and there are fewer Trust visitors out and about to look on disapprovingly. As usual, it took longer than it should have done thanks to all the gossiping, especially when I told him our retirement news. He insisted that I give him a shout about the sprayer when it's done with, as he claimed he could find it a good home very quickly.

I had a long drive round in the afternoon checking all the barley, thinking how much better it would look if we got some rain. Pipe for the pipeline is being delivered in gorgeous steel tube lengths, and I was busy cuddling one in Dell Close when one of the minions wandered over to see what the hell I was up to. I gave him a long speech about how in another life I would have been a civil engineer instead of an agricultural engineer, and then realised he was Spanish and hardly had a word of English. He must have thought I was the local nutter. He was right.

My Tuesday evening phone calls to Robert to organise a pub trip went unanswered. I assumed he was busy elsewhere, and set off with the dogs for a long walk. The phone rang just after I left; it was Robert ringing from Basingstoke hospital. His breathlessness had got so bad that he had checked into Winchester A&E, where finally someone decided it was a heart problem and not a lung problem at all. Next thing he knew he was being whisked off to Basingstoke in an ambulance. He was due an angiogram imminently, and then a date with the heart surgeon at the Brompton. Blimey.

What was astonishing was how cheerful he sounded. But when he explained that ten years of breathlessness would appear to have been misdiagnosed, and he was thrilled to find that something could be done (even if the cure was fairly dramatic), it made sense. It brought back memories for me of twenty-one years of tummy unpleasantness until a chance reading of an article in the *Mail on Sunday* medical pages produced an instant cure. Funny old world.

May 11th

It made a nice change to be mosquito-free for a night – Hazel had bought some netting and put it over the windows. It is obviously working splendidly. It meant an unbroken night and a bit of an oversleep. We may have been free of mosquitoes, but the animal magnet had been left on again, and a dramatic swarm of bees arrived early in the morning on the trunk of one of the holly trees outside the back door. The traditional phone call to Robin the Beeman was made, and he promised to come and have a look.

I suspect the bees were restless because of the change in the weather. Rain was finally imminent. As I set off to Alresford to take another half a dozen copies of Book One to Oxley's bookshop, hand in my cheap and cheerful suit for a dry clean after lots of sweaty speeches, and pick up another huge bag of prescriptions, it finally started to rain. Quite hard rain, too.

That could only mean one thing: time to sit down and do the online single farm payment forms. After a quick phone call to Chris the Land Agent to check on the procedure for fields that had been patched up and re-drilled, Hazel and I sat down and polished the whole thing off in just under an hour. Bearing in mind the five-figure sum that we should get at the end of it, it is still the best paid hour's work a farmer can do, even if its days are numbered.

The rain cleared in the late afternoon, having done some good, and I set about the swimming pool with a new-found enthusiasm. I have promised myself that this year I'm going to get in as much as possible. I suspect the end result will be a long wet cold summer. Still, you can't beat a long day adapting farm plumbing bits to get a pool going.

May 12th

The world looked a lot better after yesterday's rain, or perhaps I was imagining it. Or perhaps it was because I was up early, unusually well-slept, at five thirty. Unheard of for me. Even better, I managed to sort the visit of all the students into an article and send it off to *Farmers' Weekly*.

I was waiting until eight o'clock before ringing Yara to give them an earful. The fertiliser I ordered a week ago still hasn't arrived. But on one of my many shuttle runs back and forth through the kitchen, I noticed that my phone had a batch of missed calls. For some reason, it was on silent, and the first call was from the Yara driver at seven thirty, saying he was on his way. I'm glad I noticed it. Just at that moment, he rang again, and it was the same chap who has done the last couple of loads. That's even better – no need to talk him in.

And that'll be the end of liquid fertiliser. The last load of arable nitrogen is on its way. (I suspect we might be using some solid stuff on pastures and shooting strips, or whatever the future holds for the fields we're keeping.) It must be thirty years we've been using it, and I still love it for its accuracy and convenience. You can really get your money's worth out of a sprayer, and use that sprayer in the rain when you wouldn't otherwise be out in it. I remember old Ken being thrilled when I told him that he would no longer be spinning on the white prills with the Amazone; he never got on with the job properly, even at piddling 12m widths. I've ordered enough N35(S) for 50kg/ha on all the wheats, and a couple of extra cubic metres for the shooting strips, and then I'll ring Yara and tell them they can have their tank back. That really will mark the beginning of the shutdown. Cripes.

Some jobs are still more important. The swimming pool was filling far more rapidly than expected, which meant a trip to APM for some plumbing bits. Which they didn't have. I came back with some zip-ties and a sore back from driving the i20. The internet beckons.

Over lunchtime, Yara rang. Would I be needing that outstanding order of fertiliser? I said I wouldn't, and that I hoped that it wouldn't be a problem. They said it wouldn't, but I really should think about having it, ready for next year. I didn't dare tell them that I wouldn't need any next year, or that I suspected the price was about to plummet – which would certainly explain their enthusiasm to get me to take the last of the hyper-priced order.

After all that, getting two tanks on the Stanmore block was rather dull. It has made a great recovery, with Broom Field looking as good a crop as I can remember. Fingers crossed that take-all doesn't rear its ugly head – as it used to with second wheats up there.

The yard looked suspiciously tidy when I got home. Hazel had decided to start gathering all the seed bags and stuffing them, a dozen at a time, into another seed bag, ready for transporting to the recycling place. She was somewhat tired and grubby as a result. I wonder if she'll miss little jobs like that.

May 13th

A quiet morning. Hazel went off to the stables for some book-keeping, and I did a spell in our office. They're on about rain at the weekend, and I've got a tank full (ish) of fertiliser, so I thought I'd make the most of a dull but windy afternoon and keep doing the final round on the wheats. I did the lovely looking block of Gleam in Godwin's.

It meant I missed the first of the – what's the best name for them? – schadenfreude calls. It was from a neighbour with whom we've crossed swords about walking across our fields. The field near them has already been returned to the Trust under the Big Plan, and, guess what, there are now people walking all over it. The neighbour was not very happy. Hazel gently pointed out that such issues are not our problem anymore. It was lucky I didn't get the call; I'd have said, "I thought you wanted public access?"

May 14th

Talking of public access, there's a job that's been niggling away at the back of my head, and if I don't get on and do it, I'll be in trouble: spray off the footpaths. The grumpy locals are very hot to fire off a letter to the Council if I haven't marked them out by the time the crop grows. If they stuck only to the footpaths when they were out walking, I'd be happier, but there we go. Or they go. Quite literally.

I confess I'm a bit behind with the job – it has been such a wonderful frantic spring, and faffing about with Pig with its DIY sprayer on the back has been some way down my list. But the wind had dropped, it was too hot to do fertiliser, and the weather looks like it's going to be unsettled for a few days. Let's get on with it.

Pig needed to be reversed out of the calf pens (where it lives now to avoid rats) and have all the 20-litre drums lifted out of the back; enough rain is promised to keep the pheasants supplied with drinking water for a few days. Then all the parts for the sprayer need to be found. There's a cut down pallet, which fits nicely in the Kubota bed, and has the four-metre boom attached in a fairly rough and ready way. A sturdy ratchet strap keeps that in place.

I found the yellow tank tucked away in the calf pens, and strapped that onto the front of the pallet. The rats had had a bit of a party with the wiring under Pig's seat, so half an hour with the trusty crimping kit was needed. And once the pipes were connected, I was ready to go. I filled the tank with about fifty litres of water, gave it splash of wetter and a splash of precious Roundup, and set off across the diagonal in Middle Broom.

About twenty yards in, I realised I was getting wet, and ended up doing the rounds with a screwdriver on all the jubilee clips. I think I'd been squirting a strong mix of glyphosate in multiple directions, so God knows what the finished product will look like. It's bad enough that the wheat is almost over the height of the booms, so I've no idea if I was getting enough chemical on it. I did the shorter path across Big Broom, the two in Godwin's Park and the long one cutting the corner in Roe Hill.

There was plenty left in the tank, so I reconnected the whole boom (up to now I'd only been using two nozzles – which made the pump grunt a bit; you could tell by the smoke coming off the black tape wound round a connector) and started on the shoot strip at the bottom of Chalks. That idea didn't last long. The ground is rock hard and rough as hell from the last cultivate. I was relieved when the spray ran out.

It made me realise that there's another job on the 'to do' list: getting the shooting strips ready. Like everything else at the moment, plans for the shoot are in chaos – we don't know if we'll get any of our 'ex-layer' pheasants from our usual supplier, we're not sure exactly how the new shoot will look on Dead Dog Farm and (more truthfully) I haven't got my arse in gear. So, fired up with a new enthusiasm by the foray across a shooting strip in Pig, I put the Terradisc on the Massey and set off to blitz some other strips.

Folly and Bob's Wood went beautifully, of course (being chalk), and the full-width cultivation by the Terradisc should take out the healthy crop of docks. Roe Hill was bit tougher – and bigger, with all the extra strips that have been planned as part of the SFI Pilot Scheme. I was ready for a cuppa when I finished it.

The pool beckoned for the first time this year, and very nice it was, too – even if it took some time to adjust to the cold water. And then, after half an hour of flailing whale impersonation, it did get too cold, and I headed indoors for a warm shower, and to get ready for the event of the year: the Eurovision Song Contest.

We hadn't bothered rounding up the usual suspects to join us for the evening, so it was just the two of us. This was a bit of a shame, because it was an absolute classic. Terrible presenters (one of whom vanished for twenty minutes just after doing a link with body language that suggested she was on the point of throwing up), technical problems, and a nail-biting conclusion. The songs have all gone up a gear or three over the last few years – even the Moldova entry, which was perhaps the last relic of bing-a-bong eurocrap, was brilliant. I rang in my vote for them.

Our boy was on the point of winning until the phone-in votes came in, when Ukraine, of course, got a million billion votes and stormed into first place. (Odd to see us in second place; has Brexit been reversed? And France and Germany last and second-last – have they left the EU? I get confused.) It was a vintage evening.

May 15th

A quiet Sunday. The much-promised rain rolled in late morning, and did a lot of good. It rumbled occasionally too. The aerial cable promptly started messing about with the TV reception, and what should have been a long day drinking tea and watching the BTCC was slightly ruined, although what I could see through the dancing pixels looked much more exciting than usual, thanks to the wet track.

May 16th

Some very lively thunderstorms arrived in the night, which made for a slightly broken night. They'll be doing some good, though. It did mean that I set off for the last couple of tanks of fertiliser in fairly challenging conditions.

Hurst Down and JA/DC were a bit slippery but went well, but somehow I overfilled for the Folly, and had to run it out on the headland. I'm not sure the external gauge on the sprayer is very accurate in the middle of its range – I was putting 2,350 litres on 14.5 hectares. I had a rinse out and came home. And that, ladies and gentlemen, is (in theory) the last ever bit of arable nitrogen to be applied to this farm. It's quite a thought. From this September, the field will be full of organic beavers and free-range wildebeest, clumps of trees and regen grass. And all this on the morning that wheat price went mental in response to India's export ban, and the head of the Bank of England promised 'apocalyptic' food price rises. Imagine the fun we'll have if the Trust ring us up in a couple of years and ask us to return it all to arable in response to the world food crisis.

It seemed particularly suitable that this historic day was also Dad's 100th birthday. I wonder what he'd make of it all.

May 17th

There was nothing to spray, and nothing to put fertiliser on. Time to really commit to the shooting strips. I put about five hectares' worth of Roundup in the sprayer, and had a drive round doing most of the strips. I left Long Field and the White Hill side of Barracuda because we are due a visit from the expert at Bright Seeds, who I hope will tell us whether we should get rid of the four-foot-tall yellow vegetation that's out there. I suspect he'll tell us to leave it as it is.

I had a call from a rep from Adama. I half expected it after Friday's *Farmers Weekly* in which I gave the chemical companies an earful for selling stuff that won't rinse out of the cans. He tried the old 'we've never had that before' line, which once upon a time would have worked, but in these days of social media it doesn't work at all. I invited him to scan the spray operators' Facebook page where numerous fellow sprayer operators have been cursing and swearing about Arizona refusing to come out of its can. I promised I would dig a can out of the recycling bag and send him all the numbers I find on the packaging.

There was a long phone call from neighbour Robert, now tucked away in the Brompton Hospital awaiting a heart valve procedure. He still seemed astonishingly cheerful, but he explained (again) how he is so happy to have a proper diagnosis for ten years' worth of breathlessness. He must have chatted away for about half an hour, so his lungs have obviously improved already. I wished him luck.

The band rehearsal was cancelled as no one was available. Ian the drummer was ill with a chest infection, Dan was too busy working, Tod was stuck on the Isle of Wight, and I'm not sure what John was up to. So I put some wellies on and went for a walk before the next batch of thunderstorms arrived. My word, the crops are looking good – but let's hope the rain knows when to stop.

May 18th

Arthur from Bright's arrived mid-morning for a consultation on our present shoot and our plans for the shoot on Dead Dog Farm. He promised he'd do it in exchange for the speech to the gamekeepers' conference I did a few weeks ago. We jumped in Tigger and had a good drive around. You could feel him processing information and ideas as we surveyed the fields that we're going to be keeping this September. He sounded very positive about what we would be able to do with it and said he'd send us a report in a couple of days.

Once that was done, it was time to get into motoring mode, and get ready for the trip up to Malmsbury for the Range Rover launch. It was hardly worth a shower as I knew that two hours on the motorway network is enough to work anybody into a sweat these days. I promised myself one once I got there. Range Rover had commandeered a chi-chi hotel in a small village, even renaming it Range Rover House, and about sixteen of us gathered for pre- dinner drinks in the bar. Our two hosts held a mock and not terribly convincing press conference, discussing the new Range Rover, their hopes and dreams for it, and its astonishing internet sales. They had sold one every eight minutes in the first 24 hours after the dedicated website went live. It's certainly not how I remember buying a car.

Dinner was excellent – a good bit of beef done nicely, and I was lucky enough to be sitting between the president of the AA, who turned out to be yet another Newcastle graduate, and the marketing manager for Land Rover. I mentioned to him that I'd Googled his name and come up with an almost identical looking chap who was an orchestral conductor. "That's me too," he said, which provoked an hour-long discussion covering a thousand aspects of music. It was lovely to see him drop his professional marketing mask for a moment and talk about his passion, and it was great for me as an amateur Z-list musician to talk to a professional.

Most of my fellow guests piled into the bar after dinner. I headed to my room and tried to get some sleep.

May 19th

So much for the 'I can sleep in a strange bed without any trouble' theory. It was too hot, more thunderstorms rolled past in the night, the closing mechanism on every single door in the hotel woke up the rest of the hotel as it slammed the door shut, and dinner was sitting pretty heavy. The situation was different, too. In all the hotels I've enjoyed over the speaking season, I've adjourned to my room with my job done, and I can relax. In this case, I was psyching myself up for a very early start and a long drive, which can still be a bit intimidating. Yet more lurid dreams didn't help either.

I was first into the breakfast room at 6.45, half hoping to be done and dusted before anyone else appeared. I'm not a great breakfast person. Of course, this was never going to happen, and my fellow guests appeared in varying degrees of brightness, but all of them wanting a chat and a 'who are you and what do you do' discussion, which is lovely.

After three-fifths of a full English breakfast, I did my traditional stroll down to the church to survey the architecture as if I knew what I was looking at, check out some melancholy gravestones, and take a picture of a white pheasant that was sitting on the wall of the churchyard. I sent the picture to Hazel and the ex-Editor.

I was so busy enjoying the misty morning that I was late back to the hotel to check out and attend the very important briefing in the yard. It was all trivial stuff; most of it based around not upsetting the locals as we set off – there was a primary school just round the corner, and the last thing all the Cotswold yummy mummies in their Range Rovers needed was to have drop-off interrupted by hungover journalists in *their* Range Rovers.

My co-driver, chosen by chance (I assume), was Tim, and as luck would have it we hit it off immediately. Within moments we were completely ignoring the merits of our vehicle and were discussing life, the universe and everything. We also agreed that we were there for a jolly day out and both struggled with the intensity of those who spend a whole evening discussing the merits of different exhaust systems. Mind you, that's probably why we end up being Z-list journalists.

I did the first stretch down the M5 and over to the Severn bridge, which was stunning in the early morning sunlight. We swapped over in a layby opposite the entrance to Chepstow racecourse. It was bloody handy that there was a Portaloo in the huge car park on our left, and we were able to hop over the fence and make the most of it. I'm not sure that the Chepstow authorities had left it there for our benefit, but it was a most convenient convenience. Tim drove up the beautiful windy Wye valley as far as Eastnor Castle which is where Land Rover have their off-road experience. After coffee and pastries we swapped seats again and set off in convoy through the woods, up and down steep tracks, nicely sticky and slippery after the weeks of rain.

There was a top moment when, after another series of radio instructions telling us how to set up our vehicles for the next obstacle, the lead vehicle (which was a Defender with the knobliest tyres you ever saw) failed to get into it at all, and had to back out. There was a quick reissuing of instructions, and we set off using a slightly different bit of track. I think they thought they'd got away with it. The Range Rover was brilliant, of course, but I still yearned to be at the wheel of my Terracan with just the one four-wheel-drive setting. Our vehicles were jet-washed by a team of minions before we were released back onto the main road, so Tim took over again and we headed east into the Cotswolds for lunch. God knows where – I got completely baffled by the satnav instructions. All I know is that we ended up going through security gates, down a beautiful track, and arrived at a spanking new house/barn conversion in honey-coloured stone. The Land Rover team told me that it was a private house, and they were the first people to rent it as a venue. It was beautiful.

A celebrity chef had been hired for lunch and had come up from Cornwall with a whole bunch of local recipes. I'm afraid I haven't got a clue who he was, and his habit of lacing his mockney speech with 'like' every third word didn't endear him to me much. I skipped his garlic-laced starters and could have done with a proper plateful of lamb, even if it was delicious. That's the problem with being brought up in a house where food is nothing but fuel for the day ahead.

On the drive back to the hotel, Tim pointed out that those of us who were there planning to write up the event were in the minority. He'd enjoyed lunch with some 'influencers' (whatever they are) and a rapper. We agreed that that said more about Range Rover's hopes and dreams than anything we could write. After we'd said our farewells and picked up our goodie bags (laden with Daylesford organic grub – what a shame), I headed back down the M4, straight into the now traditional A34 traffic jam. This time a lorry had shed its load, and while it's true that we were moving, two lanes were being merged into one and it was a crawl for four or five miles. Not altogether surprisingly, I called in at Winchester services for another McDonald's. Curiously, it didn't taste terribly good. It could have been because they were very busy – or have I been converted to poncy food by a mockney Cornish chef? I do hope not.

May 20th

Tod had been round while I was away yesterday, and vans were delivering his massive order of chemicals very early in the day. It was wet again, and I didn't have to jump straight in the tractor and start putting them back on the fields. I had a bit of an indoors day instead.

The Field had agreed to give me two pages for the Range Rover write-up, but the only issue that had two pages available was the next one, which meant they needed the copy as fast as possible. It'll be going to press within a matter of days. I sat down in the office and gathered my thoughts – most of which had been put together in the A34 traffic jam – and managed to get a thousand words done by late morning. They were very grateful to get it so quickly. I bashed off a couple of emails to Range Rover asking for photographs, and that was 'job done'. I felt very pleased with myself – it's been a fun couple of days.

It turned into a bit of a coffee afternoon, with the ex-Editor dropping in for a long catch-up after his numerous holidays in Malta and Slovenia. Much of the conversation, once we'd done with holiday snaps on his phone, involved Eurovision and what a success it had been. Then Jeffrey from APECS called in to hand deliver a quote for finishing the north-facing doors on the tractor barn – a job that's been outstanding, and a bit of a bone of contention, for some years. It didn't help that his recent quotes had got stuck in my AOL spam box, and AOL quite inexplicably have stopped notifying us that there's anything in the spam box. I had possibly half a dozen important emails that I should have answered, and when Hazel went looking in hers, she found five times as many – and many of those involved the Alresford Show. She spent some time at her computer doing damage control. What AOL think they're up to I don't know. We've stuck with them as our email address suppliers for the best part of 25 years, and I suspect it will still be too much trouble to change.

May 21st

There is nothing so pathetic as a mob of flatcoat retrievers as they watch Hazel set off somewhere without them. It was made infinitely worse by the fact that she was in all her shooting kit. She had agreed to be a helper at a retriever training day in East Sussex, which meant an early start – and no dogs of her own. All the khaki kit went on, and the chunky boots, and the sleeveless jacket, and just as the excitement was reaching fever pitch (and the clock read 6.50am) her lift arrived and she was off, solo. The shock! The outrage! Mind you, it only took then five minutes to come to terms with it, and head back to their beanbags.

I could/should have had a day in the sprayer – the chemical was in and the weather was fair. But I had a lazy morning and watched some stunning Premiership rugby in the afternoon. (Quins vs Gloucester. Another great game for that Marchant lad; I briefly overlapped with his father at Winchester RFC in the mid-eighties.) There were lambs to feed at lunchtime, dogs to walk – twice, although Bella refused to leave the house the second time. And a surprisingly warm swim in the evening.

Hazel was home well after seven, having had a great day in the secret depths of the East Sussex forests. The dogs forgave her, just, but as we all set off to bed, I found Tim forlornly sniffing out her shooting kit on the coat hooks, wishing it had been his turn today.

May 22nd

A few days ago, the ex-Editor texted that we should get our huge weapons out and shoot some clays. I agreed that it was a splendid idea, not least because my new Rizzini was hardly put to the test last shooting season, and it needs some squibs through it. We agreed to set off to Chalky Hill at eleven.

We anticipated a very busy shooting ground, thanks to the lovely weather, but it was just right. We had to wait for a bit at some stands, but on one or two we walked straight into the cages. We both shot well (36/50 and 32/50) but my BR110 did another 'double discharge' which entertained onlookers and pulverised the clay, even if it did give my shoulder a bit of a nasty thump. I must remember to email ASI as soon as I get in. It was interesting to eavesdrop on numerous conversations about supply of pheasants; the consensus has now switched from blaming the French – which is traditional – to DEFRA, who, according to numerous well-informed keeper types, are deliberately dragging their heels.

We passed the Three Horseshoes in Bighton just as the lunchtime punters were leaving, and got ourselves stools in the tiny but cool bar where we enjoyed a pint and some peanuts – dry roasted was all they had, but they'd have to do. The Shoes looked like it was doing very well – it wasn't long ago that it was another country pub surrounded by HERAS fencing, with property developing vultures circling overhead, drooling with anticipation of filling the car park with yet more luxury homes. How that was prevented, I don't know, but it was good news. When someone arrived in the bar and asked for two buckets of water for her shire horses, the staff hardly blinked. We were on our way out by then, and I couldn't resist a sweaty cuddle with one of the monumental greys, standing patiently in the car park. Right eye to right eye, and let them push a nose and nuzzle into your (still sore) right shoulder. I miss horses sometimes.

I got back to find Hazel in the middle of the lawn, and in the middle of a phone call to Robin the Beeman; yet another swarm had arrived in the garden, and after trying the holly bushes and a chimney for size, had settled down noisily in a shrub at the end of the old garden wall. He said he'd be over later to fetch them. I went and had a wallow in the pool, carefully avoiding the humming masses.

May 23rd

Half a weekend's worth of weapon waving made me realise that it was time we did something about our shooting strips – even if we don't manage to source any birds.

The Roundup I put on most of them the other day is working well, and they're looking ripe for some cultivation. I helped Hazel put on the massive rotavator, and she set off to give the strips that had had maize a good mullering, in the hope that the old stalks get smashed enough to go through the little Fiona drill's coulters.

And while it was fresh in my mind, I thought the time had come to sort out the new Rizzini's double-discharging. I exchanged friendly emails with their tech man (he's a keeper, too, so most emails discuss wheat supply and pheasant availability, and only then get to the business in hand) and we agreed I'd pop my gun in the post. No idea how I do that, but there we go.

Over lunch, Hazel and I ran through the list of strips, consulted the list of what Arthur from Bright's had recommended after his site visit, and got everything ordered. Hazel had done with rotavating, so I hitched it off and put the deep leg/disc combo unit on. I did all of Chalks, Big Field and the old bits of Roe Hill, and they all went down beautifully. More rain is on the way overnight, which won't do any harm. What a strange spring.

Neighbour Robert rang, now back at home after his heart valve job. He was back to normal – spitting teeth about the delays, the paperwork, the misdiagnosis, the food, the paperwork – again – which all seemed to be a very good sign. He must have been a terrible patient; all he wanted to do was jump out of his bed at the Brompton and get home to his Land Rover.

May 24th

There were still vans arriving in the yard, delivering the spray from Tod's big visit last week. Also arriving through the course of the day were heavy storms, which messed up any plans to get the spray on the fields. There was hail, a rumble or two of thunder and a spectacular outbreak of measles on the rainfall radar.

The proof came through for the two-page Range Rover review, which only had a couple of things that needed tweaking. It took an age to get an insurance group out of Land Rover, and it was, inevitably, 50.

The Rizzini importers suggested I take the BR110 down to the gun shop in Botley, and they would organise a courier from there. I packed it up in its nice new travel case and set off through the lanes – now becoming overgrown and a bit dangerous. Through Kilmeston, up over Lomer, (pausing to be amazed at the view of the Isle of Wight in the clear air; have they really towed it fifty miles closer, or does it just look like that?) and onto the Corhampton to Bishop's Waltham road. Then on down through Curdridge and into Botley, parking in the yard of the old mill.

The car park was surrounded by aggressive signs, all in small print, warning of confusing and seemingly contradictory parking regulations. They made no sense at all to me. My first question on entering the gun shop was "Am I alright to park there?" I had an hour free, apparently. But you just don't know, these days.

There was a lot of paperwork to do, and I browsed the racks while forms were filled in. In another life, I'd have been in the gun trade, and going through racks of shotguns is my very favourite thing.

My next favourite thing is, of course, playing in the band, and we had a very noisy and somewhat chaotic rehearsal. Tod was stuck on the Isle of Wight, Dan was late, Ian was doing his epileptic octopus impersonation, and I got cramp in my right arm. Apart from that, it was brilliant.

May 25th

Another non-spraying day, windy and showery; very frustrating with bank holidays on the way, a pile of chemical in the store and the crops approaching their 'ooh, they could do with another dose' stage. I did office stuff, and Hazel did admin at the Alresford Show office and at the racing stables.

I kept going with the discs, working down Chalks and Roe Hill again. I'm determined to get them as good as possible this year, even if we don't have any birds to populate them.

In the evening I popped down to Cheriton to visit neighbour Robert, now back at home after his new heart valve job. He had lost a whole heap of weight but had colour in his cheeks and was breathing freely. We had a beer in his conservatory, got mugged by a cat (once the comedy poodle had stopped barking at me), and I even had a small tour of the garden, almost as if he wanted to show he could walk up the garden a bit – something that was impossible only a few weeks ago. It won't be long before we're in the Pots again.

May 26th

It was time for a long overdue review of the farm insurance. It should be done every year, over coffee at the kitchen table with the NFU agent, but the last couple of years have made that routine somewhat difficult. He was here by eight thirty, and there were a few tweaks to be made, but most of it stayed the same. Come October, of course, it will all be different. We agreed we'd meet again for a bigger review then.

The seed arrived for all the shooting strips, and – even better – Hazel got wind of some pheasants that might be available. That was my cue to continue with getting the strips ready. I sprayed off Barracuda and Pipeline a few weeks ago, and was contemplating ploughing them, but decided that the discs/deep leg combo would do the job. A couple of passes made a fairly good impression, but I think another pass with the rotavator will make them better. I also did the Folly and Bob's Wood, which, being chalky, were ready to go – apart from yet another flush of what look like docks coming through.

May 27th

Hazel volunteered to give the shooting strips another (final, we hope) pass with the discs. I reckoned we could do it without the Opico Varitilth that's on the front of them and had a long session splitting the two. There was enough time for her to do a Friday Tesco run, and yes, traffic is back to 'stupid' at Winnall.

I couldn't wait for the wind to drop any longer. I decided to go and do the wheat in Hurst Down and JA/DC, which, mysteriously has failed to have any fungicide on it so far – and it's well in ear. It's fortunate that it's turning out to be a low-pressure year for disease.

Something told me my sprayer wasn't well almost as soon as I started in Joan's Acre. The pressure was setting itself at around 3 bar to get a flowrate of 134 litres/hectare at a forward speed of around 10 kph. That's too high. And when I finished Dell Close, there was too much spray left in the tank – far more than the on-board computer suggested there should be.

Mind you, that was actually the least of my problems. The pipeline gang had been out and welded the vast majority of the pipe sections together – and very nice welding it was too. But it meant that access from JA/DC into the bottom of Hurst Down was impossible. I could get into the top of Hurst Down, but only with some very careful and tight turning – remembering to switch off 4WD to tighten the turn radius. There was once again still too much in the tank when I finished, and I started trawling the memory banks; I'd had this issue before.

My latest sprayer has got a very clever recirculating system. When not actually spraying, chemical is pumped backwards through the pipes, in theory filling the booms with chemical ready to go. When you turn the nozzles on, the flow is reversed, but a one-way valve means that the chemical now comes out of the nozzles. All very simple, and makes you wonder why they didn't do it years ago.

Unfortunately, on my sprayer the system has never worked properly. I still have to wait for chemical to reach the end of the booms once I've turned the nozzles on, whereas in theory you should be able to start off at once with a boom full of the correct chemical, rather than clean water – or whatever's in the booms from the last job. The original one-way valves, despite being brass, seem particularly fragile – I wonder if it's something to do with the liquid fertiliser. When these disintegrate internally, some of the chemicals sent to the nozzles makes its way back to the tank unmeasured by the many flow rate meters plumbed into the system. You end up not putting enough on. I bet that's what had happened this time.

I wanted to finish Hurst Down anyway, and did the last half tank having put the flow rate up on the computer to 150 litres per hectare. It still wasn't quite enough and there was a couple of hundred litres of mix in the bottom of the tank when I reached the top corner. I set off home for repairs.

I had a new one-way valve in stock – a nice cheap-as-chips plastic version – and it took me all of five minutes, with the monster booms unfolded in the yard, to replace the malfunctioning brass version. It helped that I remembered that when cleaning all the nozzles the other day, the flow rate to the inside left boom seemed pathetic. Sure enough, the spring and the pressure plate inside the valve had disintegrated. It took longer to find a useful roll of PTFE tape than it did to do the repair. I called it an early night, helped by a phone call from Graham Tosdevine to say that George would be in early in the morning to do a couple of tanks. If that goes well, all the wheat will be done exactly on time.

Hazel had done a splendid job on the shooting strips with the discs and they looked absolutely perfect – ready for drilling. Not tomorrow though; she's away all day with the dogs, and I'll be doing spray support services for George, and maybe getting a tank on myself.

May 28th

Hazel was off quite early with all three flatcoats, down to the edge of the New Forest for some 'water work', which is a grand name for playing in the River Avon for a day. I consoled Sasha for a bit, and then opened up the spray store and the gates for George. I got my tractor out of the yard and parked it round the back to give him enough room to turn his massive John Deere self-propelled machine. He arrived on the dot of nine thirty as promised, and once we'd done our usual gossip and moan about the madness of the day, he set off to do the rest of the wheats.

I fancied the morning out of the tractor and gathered up all the bits I needed to repair the DIY heat exchanger that I plumb into our pool. I needed a hacksaw with a blade that was a tiny bit sharp, some solvent cleaner, some solvent welding glue, some fine sandpaper and a bag full of bits that had been delivered from eBay during the week. It only took an hour or two, and when I'd finished, my grid of eight two-metre black PVC pipes were once again all plumbed into one unit, ready for water to be pumped through them. I'm not sure just how much it raises the temperature, but it does seem to work. The hot sun on my neck as I wielded the glue-filled brush made me wish I'd got it up a bit earlier.

After George had been in and refilled and set off for his second tank, I brought my tractor round into the yard, put 17 litres of fungicide in, and did White Hill and Cheyney. The blackgrass in White Hill was embarrassing, and nearly had me reaching for my chemical bills to see how much I paid for a chemical that had done the square root of bugger all. If we had been continuing to farm this autumn, White Hill would be a candidate for some dramatic rotational changes to try and sort out the blackgrass.

Three drenched dogs and a very happy Hazel came crashing through the back door and into the sitting room where I was snoozing through an uninspiring rugby final. We'd got 260 acres of cereal sprayed, too. That's officially a good Saturday – especially as the forecast for tomorrow is heavy showers.

After a busy day, I was looking forward to a proper sleep. Unfortunately, someone over Bramdean way decided that a hefty display of fireworks was in order at eleven o'clock. And I could have sworn that their music got louder after that finally finished. God I hate fireworks. God, I miss lockdown... sometimes.

May 29th

Heavy showers were promised, so it was time to get on with the strips, and actually put seed in them. It took an hour or two to get the Massey hitched onto the vintage Sulky box drill (eBay special a few years ago) and get it set up and calibrated. I had to take a break for the first BTCC race of the day, but set off to the Folly after lunch. I got the U-shaped strip around the trees done, the Bob's Wood strip, and then drove back to Roe Hill. The new strip along the northern headland is pretty big, and I did worry that I might not have enough seed – good old Pheasant and Finch from Bright's.

I should have had more faith in the old drill's calibration consistency. By the time I'd done the West and South strips in Chalks, there was a thin line of seed in the bottom of the drill, and the first of the eight spouts (all the rest get shut off) were making an appearance. Perfect.

It was hotter and sweatier than the forecast had suggested, and a warmish swim beckoned after the last of the BTCC races. We did eventually get a shower of rain – a tiny one just as we were having supper. I could have gone spraying after all.

May 30th

Fired up with enthusiasm for sowing shooting strips, I cleaned out some of the dregs for Pheasant and Finch from the old box drill (leaving a bit at the bottom in between spouts to act as 'buffer') and calibrated for 'Grass Buster'. The heavens then opened. Proper rain. Good rain. It did mean that Hazel and I had to spend an hour clearing the down pipe outside the back door, which despite decades' worth of time and effort by the Trust to get it sorted, still overflows and floods the house at the first sign of heavy rain. Rolling the strips that I'd sown yesterday was right out of the question.

The gig season is about to kick off, and we had a good-ish rehearsal. I struggled with cramp in my right forearm – not good when your piano playing is amateurish at the best of times. When we were an eight-piece, I could hide my incompetence a bit – not so easy these days. I blame the cramp on all that drill calibration, cranking the home-made handle on the side gearbox.

May 31st

That little drill isn't as rainproof as some modern ones, and it had half a dozen bags of very expensive 'Grass Buster' in it from yesterday's calibration. The quicker that seed goes in the ground, the better. I walked down to check the pool, fling in some more chlorine, and then on out to the strip at the top of Chalks – one of the strips due to receive Grass Buster. It was perfect, crumbling nicely under the boot.

I thought I'd start with the strips in Big Field first, and they went nicely, too, although the maize stalks did get in the way once or twice. I lifted the drill up a couple of times to let them flow underneath. I'll call the resulting gaps 'flushing points'. My technique of going very slowly to ensure a nice even seed placement went to pieces as a massive black cloud appeared in the south-west. I went up a couple of gears, and finished the last of the four there-and-back turns just as heavy rain started. Good timing. I headed home for lunch.

Hazel went to pick up Diana from Winchester station. She is coming down for a few days of R 'n' R after some intense months at her video game company. She's certainly looking well on it though, but a few days of dog/cat/cattle/lamb therapy is always a good thing.

After an hour to two of hot sun, I thought I should check the Chalks strip again, and found it had dried amazingly. Off I went again – pausing briefly to help a mother and son team struggling with an old-fashioned OS map. They were trying to walk back to Ropley, so I despatched them towards Bramdean. I commented that it was lovely to see someone using an OS map. "And yet somehow we're lost," she said. Fair enough.

Chalks went nicely, although with the same maize problems as Big Field. It was very satisfying to finish 15 acres of strips with only a few pounds of seed in the bottom of the old drill. They went into a bag, ready for patching up, or using next year.

Just as I was finishing flushing out the seed, the vicious black line of clouds that had been lurking to the north for an hour decided to move south, and bring its lightning with it. Another proper – and very handy – deluge was perfect on the freshly sown work. Fantastic. And all in May. (I'm ignoring the Stanmore block, of course. That's for another day.)

A late afternoon text to Rufus resulted in a trip to the Thomas Lord in West Meon for a long-overdue catch-up. He's suffering from 'long Covid', struggling with what was once a routine lifestyle that involves hectic trips back and forth from London – mind you, he had the Kung Flu proper: several days in intensive care and all that. I told him that it wasn't 'long Covid' at all. He's just a fat bastard. And old. Bit like me, really.

The really good news was that, just before I left for West Meon, neighbour Robert rang suggesting a trip to the Pots. It was bad news that I couldn't come, of course, but great that he's feeling fit enough for a beer already. We agreed we'd give him another week to get that bit stronger. For a brief moment, I thought Rufus and I should divert to the Pots and join Robert, but Rufus in full voice might be a bit of risk to a senior farmer having just had a heart procedure.

June 1st

If you haven't seen _No Time To Die_, skip a couple of pages (spoiler alert).

Farmers Weekly have given me an interesting task: like all Remainer institutions, they're still fighting the EU Referendum, and they thought they'd do a 'two letter debate' to mark the sixth anniversary of the historic result. They've asked me (Brexiteer) and fellow columnist Will Evans (staunch Remainer) to write letters, setting out our views on Brexit. He starts, I reply, then he replies, and I get the last letter.

FW had sent Will's first one through, and I sat down this morning to do my reply. His main thrust was that the promises from Brexit politicians haven't come to pass, so my main reply was that neither had the doom-laded promises from the Remain camp. Neither of us touched farming, but I suspect that will be the main point of his second letter – probably based on the crisis in the pig industry. We'll wait and see.

Tod was round just after lunch for one of his last visits. He had no new recommendations – just confirming his last batch, and a thorough check of the spray store to make sure we get it as clear as is possible for the end of the season. The weather cleared enough for me to pop out and get a tank on Drier Field, which looks a picture – as does the whole farm from the top of the hill. I took yet more pictures through a filthy windscreen.

And after a large tea, the three of us decided we'd fire up all the CD players and the aged surround-sound system and watch the latest Bond film – _No Time to Die._

I was genuinely unaware of how it ends. It has to be one of the best-kept secrets in media history. I've been to plays and films where the producers beg you to keep the plot to yourselves – but these were all in the days before social meeja. And I've followed the debates about 'the next Bond' and where the franchise will go next with great interest – especially as this latest film was unlucky enough to coincide with the Kung Flu and the lockdowns.

But all that debate was a clever ruse – a red herring. Bond dies, for fuck's sake. It was a real shock. My whole life has been punctuated by the release of Bond films – some good, some bad, some terrible. But there has always been, for an amateur film buff like me, the next Bond to look forward to. No longer. Two and a half hours flew by, and it was a real tearjerker at the end – made worse when the lead up to the end was a clichéd gun battle in which Bond has limitless ammo and all ten thousand baddies are woeful shots. He manages to survive impossible odds – and then suddenly, he can't escape his fiery fate. In fact, the whole film was lighter than normal, with genuinely funny one-liners. But then he's dead. It was quite an event. Hazel said that when she watched it – I was away on a speech – she blubbed uncontrollably.

Where do they go from there? Nowhere, I suppose. I went to bed in a state of some sadness. I must get out more.

Mind you, it had the worst theme song in film history. Does no one _sing_ anymore?

June 2nd

The Queen's Platinum Jubilee. I had forgotten that today – a Thursday – was a bank holiday as a result. I had a full day's spraying planned. The weather was fine, but my job was all the spring barleys, and they're mostly next to paths that were likely to be very busy on a fine June bank holiday.

I was busy finding more excuses not to set off in my tractor when there was a clattering from the gate outside the office. The first job is to stop the dogs rushing out to kill whoever/whatever is there, and the second is to find out who/what is making all the odd noises.

It was one of the old shoot syndicate, now an Iron Man triathlete, doing a tour of the county on his bike (a routine ride for him), who thought he'd drop in for a cuppa. Splendid news – not just because we had a lot to catch up on after what must be ten years, but also because it made the decision on my morning plans. We covered life, the universe and everything, and parted with a half-certain plan to get everyone together from all those years ago for a reunion. We'll see.

Never mind Her Majesty's big day; the first Test match of the season started today, and once I found a way to listen to it (BBC won't cover such a sport, of course) it very quickly turned into prep school cricket, with wickets tumbling. It's sad, in a way, that it's all crash-bang-wallop cricket. I miss Tests when the tumbling of wickets was a rare event.

The first of the weekend's gigs was looming, so I had a nice snooze – another excuse to not go spraying. Tod, John and Dan arrived to get all the kit into assorted vehicles, and off they went to Privett church. I had a quick shower and was on my way to join them when John rang, urgently requesting more extension cables. Good thing I was hanging around being late, eh?

The venue – the church at Privett – was astonishing. A view south towards the Meon valley, the enormous steeple, and, of course, the good people of Privett losing their inhibitions as the evening went on and getting their boogie shoes on. I didn't get home until midnight – and even then bedtime was delayed further by a text saying that Alexa Cheung was in the audience, and had been sending pics of us setting up to her five million plus followers. I think she only took the pic because Dan was bending over in the background.

A great evening.

June 3rd

Inevitable, I suppose, that today's gig would be a bit of a comedown after last night's. But even so – none of us was ready for what was a very odd evening.

It was another Jubilee gig, in – we'd better say – a local village. On a recreation ground, at the end of a long day of celebrations. And, more importantly, we were playing as the third of three bands on a cold drizzly evening – hardly conducive to a cosy and intense evening of hits.

But the early bit went well. The clouds cleared for a bit, and we had a couple of dozen dancers trying to fill the huge gap between us and the first row of straw bales which served as the seating.

And then we took a short break. It had to be short – any longer than ten minutes would have resulted in us freezing to death. (Pause to check the date and global warming predictions.) Suddenly, there was an emissary from the audience, who homed in on Ian the drummer. There was a nipper in the crowd who really *really* wanted to have a go on the drums. Would that be OK?

Ian was, of course, the very model of diplomacy. Not tonight (he explained). We're only on a short pause, and he didn't want his kit all messed up. But feel free to drop into the music shop he works in in Guildford and the nipper can play all the drums he likes.

The emissary beat a hasty but reluctant retreat. Next thing we knew, the nipper's parents arrived, somewhat more belligerently. Ian the Drummer's polite refusal cut no ice with them. It got a bit heated. Little Tarquin (not his real name) just *had* to play the drums. Now. Once again, Ian said no, gently and politely. This undignified spat went on for some minutes. "Let's see what happens at the end of our set," said Ian, somewhat exasperated. The posse of pushy parents finally backed off.

As it happened, our set finished earlier than expected. It got colder and damper, the crowd dwindled to about a dozen, and the mood of the evening had changed dramatically. We went to Jumping Jack Flash and said our goodnights.

Team Tarquin descended on Ian's drum kit. The first thing Tarquin the Drumming Prodigy did was pick up Ian's sticks and sneer at them. He then launched into a hideously complicated solo, with pushy parents baying at his brilliance. I'm not a drummer, but I thought it was shite. Someone said something to Ian – it's hard to establish what – and he had had enough. Tarquin was asked to get off the kit and go away. I don't think anyone had ever spoken to Tarquin like that in his life, and he spent the rest of the evening sobbing with his adoring coterie. "It's all about making memories for the kids!" was one of the lines used by the pushy parents earlier. Perhaps Tarquin will remember this night as the one he found that he doesn't always get what he wants. Bless.

We tidied up, packed up and brought all the kit back to Shed 3b. Another 1am bedtime beckoned. We'd missed the rain, played well, and had a whole new story to add to our long list of stories. God Bless Her Majesty.

June 4th and 5th

A couple of snoozy, drizzly and cold days. I didn't feel terribly well, either. Probably two late night gigs getting to me. I was cross, too – I should have done that spraying over the fine start to the Jubilee weekend. Still, that's what happens when you believe the 'fine next week' forecast that the BBC serves up as default.

June 6th

A casual glance at *The Field*'s page which details all our commissions showed that the two-page article I'm supposed to be writing about ATVs and UTVs was due in today. It was wet and cold again, which meant I could abandon plans to get the last bit of spraying done (again) and hit the keyboard. All day.

I didn't just write – I had a curious flurry of books to post, pills to order (God, we're getting old), a *Farmers Weekly* article to proof – and a message saying that I should listen to *Start the Week* on Radio 4.

Now, if the BBC is a hostile foreign country, then Radio 4 is its capital. And *Start the Week* is one of its seats of government. But today they were discussing farming, like we all are at the moment. Three authors with farming connections and recently published books to match had been summoned for a round-table discussion (one of the ones where everyone goes 'nimnimnimnim' in a weird nasal way that you never hear anywhere but on Radio 4). One of the three was my niece, who has written a book on farming (like we all are at the moment). It's the follow-up to her stunningly successful book on her life as a barrister, and is all about her first steps towards becoming a farmer. She and I disagree violently about what 'becoming a farmer' actually entails, but her book is getting good reviews in the strange world of the Guardianista – even if it does have a full chapter about me.

Anyway, she was live on Radio 4, sitting round a table with the interviewer, a poet (really?) and the High Priest of Agriwokeness George Monbiot. GM of course could hardly sit down for the interviewer's tongue being so far up his arse, but Sarah was eventually allowed to speak. She'd studied GM's claims about farming. Using her lightning-quick barrister's mind, she'd been through his arguments, and told him, live on air, that he was wrong. Oh, to be a fly on the wall in Broadcasting House as every single employee of the BBC dropped their breakfast tray and collapsed to the floor in shock. Someone telling George Monbiot he's wrong? Good God! Sarah and I may not agree about much, but I reckon that was a great moment in modern broadcasting. But I'd love to know how much of the billions of pounds the BBC extorts from licence-fee payers had to be diverted to counselling services.

I failed miserably to write the ATV/UTV piece.

June 7th

There was annoying drizzle all morning. It would have been perfect if I hadn't had a complete block on inspiration for the ATV article. It's my first listicle, and I hate listicles. 'Ten best ATVs' was the commission. 'Best'? Define 'best'? It's like the page-fillers that smother the Saturday edition of *The Times*: '20 best pubs near towns that have a 'w' in them'. You then read twenty glowing write-ups of pubs that the writer has obviously never visited. Still, this sort of thing might be my job in the near future, so I knuckled down and got on with it. Well, some of it.

The afternoon was much more productive – in the traditional way. Hazel and

I did some long-overdue fence repairs in Springshot, and I took a chance on the weather clearing to do some spraying. Which it did, and I got two more tanks in. The little i20 went down to North's for two new tyres (Jonathan drives with a heavy right foot, I think) and neighbour Robert was better than ever in the pub. A good day in the end.

June 8th

No spraying today, so I persevered with the ATV article. Hazel vanished off on a coffee round. First to picker-up Nessa, who managed to go arse-over-tit down a badger hole (not a euphemism) a few days ago, and broke her ankle. Unbelievably inconvenient at the best of times, but when you've got a wedding imminent, it's really bad timing. Not just any old wedding, too; it's the one that has been delayed for years by Kung Flu, and is a double-header – one service in Hants, one in Italy. Poor old Nessa. She's been learning Italian specially for the trip abroad. What is the Italian for "I fell down a badger hole. No, it's not a euphemism." Google says it's *"sono caduto in una buca di tasso. No, non è un eufemismo."*

By the time she'd called in to see picker-up Suzi to inspect another gorgeous litter of flatcoat puppies, Hazel had had quite enough coffee and cooing. I managed to grab her to give me a lift down to pick up the i20 with its smart new tyres before she set off round the farm to clear her head.

June 9th

A calm (as in demeanour rather than weather) morning was needed. I was due to go to a meeting that had been organised by the Countrywatch police team near Petersfield. The Police and Crime Commissioner was coming along to address assorted farmers and hear their concerns. The last thing I needed was a sweaty morning doing stuff.

Of course, it didn't work out like that. There was an early text from Brad saying that he had seen three Dexters loose in Dark Lane. This didn't make any sense at all. Between us, Hazel and I can place most makes of cattle within a few miles and Dexters don't feature on the radar. Could they be Nicola's Gloucesters from Hinton Park? They'd been unsettled and bulling when we were fencing in Springshot the other day. Hazel texted her anyway just in case, and then set off for a dog walk with Mrs ex-Editor.

Then, my phone rang, and this time it was the transport company delivering another pallet-load of cattle feed. All very nice to get some forward notice, but he said that the lorry was twenty minutes away. Hazel was still dog walking, so it was up to me to get out, unlock the gates, and get the tractor all set up for pallets. The lorry arrived on time and was on his way back down the hill three minutes later.

By then Hazel had finished her dog walk and had jumped in Tigger to go and play 'hunt the Dexters'. I'd had numerous phone calls from dog walkers all pointing out that there were three stubby cattle doing the rounds of the farm, but no one gave a specific location. I said to Hazel that they were bound to end up in our farmyard – lost livestock always does – but she set off around the farm anyway.

I was nearly right; they ended up in the Drier Yard instead. Hazel rang (what did we do before mobile phones?) to ask if I could get down there and help them into a lean-to where we could shut them in. I went down in the i20 to see what I could do. Three stubby little cattle were stubbornly refusing to be herded anywhere, and after ten minutes of circling in the grain store yard, they set off through the winter barley. Not sure where they were going, but they seem to have some idea.

By this time a proper June sweat had materialised, and a quick shower was in order before setting off to meet the new PCC. The meeting was interesting, in a very smart grain store near Petersfield, although police staff and personnel almost outnumbered the farmers. It was a bit like one of those 'flash mob' videos that were all the rage some years ago; a thousand members of the public in a railway station, and four hundred of them get up and dance/sing in stages. By the time all the PCs and their assistants had stood up and introduced themselves, the audience was somewhat depleted.

It was a good meeting though. We all had a rant about something; for me, it was noisy bikes. The PCC was very positive (even if she said that wading into the bikers' café with a decibel meter was impractical), crowing about new recruits and technology. Normally such announcements are greeted with barely suppressed scoffs from surrounding plods, but they got appreciative nodding this time. Good news.

Back home, Dextergate had nearly resolved itself. Owners and assistants had been found, neighbours were all chipping in to help, and the three weary cattle were making their way back to Kilmeston. Should make a good article, anyway.

June 10th

The next column finally arrived in the night – Dextergate, of course - displacing the one about fertiliser that I'd started and stopped a dozen times. But, once again, it was not a spraying day, with a howling hot gale blowing, so I continued my mission to get the Lupo up and running.

Its old battery had failed to charge, but once connected to Tigger's with jump leads, the engine started after just one turn – amazing after all these years standing idle in the yard. I listened carefully for any signs of the engine being about to explode, but there were none. The dodgy hydraulic tappet was still ticking away, but there were no warning lights to be seen.

I drove it carefully and slowly across the yard to the tractor barn to pump up the tyres. It was a great relief that the brakes weren't seized on – if anything the problem was the other way; they were rusted to almost useless, and I nearly went straight into the sheeted doors. These cheap and cheerful tyres were all hovering at about 20psi, and, being so small, needed very little air to get them back up to 32psi. The engine was warming up nicely, but not overheating, so that was my cue to do lots of laps of the yard, trying to shine up the brakes with some left-foot braking. After about five minutes, they failed to feel any better. If a big restoration job is in order (and I think I'm being stupidly sentimental in thinking I can get Granny's pride and joy back on the road), I suspect they'll be the first job. I parked it next to the drill in the yard, ready for a wash.

A quick turn of the key moments after turning the engine off showed that the old battery was in fact dead, and a new one would be the first bit of shopping – not new brakes. A call to Rod Gaskin revealed that, on the shelves among all the huge tractor batteries, there was a little one that would fit.

Then I gave the old VW a wash. I was going to use the pressure washer, but all the extension cables are running the pool pumps at the moment. A hose pipe and a sponge would have to do – and a bucket full of hot water and Fairy Liquid, as we're also out of car shampoo. It was a bit of a marathon session, getting all the grime and mould off, but the little old car came up a treat. I'll probably take it down to North's for an MOT and find it's a scrap job, but I'd love to keep it going somehow, if only for sentimental reasons. I left it with doors and boot open to air a bit and hopefully clear the slightly musty smell.

I'd had a message from the gun shop in Botley to say that my Rizzini was back from Snape, all repaired and ready to go. With a gale still blowing, it seemed like as good a time as any to drive down and get it. The team at ASI had apparently sorted the double discharge ('overlapping sears') and had kindly filled the ABS case with goodies: another cap, lanyard, some pens... Let's hope the gun works properly now.

June 11th

Yet another windy day, which meant no spraying. The forecast predicted a nice long calm spell next week – there we go, after all these years, still falling for the 'fine next week' line from the weather muppets. But it was enough to persuade us to think about cutting some hay in the Back Meadow again. There's not a lot of grass out there because it's had no fertiliser, but it's 'going to seed' and in places has quite a lot of bottom grass. I took three dogs out for a loop around the Meadow – it's on the verge of not being worth the effort, but a hay cut would tidy up the field a bit and yield a couple of dozen bales that will always be handy.

More importantly, there's another gig tonight. It's an early start and an early finish, being at a wedding venue in the middle of Winchester – which limits noise levels – and Tod and Dan were in the yard loading all the kit into Tod's Freelander shortly after four o'clock. Sasha and I went up to making encouraging noises, and Sasha decided that Dan was her new best friend – it was hard work getting her away. Because it's a small venue, we didn't need all the kit, and they set off for Winchester only about half an hour later.

Experience has taught us that it's always handy to have one person hanging back behind the main set up team, and sure enough, I had a phone call to say that they had forgotten the two main speaker stands and an amplifier stand. I went and fetched those, put them in the i20, changed into my 'uniform' black shirt, and set off for Winchester.

The Chesil wedding venue was lovely; three or four rooms overlooking the Itchen just after it has been through the old city mill, with a smart garden and a veranda. The last time I went to that building it was an undertaker's; a big change in one way, but still dealing with the inevitable stepping-stones of life and death.

We got set up in the dance room and were up and running shortly after seven o'clock. We had a 20-minute break – much shorter than originally anticipated – and, thanks to some careful set-list management, finished the second of our encore songs on the dot of 9.45. Perfect.

The dance floor had been full for most of the night, and I don't think the bride and groom had left it once. There were toddlers, teenagers, oldies and a baby wearing earmuffs being carried by his parents as they danced. He – or possibly she – had the biggest grin on their face you ever saw.

We didn't play faultlessly but we played very well, and were thanked profusely. You could tell there were proper musicians in the audience somewhere because, as we finished, a tray of glasses holding chilled Coca-Cola was proffered. Just the job – although Ian's cry of "there's coke over here" gave me a bit of a fright. We were home and dusted shortly after eleven - most unusual for one of our gigs. It will go down as one of our best ones ever.

June 12th
The ex-Editor was determined that we should do another clay shoot. I said that it would depend on how I felt after the gig. He was having none of that sort of lame excuse, and was on the phone at some unearthly hour demanding to be picked up at eleven, so that we'd get to Petersfield Gun Club at about half past. I had a bit of a thick head, but agreed.

The Rizzini behaved perfectly, even if I couldn't hit a barn from the inside. The shoot was a tad expensive, but it's a sixty bird one rather than the traditional fifty, and it's well laid out in a copse called, quite appropriately, Gunner's Wood.

The wind just kept on blowing in the afternoon, which meant no spraying, and lots of snoozing in front of the BTCC.

June 13th
Finally – the wind dropped. Perfect for a busy day's spraying. Hazel was busy, too (as ever). Her Skoda had developed a nasty crack in the windscreen a couple of weeks ago, and it's no longer a case of ringing Reg's Windscreens and them coming out to the yard. Oh no – modern screens aren't just a sheet of glass. There are sensors and electric thingies and all sorts to be installed as well.

This means a trip to the depths of Southampton (as instructed by the insurance company) and a three-hour wait. Hazel's appointment was nine o'clock this morning, so she was up and about very early doing livestock and dogs, and on the road not long after eight o'clock.

At eight forty, she was back in the yard. I tiptoed out to see what the problem was; engine trouble? Forgotten the paperwork? No – it was far simpler than that. The windscreen company had rung just as she was leaving Cheriton to say the screen hadn't actually arrived, and could they reschedule for lunchtime? We're both sticklers for not using phones on the move, and it was lucky that Hazel had pulled over and answered it – not something she'd normally do.

I proofed the next FW article and then set about the last two-and-a-half tanks of spray on the spring barley. I managed Big Field with only a couple of pauses for walkers, and BML's – still working my way round the pipeline work. A full tank on Blackhouse Road left a bit to finish there, plus Godwin's Broom and the late patching-up in White Hill – about two-thirds of a tank in total, I guessed.

It was a bit of a round-the-farm hike, and I only had enough for the bit of spring barley in the corner of White Hill, but I was happy enough with that. The spray store was empty, it was getting on for eight o'clock, and I was knackered.

Hazel's rescheduled trip to Millbrook had been smooth and uneventful, and she had a shiny new screen in the Octavia. And the weather forecast was good enough to start ringing round to make hay plans. That'll make it rain.

June 14th

Another stunning June morning. I leapt out of bed ludicrously early and then fell over. The bedroom developed a 30-degree slope to the south-east, and then started spinning. Very odd. I realised I was heading headfirst for the mantelpiece and managed to divert the fall back to the bed, where I lay for a minute or two. It was very scary. I suspect I'd leapt out of bed a bit too quickly, or the long day spraying yesterday may have left me dehydrated. Or a busy weekend was catching up with me. Or it's Kung Flu again.

Whatever it was, I promised myself a quiet day. We're up together with farm work, and even the haymaking has been put on hold by a forecast of storms at the weekend. I needed more chlorine for the pool, and drove to the little shop the other side of Petersfield to get some. I picked up a new head for the vacuum while I was there. The i20 has no air-con, so it was quite nostalgic driving along with a window open to keep cool. It was 1980, I was in a Fiat 127...

Mind you, that was nothing compared to the nostalgia inspired by the sound of two Merlin engines as I was wallowing in the pool. It took me back to prep school, which was near Middle Wallop. We would regularly get buzzed by a Spitfire that was still based there (this was the very early 70s) as we played cricket/rugger/ made daisy chains out on a windswept Hampshire down. A quick check on the excellent Flightradar24 revealed that a Spit and a Hurricane had spent an hour or so entertaining the crowds at some event just south-west of Winchester.

Robert was up for a Tuesday beer, looking even more human as his heart op fades into memory. He's driving again, and said he was on for tomorrow's lunch with a farmer 'walking group' who are coming to the Pots. I did warn him that I wasn't convinced the original letter wasn't a spoof, but he said we'd have a jolly lunchtime beer anyway. Quite right. It was a relief to get into bed without the whole room spinning again. Even after a couple of pints.

June 15th

As I was finishing a morning check of the shooting strips (verdict: hmm, not very good) I called in to inspect the new one along the bottom of Roe Hill. A couple who had been walking up the track promptly turned round and headed back down. We exchanged greetings – and then he said, "Crop good enough for a mention in *Farmers Weekly*, then?" That was the cue for introductions, and a lift home in Tigger for a long cup of tea over the kitchen table.

They were farmers up from Wells, having a couple of days away from their business, which is broiler chickens. Now, I don't know much about most farming, but the world of chickens is one that I know absolutely nothing about. Or 'knew' – after a long chatty coffee, I was much better informed. Eventually, they continued their walk, and Hazel headed off to the Alresford Show office for more talks about the next show. "See you in the Pots at lunchtime!" was my parting shot to the chicken farmers.

Why? Because I was having another one of those surreal farmer moments. I'd had a letter from a retired ICI agronomist, saying that he and some walking chums were planning a yomp round Hampshire in the morning, and then lunch in the Pots; would I join them? Silly question. I managed to persuade neighbour Robert to join me, too, and we were treated to a couple of pints and a plateful of ham, egg and chips in the hot sun.

If you thought farmers were grumpy about the future of farming, you should try listening to a gathering of retired agricultural chemists and their ilk. They were probably all in their seventies, and all had enjoyed a fantastic career in farming's glory years, but they could not get their heads round modern agricultural systems designed to reduce food output. "Where's it going to come from!" was the cry round the table – many times. We enjoyed a few pints – one supplied by our new friends the chicken farmers, who had taken my advice and headed down there for lunch, too – and I headed home with a bit of a thick head. You guessed it – the sofa beckoned. Good thing there's no farming to be done at the moment.

June 16th

Hot and windy. Not a lot to do in this weather. I found some shade and a table, and we lifted the Mountfield mower onto it, ready for the new carburettor kit that had arrived via eBay the other day. It has been struggling for some days, and the simplest method to cure it is to buy a whole replacement kit. I seem to remember doing exactly the same job for the last book, and here we were doing it again. Last time, my fifteen quid only got the carb itself; this time it got carb, gaskets, fuel and air filters and new fuel pipes. I think I asked the same question last time, too: how the hell does anyone make any money shipping that lot over from China for fifteen quid? Certainly not the poor souls making and packing everything. The lawnmower sounded perfect once it was all fitted, though.

Tod was round for a crop walk – it could be his last one ever. There will be a huge heap of earwash fungicides for the wheats and the spring barleys, but he's confident that they will justify it. We stood in the spray store, checking that the campaign to clear it right down was going well. But it was slightly sad to see. God knows how many thousand litres/kilogrammes of stuff had gone in and out through that old stable door. I pointed out the date (1989) in the cement from when Ken the tractor driver had built the hollow-block wall to turn the last bit of the stable block into a store, and had dug a dustbin down into the floor to act as a sump. Bloody good handyman, our Ken.

June 17th

Even hotter, and even windier – which somehow made it feel even worse. The first loads of fungicides arrived, but no chance of getting any of it on in these conditions. I did some office work, had a bit of swim (even that was too hot in the sun) and generally looked forward to the first 'beer on the lawn' of the year. Mr and Mrs ex-Editor were planning to walk up, and neighbour Robert had promised to make it a proper quorum.

Guy the Sprayer Doctor arrived in the mid-afternoon to mend my machine; it has been losing air pressure from its Ramsay valve for a couple of years – slowly at first, but recently it has needed pumping up a couple of times in every tank. It is done from a switch in the control box in the cab, so it's more of a nuisance than an issue. My first Gem sprayer came with a foot pump and a very long bit of tube. Adjustment was a bit of a palaver. I have to say that the modern tech is fantastic, though; dial in some info and some required rates, and off you go.

He found an air leak in the brass pipe coming out of the 12V compressor mounted in a little case right at the back of the sprayer. Getting the pump off took far longer than the little bit of work needed with PTFE tape around the join. He was confident that he'd sorted it, but time alone will tell.

We didn't really need the fire in the old lorry wheel in the middle of the lawn for the boozy evening session, but I lit it anyway. It was lovely; warm, quiet, but no satellites visible (always the ex-Editor's favourite moments). It never really got dark enough.

There was a hilarious message from neighbour Robert just as we were starting to worry that he'd got lost (as if); he'd been checking out the Raimes Rosé down at the vineyard, and it had all got a bit out of hand. He wasn't really fit to come up and see us tonight. At least, I think that's what he said – he sounded pissed as a fart. One answerphone message that I'll keep for posterity.

By the time the four of us had put the world to rights and covered just about everything that two couples all within touching distance (before and after) of being sixty could cover, it was dark. Mind you, it was nearly midnight. And I think we were all fairly pissed too. I lent them one of our super LED pencil torches to see them home through the wheat. If that doesn't provoke phone calls to the police, nothing will. Especially if Mrs ex-Editor has to stop for a traditional wee halfway down the footpath.

June 18th

Yesterday's heat bade us a dramatic farewell, and it was cloudy and cool, with occasional spots of rain. I was just heading for the sofa with a cup of tea and a thick head when a farty Land Rover arrived in the yard. It was, of course, neighbour Robert, keen to make up for missing out on last night's beer – and that took most of the morning.

The rest of the day involved some gripping Premiership rugby and watching a band of thunderstorms creep across the channel. They had the decency to hold off until the two weddings that had somehow been booked for the same day in Cheriton were done and dusted. Cain arrived on the sofa just before bedtime, dripping wet, so the storm got here in the end, although the biblical thunder seemed to have gone east.

June 19th

I couldn't help commenting to the ex-Editor, as we drove off to do another clay shoot, that our Sundays were in danger of becoming a routine: late morning start, a round of clays that produce pleasure and frustration in equal measure (always the sign of a well-thought-out shoot), a pint on the way back, and then a lazy afternoon. He agreed. But we still did it anyway.

Give us a month or so, and lazy Sunday routines will be right out of the window. And then in six months or so... who knows?

Father's Day produced the usual stream of rude cards, lovely texts and a phone call. What well-brought up children they are. And we went to bed with the distant rumble of Muse closing the Isle of Wight festival, drifting up on a humid southerly wind.

June 20th

On viewing a video clip of the band playing at the Privett gig, one of Tod's lads commented that I looked like a glue-sniffer attempting to type out the complete works of Shakespeare in three minutes. Harsh, I thought – and then booked a haircut.

And after packing a couple more copies of Book Two and getting the next FW column sorted out, I drove into a surprisingly empty Alresford to have a proper preharvest trim. I was early, of course (lots of easy parking) and spent ten minutes strolling round the old railway station, enjoying the historic stuff. It took me back to my childhood days with an OO train set. I even had one of the chunky blue diesel shunters.

A check of the shooting strips in the afternoon was a bit depressing; the pigeons have had a party out there, and the 'Grass Buster' strips have been completely cleared. In a way, it's not a problem, as there are no birds to be had this year, but I was on a mission to get the best two-year strips sown. And then I realised that the wind had dropped, and I'd missed a perfect spraying afternoon. Oh well.

We had our last band rehearsal before the ABBA gig, and finally applied ourselves to the two ABBA songs we've agreed to do. Trouble is, their songs are so good you half wish we could do more. I typed out the lyrics and annotated them with chords, perfect for the assorted musical geniuses in Shed 3b to pick up at a glance. Well, that was the theory, anyway. In the end, most of it was done by ear, as ever. Mostly wrongly.

June 21st

A perfect spraying morning, and lots to do. I started with the last fungicides on the wheat and set off to Stanmore relatively early. It was yet another very significant moment, heading off to Pipeline (I thought I'd do the long-distance stuff first), and realising that this was the last time I'd be up there doing tractor work. A quite spooky moment. But it's handy that these 'last ever' moments are coming in waves (last ever drilling, last ever fertiliser, last ever spraying). But when the combine pulls out of the wheat up there, that really will be it.

The pre-lunch tank did Pipeline and most of Long, and after lunch I finished Long, did all of Broom and most of Folly. The wheat up in the Stanmore block is looking pretty good for an early-drilled second wheat, with only a few patches either dying off or showing signs of take-all. I never could tell the difference.

Spraying stopped for another meeting with the Trust's estate land manager, who arrived waving two things: a map of the estate as they want it to be in a few years' time, and a plea for me to do all the ground preparation and sowing of amenity grass. She had emailed it to us a few days ago, and I'd had a bit of a think. Why not? I've got the kit, I know the fields intimately, etc. I said I'd give it a go – it would be daft not to try it. If it doesn't work, or we decide for one reason or another to move on, then at least we've tried. She went on her way very pleased. Ironic that after three decades of telling the Trust to bugger off every time they've suggested we 'work with them', we're now dead keen to help them out. It will be a whole new experience working as a contractor. I can charge by the acre/hour and not worry about results. All my talk of 'last ever' trips to fields might be premature.

Plans for a late tank of fungicide were scuppered by a pub trip request from some Winchester-based friends, suggesting a trip to the pub with a Ukrainian that they've taken in. He apparently has plans to set up a fertiliser business over here – which seemed curiously specific – and wanted to have a chat with a farmer. I wasn't sure what help I could be. After all, all I do is buy it and put it on the fields; I know nothing of the logistics of supply. But a beer's a beer.

We sat in the Pots garden and had a very long evening. I tried talking shop with the Ukrainian, but soon realised that he knew even less about the logistics of fertiliser import and distribution than I did. So we reverted to the UK being robbed in the Eurovision Song Contest, which was much more cheerful – and much more my specialist field.

June 22nd

Suddenly extraordinarily hot. I can't remember it being forecast. Too hot to spray – which wouldn't have been a problem based on the weather forecast as it was yesterday, but it has suddenly been rewritten: thunderstorms tomorrow and then unsettled for some time. Great job, being a weather muppet. You can say whatever you fancy. ("Oooh, look at me; I play the drums!") I was somewhat the worse for wear after last night's beer, so I treated myself to a quiet morning.

Hazel was about to abandon her training session with Tim, but decided to give it a go. It wasn't too far away, and if it got unbearable, the session would be called to a halt anyway. In the end, she lasted the whole morning and came home thrilled to bits with both her and Tim's performance. He might be a quiet soul, but he's turning out to be pretty good at the retrieving stuff.

She'd hardly had time to grab a bite of lunch when the yard filled up with vets. Lots of them. She'd volunteered her calves for a team of trainee vets to do some work experience, and that experience was castration. I like to make myself scarce under these circumstances, and let Hazel and the gang of trainees get on with it. They were all girls, and from all around the world – America, Canada, Singapore, but not the UK. The Royal Veterinary College runs courses that are considered the best qualification worldwide, and the students get sent to Hampshire for a fortnight's farm animal experience. We get our calves castrated for free, the students get valuable experience (although they're all highly unlikely to end up in a farm animal practice) and – today – they all got sunburn.

I was nicely sheltered indoors, although I did feel the heat at one stage. The dogs, already hanging out of the window at all the visitors coming and going, started barking again. I looked out into the yard, and a stern-faced woman was walking round the yard with a clipboard. I decided that this was obviously not a vet, and thought I'd better find out what she was up to.

"I'm here to inspect the building before the Trust starts renovation work," she pompously announced. I asked why I knew nothing about it. "I tried to ring, but couldn't get any signal." Yeah, right. It took some time and some more fairly tense exchanges before I got to the truth: she's the bat inspector. Truly one of the most powerful people in the history of the universe, able to stop the smallest or largest bit of work at the stroke of a pen, at the first sign of a tiny dropping. Hence the pomposity and the lack of a sense of humour. I tried to point out that although the Trust owns this house, it is my home, and she ought to bear that in mind when coming to inspect it unannounced. She looked at me with a cold hard rage, furious that I had dared to question her authority. I was glad to see her go.

The vet squad were still cutting and slashing scrotums (scrota?) in the barn, so I agreed to drive up to Bentley to pick up Anthony, who is coming down for a day or two to cuddle some dogs and do a bit of gardening. He does a day at his flatmate's parents' house, and then we pick him up from there.

Even though the day hardly cooled, I did a late tank of fungicide on the wheat, finishing the Folly and doing Big and Middle Broom. The forecast got more and more dramatic, and I kicked myself for ignoring the spraying opportunities earlier in the week. Tell you what, I'm not going to miss spraying.

June 23rd

The forecast was for biblical thunderstorms – 'danger to life and limb!' screamed the weather pages. I had an office day and generally tried to get my head around tomorrow's very unusual plans. Hazel did a long afternoon up at the stables, Anthony and I tried to get the aged strimmer up and running, and he set off round the garden with it. Sasha and I did a couple of recces out to Rough Field bearing enlarged photographs of the Barracuda being dug up in 1975. Some features visible in the background back then were still visible now – telegraph poles, gateways, and so on – but most of the countryside has greened up beyond belief. No sign of the church, Hinton Ampner House or the bungalow, which were all clear as day nearly fifty years ago. Even so, I reached a spot which I was confident to call the crash site. That was where we'd meet up tomorrow, with the lovely vicar.

The curious feeling of unease (probably too strong a word for it – 'slightly wary anticipation' would be more accurate) wasn't helped by finding 'Barracuda' as an answer in *The Times'* puzzle page, and a Wildcat helicopter doing some hovering over Rough Field late in the evening. I texted ex-FAA pilot Vee to ask if she knew anything about it. She didn't. How very odd.

The life-threatening thunderstorms arrived just after nine o'clock. Cain arrived on my lap on the sofa, wet through. There wasn't any lightning or thunder, and no threat to life and limb, and it was six hours late, but otherwise the forecast was spot on.

There was a bit of a storm going on elsewhere; *Farmers Weekly* released the exchange of letters I'd done with a fierce Remainer. I'd made my case for Brexit, he'd disagreed. I decided to avoid my Twitter account for a day or two; the bile, insults and fury really won't be worth reading. 'Kinder, gentler politics' was what they used to call it.

June 24th

After a lifetime of driving over Rough Field and encountering what could be called 'supernatural' events (some months later, the vicar suggested that 'preternatural' is the better descriptive word, rather than 'supernatural'), the day had finally come to do something about them. I'd mentioned to him some weeks ago that now we're leaving the land, he wouldn't be called upon to lay the ghost of Sub-Lt Daley to rest, all those years after he died in his Fairey Barracuda in 1943. The vicar took the opposite view, went away to do some homework, and came up with the idea of a short service at the site.

Hazel picked him up from Hinton Ampner church just after eleven o'clock, and they drove down to the entrance to White Hill. I was already there with Vee, who had volunteered to come along to represent the Fleet Air Arm, and the sheep trailer – washed and sterilised by Shepherd Ella after using it for lambing – connected to Pig. We climbed in and set off along the headland tramline.

The four of us stood in a semi-circle around what I'd decided was where Norman Daley had plummeted, possibly unconscious, to his death, and we held a short but very intense ceremony. I read out a selection of the 'incidents' that have happened over the years (electrical failures, mechanical failures, small fires, punctures, bolting horses and the tailgate of my trailer coming open in about 1977) and, as he'd suggested, explained to the Rev Christopher that these were why I had asked him here today. Vee read out the FAA version of 'For Those in Peril on the Sea', Hazel put one of Dad's old trugs filled with forget-me-nots on the ground, and then, and only then, did we notice the single poppy growing a couple of feet from where we were standing. Once we were done, I took a photo of it for the article which I know will be too difficult to write.

We spent a good ninety minutes back at the farmhouse having coffee and cake, which rounded off the event perfectly. Both Hazel and I spent the rest of the day in curious contemplation. We're both militant agnostics, and yet we both agree that there's something 'afterlife' going on out there, and we were happy to summon an official representative of a deity we are not sure about to sort out a troubled soul and ease his path to the next life. No wonder it took me ages to get to sleep.

Although it could have been the cake, of course.

June 25th and 26th

A quiet weekend. Anthony had gone back, there was no shooting, and the weather meant no spraying. The cricket was quite phenomenal, though. If I were a cynical old git, I'd say the whole thing was a fix. Luckily, I'm not.

June 27th

Just as I was beginning to regret having booked a morning appointment with Jane the Physio, the bright blue sky vanished and several deluges came through – once again, no spraying. It meant I could go and have my hand sorted out.

It's becoming a bit of a nuisance. About ten minutes into every gig and rehearsal, the tendons down the back of my right hand start to burn. My piano playing is poor enough anyway, and the last thing it needs is an unusable fist making even more of a mess of our setlist than we usually do. I set off to Jane's with full confidence.

Just for once, there was nothing mechanical she could do. The knuckles and joints are becoming stiff and swollen (classic arthritis), and the tendons are obviously finding it hard to make fingers move. Combine that with a lack of proper warming up and stretching, and a sudden flurry of gigs after lockdown, and the result is some boxing-glove piano work. Ho hum.

She suggested lots of ice/hot baths treatment, lots of stretches and exercises, and a lump of Voltarol pre-gig. And if all that fails, go to the doctors at Medstead, tell them she'd sent me and get some blood tests.

The third Test against New Zealand finished in the same dramatic style as the other two, and left us all cursing that we only play three Tests against them. I had time in the afternoon to do a convoluted loop round as many shooting strips as possible with Sasha, which did little to induce optimism for the forthcoming season. Mind you, we've got no birds anyway. Ho hum. Again.

June 28th

We had an early meeting with our landlord to discuss more details about the Big Plan. Something tells me there will be quite a few of these over the next few months and beyond. Funnily enough, now that we've agreed to help them and 'work with them', these meetings are great fun, and very positive. We asked how she was getting on with all the neighbours who are (we hear) desperate to get their hands on the block of land that we're vacating. Poor lass; she rolled her eyes and said the phone lines were busy. One particularly posh neighbour (the one I really did say "I don't care who you are – please return to the footpath!" to) had been in touch demanding a small field next to his house to keep llamas on. Yes really. How we laughed.

The gale refused to stop blowing – still no spraying. I decided a spot of gardening was in order instead, and dragged the 'chainsaw on a stick' out of the old larder. Off came the 'chainsaw' bit, and on went the 'hedge trimmer' bit. The beech hedge in front of the house desperately needs a trim, and I haven't got the trimmer on the tractor yet.

An hour later, I felt very old. The carburettor was playing up (most unusual for a Makita), and extensive tugging on the recoil starter hadn't done my shoulder any good at all. I managed to get it going by refusing to let it idle, and it screamed its way down the roadside hedge for twenty minutes. It did a good job, but I could have sworn it was ten pounds heavier than it was last time I used it. In a huff, I came in and ordered an 18V battery version. It'll be here in a couple of days.

An evening in the Pots with neighbour Robert was great fun, but didn't make me feel any younger.

June 29th

Yet another non-spraying day. The beer and peanut combo wasn't sitting very well for some reason, so I was quite relieved to not be in the tractor. I had a quiet morning, and then we went off to Four Marks to look at wood-burning stoves.

Last winter, our chimney sweep announced that we really shouldn't be using the sitting room fireplace. Despite years of using the driest wood, the huge chimney was getting a bit dangerous – too much tar had formed on the brickwork. Something to do with the fact that the piddly little 1960s hearth never got the rest of the stack warm enough. Her suggestion was a major overhaul, with a liner and a wood burner. We spent an hour or so at the showroom, being treated to a lot of tooth-sucking and buck-passing, but finally managed to get some positivity from the man in charge. He knew someone who could do all the building work, and he'd get them to get in touch. For some reason I decided I wouldn't hold my breath.

June 30th

The wind had dropped – at last. The sun was shining. Perfect. Just the sort of day to get to grips with the huge backlog of spraying – or it was until about ten o'clock, when the heavens opened. Somehow a shower is better than high winds when it comes to calling off spraying. It's more definite.

We went kitten hunting instead. There is a semi-wild cat that lives down at the grain store, and every couple of years, it has another litter of kittens. Very rarely do any of them survive, but the latest litter has been turning up at the back door of one of the houses down there. They, of course, have succumbed to the moral pressure of a litter of hungry kittens, and started feeding them. And then stopped. This isn't the ideal scenario for a litter of wild kittens – you either feed them non-stop or you let the poor mother support what she can naturally.

Hazel had been tidying up the long grass round the Drier Yard with the topper and spotted the litter – about seven of them, she guessed – and was worried about the state of them. We drove down to the yard and found nothing. The mother had obviously managed to take them somewhere else, which was a bit of a relief. Of course, had we been inclined to, we would have trapped them, tamed them and flogged them for a small fortune; kittens are rare and expensive these days.

The day dried up, and I started shifting tractors around ready for a long evening spraying. Both needed refuelling, and once I'd done that, the main tank was empty. Curiously, it ran out 150 litres short of what the meter suggested we should have in the tank. Were we short-delivered in the spring? Is our meter playing up?

I rang round our three suppliers for quotes, and got two at about 125p/l and one at 117p/l, which I took. Extraordinary prices – prices I've never seen before. (My last order was the day before Putin invaded Ukraine – 80p/l.) But there's no other option. Harvest is on the way, and I'll need it. I'm glad Hazel is putting the word out about selling all the straw, which should save a small fortune in chopping costs as well as raising some harvest cash.

The phone stayed busy. A chimney company rang saying they'd been given our details by the stove company, and they were dead keen to send a surveyor round. That's a good start to our project. I tried to get another press car sorted out, but failed miserably, but was cheered up by the arrival of Jonathan from London, looking fit and well, and incredibly full of beans. His placement year at the Bank of England has been a stunning success. We were lucky to get a couple of days in his busy schedule to try to bring him back down to earth. Forty-eight hours with flatcoats is all you need. I suggested he have a go with the new Makita battery-powered hedgetrimmer which arrived safely today – but got a very un-Bank of England-like response.

Graham the contractor sprayer rang in the late afternoon; he had a spare evening – should he come over and bash off a hundred acres? I took one look at the rainfall radar and said, "not on your nelly." An hour later, the sky went black, with thunder and lightning, even though the bulk of it went just south of us. Good call.

That left one more thing to round off a busy day: the Bat Police. After the visit last week, I'd had emails from the Trust saying that the BP would like to come and sit in the garden for two consecutive late evenings – nine till after eleven – watching and counting bats. I threw my toys out of the pram and said no. We all go to bed, with much slamming of doors and locking of gates, just after ten. Tough titty. I then had a flood of pleading calls and messages from the buildings manager, pointing out that the BP are the most powerful people in the world, and nothing can happen until they've given the go-ahead. If we wanted those windows done, we would have to endure the visit. We did want the windows done, so I agreed to it.

For three slightly spooky hours, we went about our evening routine in the knowledge that the garden was full of people watching the house. One of the many joys of our farmhouse is isolation. But not tonight. We were drawing curtains, shutting all doors and keeping dogs well tucked away. Very odd. Luckily, *Casablanca* was on till late. Even Hazel stayed awake through it. I was mighty glad when the BP drew stumps and buggered off.

July 1st

Last night's visit from the Bat Police provided enough material for the next Flindt on Friday, which I managed to get written and sent off by eight, and we then had a fairly chaotic morning. Neighbour Robert Jnr rang about hay – did we have any, and were we planning to make some this year? Answer: not a lot, and yes, but not a lot, which probably wasn't much help to him. I handed the phone to Hazel to discuss it just as she was coming back from getting the papers.

The dogs then all went mad, barking furiously. I went out to see what was going on, and saw Hazel trying to finish her phone conversation with two surly looking lads standing next to her. It all looked a bit odd. I asked if I could help.

It turned out that they were part of the wedding crew setting up for tomorrow's big event down at the old rectory. They'd driven their lorry onto the grass and were stuck. They'd been told to go and find the farmer and he'd pull them out. Just for once, I said I wasn't available; the morning was busy enough (a rare thing for me) without having to free up a tractor and drag lorries around. It didn't help that they were both Poles, only one of them spoke English, and that they wouldn't take 'sorry, no' as an answer. "But those are your tractors," said the one who could speak English, gesturing at my machines indignantly. At this point, I got a bit cross, and sent them out of the yard. Not sure I did much for the reputation of British farmers, but there we go. Maybe next time, they'll think twice about venturing off road in their lorry.

They'd only just sulked their way off the premises when the latest National Trust employee arrived in the yard. She is part of the team running 'our' land from now on, and now we've agreed to help them with tractor-based jobs, there's paperwork to be signed – lots of it. They'd seen our public liability insurance, so that was fine, but we needed risk assessments and declarations of hazardous substances. Just for a moment I thought we'd made the wrong decision to 'work with them'. I banished the thought and signed the forms.

Another very significant moment followed. Hazel climbed into her Massey and set off to Kilmeston Road with the Major flail mower on. Off to a field that we thought we'd seen the end of. A field that we thought we'd never set foot (or tyre) on again. And we're now out there again. And being paid to work it. Funny old world.

For some reason, it cheered me up immensely, and I did a load of late fungicide on Top and Bottom of Hurst Down. It was on the cusp of being too windy, and the pipeline gash through the wheat makes it all incredibly awkward. The wheat itself looks a treat (if you ignore the deer damage), and it's the last time I'll be up there in a tractor. Mind you, I said that about Kilmeston Road.

July 2nd

Windy and showery again – no chance of getting any more fungicides on. Sasha and I had a long walk instead, as I got my head around tonight's gig in Bramdean. As we walked, I could hear sound checks being done halfway down Hinton Hill, where a long-overdue wedding is taking place today. There's only so many times you can hear the thumping opening bass line from *Seven Nation Army* being used to check the speakers before you shout at the sound man from half a mile away to try something else.

The gig at my old mate Graeme's Mamma Mia-themed party went well, even if we did make a right hash of the two ABBA songs we'd carefully rehearsed. No one seemed to mind, and the singalong could have taken place without us. That's the joy of ABBA.

We finished just before midnight, and were back at Shed 3b, unpacked, shortly after that – Bramdean isn't far away. And we'd all got snarled up in the queue of taxis picking up revellers from Hinton Ampner Place. Our gig warranted a good forty minutes of wind-down in the shed before we finally went our separate ways, which is the sign of a successful evening. The wedding party was still in full swing while all this was going on, and I was all set for a long evening watching TV, waiting for the music to stop, but it did stop – right on the dot of one o'clock, as promised. Phew.

July 3rd

It was a very lazy Sunday – for me, anyway. Hazel, keen as ever to get out and do something, continued topping Kilmeston Road.

July 4th

I didn't sleep well, with an odd itchy scalp and even odder dreams, and when the phone rang just after seven, I was still snuggling under a hot duvet trying to catch up a bit. The phone went to 'message' before my lame attempts to sound wide awake could be heard. It was the diesel delivery man on his way, and leaving an early warning as requested. That was my cue to get up and get everything unlocked for him.

The rest of the day was busy. I proofed the latest *Farmers Weekly* column, and made an early start on the last doses of fungicides on some wheat – possibly the last bits of spraying ever? The lack of sentimentality about this moment was significant. And when the rude email from NRoSO (the bossy body that regulates all our spraying licences) arrived at lunchtime demanding to know why I hadn't renewed my membership, it made my day. I typed an even ruder reply and then deleted it.

Spraying was interrupted by neighbour John bringing some farmers down from Lincolnshire to look at the Turner grain cleaner in the main Drier barn. It has been there since Dad's big overhaul in the early 1980s, but we stopped using it at the beginning of this century, when we joined Hampshire Grain. There was no need to clean our grain or store it – it was all done up at Micheldever. It's a system that has suited us perfectly over the last two decades.

All the plant in the Drier building has now got to go – either in assorted skips or to better homes. The two Lincolnshire farmers were very keen to have the old Turner and all its sieves, and we agreed a bit of beer money would cover the price. How they get it out is another matter, of course. I'd leave that bit to them.

Hazel finished topping Kilmeston Road, and it was now ready for a good plough. Unfortunately, I've agreed to plough it, so it might not be 'good'.

There was slightly concerning news from the world of test cars. I'd been trying to get the pre-Christmas tests lined up nice and early, only to be told by two huge groups – VAG, who include VW, Audi, SEAT and all that lot, and Stellantis, who have a dozen brands in their portfolio – that *The Field* is no longer significant enough to qualify for test cars. Blimey. That might throw a spanner in the works.

July 5th

Time to cut some hay. We're only making the Back Meadow, and we haven't sprayed it or given it any fertiliser, but it has got too long for the calves (when they eventually get out there) so it makes sense to knock it down and see what we get.

That was the plan, anyway. As usual, it didn't quite work out that way. I still had an article to write – the review of the Volvo XC60, which was here months ago. So long ago, that the version we were testing has been renamed – 'Momentum' is now 'Core'. I managed to write it up without referring to what version I was driving.

I took the flail mower off the Massey and hitched it onto the drum mower. Mid-change of blades, the Landlord turned up for a cuppa with another NT agent, over from Northern Ireland – there was another ninety minutes wasted. (Not wasted at all, of course – it was an interesting, if occasionally challenging chat; it became clear very early on that he and we would see eye-to-eye on very little. I do hope he doesn't end up in the Hinton Management team.)

Finally, I could get out into the Back Meadow, and start the long slow process of mowing. 9kph with a 1.86m mower is never going to be a quick job. And then George the sprayerman arrived, ready to do the last ever tanks of pesticide. I'd booked him ages ago, but I was glad he came, now that I can no longer spray. I gave him a complicated map of the remaining spring barley and sent him on his way. He'll be back to do the Roundup, of course. Does that count as a pesticide?

There were more interruptions when, after a bewildering barrage of phone calls, a lorry arrived with our stolen trailer, bringing to an end a most bizarre series of events that started when we realised it had gone missing, nearly sixteen months ago. I'd spotted it in FW's classified pages, driven to Devizes to identify it, failed to get any joy from the police, told the NFU about it, given them back the grand they'd paid us, and then been chasing up its return for some weeks.

A recovery team had been given the job, but had no idea what they were picking up – hence the phone calls about air brakes and how we'd get it on and off. In the end, the big yellow lorry had a fantastic bed that slid 'off' the lorry, and I simply picked the trailer up on its hitch using the tractor and took it away. I could get back to my little mower at last. It was tempting to keep going long into the evening, but by about seven, I was done, and persuaded myself that the last remaining block of land work was going to take too long. I called it a night.

Half an hour sitting outside the back door watching a mother deer nervously supervise her two fawns as they played zoomies in the orchard made the early stop worthwhile. Seeing hornets nest-building in a hole in the house's brickwork was a little less bucolic. Might have to give the pest control people a shout.

July 6th

I think we're going to be seeing a lot of George the Trust's building manager over the next few weeks. He's got a flood of builders coming in to do quotes for our falling-out windows, and he came round early this morning to discuss our chimney plan for the sitting room. I'm getting used to the routine now – and it's not just with George. You describe your plan: take out 1960s chimney, rediscover Georgian original, renovate, install wood-burning stove after lining the chimney, Bob's your uncle.

The response is an inevitable and predictable word salad of planning applications/ listed/bats(again)/how big's the stove/sucking of teeth… It could be so easy to just not bother. But then George got more positive; it's perfectly possible, but it might take ages. The first thing he would do was hunt down an early photograph of the sitting room which features the fireplace. I expressed astonishment that such a thing existed – but he seemed sure that there was one. I'd love to see that.

Then it was back to the hay mower. I could have finished it last night after all, as it only took ninety minutes. I folded it up (tweaking my lower back in the process, dammit) and hitched it off in the yard. Somewhere in the brambles in the estate yard was the haybob, and it only took a couple of new tines and a grease up to get that going. I did a turn or two and left the tractor parked in the field. Hazel said she'd get out there after she'd done another long afternoon's training with Tim.

After lunch I set about the five-furrow Kverneland with the angle grinder and my new Norton 'Blaze' sanding discs. Very impressive they were, too, taking off six years of rust and not scratching the metal underneath. It was a good workout in some very hot sun, and everything hurt so much by the time I'd finished I didn't notice the pain in my lower back anymore.

I gave the pool a long overdue hoover, chucked in some chlorine and enjoyed a bit of a wallow. It was all very lovely, with Hazel trundling up and down the Back Meadow spreading the hay. I did feel a bit off, though. Must be all that angle grinding. I had a shower and suddenly started to shiver. Huge, violent shivers. Bone-shaking shivers – the sort that will really put your back out. All very odd.

July 7th

Shortly after I'd written up the grumpy Polish delivery men (the ones who got their lorry stuck and were most upset when I was genuinely too busy to help) for *Farmers Weekly*, I got a text from George the NT building manager. He wouldn't be round with the first of the builders getting quotes for all the external work on the house; he'd tested positive for Covid. Bearing in mind last night's shivers and yet another hallucinatory broken night, and the fact that my eyeballs now hurt almost as much as all my hair follicles, I did a dreaded Covid test. The 'positive' line shone like a beacon in the little plastic strip within a minute – no need to wait the full thirty minutes for the result. Oh bugger. Now what? Not a lot really. I grabbed a duvet, took the first of the day's paracetamol, and hit the sofa.

It all got a bit blurred from there. The first T20 was a bit one-sided, but I felt a bit better come evening. Well enough for a can of ginger beer before bedtime.

While all this was going on, Hazel turned the hay again, and took Evie on another training day. The heatwave is beginning to build, and she said the dogs were all most unenthusiastic.

And Boris resigned. Curiously, I've not mentioned the turmoil in the world of politics. All I need to do is congratulate Team Remain for finally getting their man – and all over a bit of cake.

July 8th

I had a decent sleep – the first for several nights – but the dreams didn't get any less bizarre. Much of the day has vanished from memory. It was unbelievably hot. And I took lots of paracetamol.

July 9th

Another day that passed in a bit of a blur. Apparently Mac brought in the enormous twin-rotor rake and left it here while he went baling in Bramdean. I dimly remember showing Hazel how to use it once she'd hitched off the haybob. (That rake is a delight to use, sweeping six metres of spread hay into a single line almost silently, with the tractor cruising along barely above idle.) And then Mac arrived late in the afternoon and round-baled 53 lovely bales; an amazing amount, bearing in mind that cutting the Back Meadow was a bit of a whim in the first place. We hadn't done any rolling, harrowing, slitting, fertilising or spraying.

I'd felt another twinge in my lower back when I'd been helping Hazel with the rake's PTO shaft, and a twinge turned into a lightning bolt spasm when I was putting on my post-shower socks. Fuckitty fuckitty fuck. And just as I was beginning to feel a bit better, too. And yet another music festival is tonight, which – they say – is a 2am finish. Mind you, it was nice and quiet when we went to bed – once the now-compulsory 11pm firework display was done.

July 10th

I knew I'd spoken too soon about the nice peaceful music festival. I was jolted awake just after midnight by a hideous thumping beat, which was my cue to not bother trying to get back to sleep. I got up and found a bizarre horror film on the TV Digibox – *The Cube* – and enjoyed that. The music did stop at two, but my back didn't stop hurting and it didn't get any cooler, so it wasn't a brilliant night.

The day was somewhat lazy as a result. I was beginning to feel slightly more human, which was handy when Mac rang from Blackhouse Farm to say that some builders' debris had got mangled up in his disc mower, and did we have some sockets he could borrow. He would have popped home, but yet another pile-up at the West Meon Hut meant that the road was closed. I just about had the wherewithal to gather a few sockets and help him untangle a length of rope once he'd got a disc safely off. We had a gossip in the hot sun for a minute or two and he set off again, back through the lanes to Blackhouse. Where he hit something bigger and the mower gearbox exploded.

I felt I was making the right call sitting indoors again.

July 11th

I took another Covid test, confident that it must be over; I certainly felt better. It was positive. A period of self-isolation in a tractor cab in Kilmeston Road with a plough beckoned.

God, it was odd to be out there again. I'd resigned myself to never again doing the long drive through all those locked gates, and here I was, jumping in and out of the cab, locking and unlocking padlocks, and with the added awkwardness of the electric fence that Shepherd Ella has strung north-south across Springshot.

Still, we're being paid good money to help the Trust with their plans for Kilmeston Road, so shut up, Charlie, and get on with it. I marked out the north, west and south headlands, and started the land work in the south-east corner, next to the old shooting strip. It was unbelievably tough – the last time it was ploughed was, I think, 2011, just after Dad died. Once or twice the points simply refused to bite into the earth, and I was scraping my way across the surface. An inch of rain might help, but we really don't want that now.

It was well past five when I decided to call it a day, having surprised myself with lasting that long. What was also surprising was how little setting up I'd had to do; the old Kverneland has slotted perfectly on the back of the new Deere, and the furrows were matching up perfectly – where the plough could get into the ground, anyway.

There was more good news at home, where Hazel had had a call from our pheasant suppliers, saying that they did after all have ex-layers if we wanted them. Of course we did. It would mean some fairly late-in-the-day pen preparation, but if it means we get a shoot this autumn, that won't be a problem.

July 12th

The house was full of thoroughly pissed-off dogs when I got up; Hazel had set off very early in Pig to check on our pheasant pens (actually old partridge pens that act as a two-night dormitory for the ex-layers when they arrive) and left them all behind. 'Indignant' wasn't the word for it.

Apparently, all the pens had survived another season and with a bit of lopping and application of string, would be fine for another one. This is great news. It does mean I'll have to get back to renovating the strips, which had not grown well, but there we go.

My long haul out to Kilmeston Road to do a bit more ploughing was less than successful: the ground is now just too hard. I came home after a few turns and dropped an 'update' email to my new bosses at the Trust. There are days when you realise that the Big Plan was a good call. And I still felt like shit.

George the sprayerman arrived to do what must surely be the last bit of spraying ever: a splash of Roundup on Drier and Cheyney to try and even it up a bit before harvest. And my positive Covid test ruled out an evening with neighbour Robert. Bother.

July 13th

Another positive Covid test, which didn't improve my mood. Still, there was lots to do. Hazel wanted to get on and bring in the hay from the Back Meadow – there's no rain forecast for a hundred years, but it ought to be in anyway. We had a brief chain-sawing session down at the entrance to the cattle barn to ensure the gates opened fully, and were interrupted by Paul the ranger and his new sidekick; I think the Big Plan has done more to reduce levels of unemployment than any grand political scheme.

We towed the aged bale trailer out of the tractor barn, decided it would just about do one more season of bale cart, and went hunting for the front and rear ladders. We found one outside the old calf pens, and one down at the grain store, and with a bit of careful manoeuvring, got them in their slots, ready to go.

Now that ploughing seems to be off the agenda for a bit, I took it off and spent a careful hour in the hot sun getting connected to the hedge trimmer, which is traditionally the main pre-harvest job. I managed it without injury, and that's a result these days. To celebrate, I went and collapsed on the sofa.

It didn't last – Hazel got a text from our pheasant supplier; he was on the way, and he'd like the empty crates back tonight, if that's OK. We are so lucky to get any birds that little conditions like that were nothing to worry about. It was lucky that Hazel had done vast amounts of work on the pens getting them ready, cleaned up and well stocked with food and water; all we had to do was load up Pig with half a dozen crates and set off for a pair of pens. The birds tumbled gently out of each crate into a ten-foot by ten-foot by five-foot environment of weeds and grass, with wheat in a feeder, bowls of water, and, more importantly, all six sides of each pen safely meshed over. Mind you, we haven't seen or heard foxes or badgers for ages.

A very satisfying evening's work, helped by a stunning July sunset and a feeling that a shoot that a few weeks ago had been written off is now 'on' again.

July 14th

I'm not saying that Hazel takes her animal husbandry seriously, but she thought she heard suspicious activity in the night, down at the pens just below the old tennis court – much fluttering and squawking. It was enough for her to get up in the small hours, grab Sasha and head down to move on whatever was causing all the birds to panic. Sasha chased something away unconvincingly but thoroughly enjoyed the bonus bit of guard dog duty.

It was too hot, I felt grim, and managed three hours of hedge trimming from Roe Hill down to New Pond before calling it a day.

July 15th

I had managed to get an extra day for the FW column but didn't want to push it any further. I came up with a sob story about the virus and sent it off. All a bit lame, but under the circumstances, it will have to do. The nearly-new Proforge discs arrived from Agrilinc. They're part of the new toolkit I'm getting set up with in my new role as 'custodian' of the fields we're giving up. We're going to be paid by the acre, so the quicker we work them the better. And the new Deere should really have bigger discs than the old 3m ones. All I had to do was stand and watch, as the young man wielded his huge HIAB to lift off what we'd bought and load up with the trade-in 3m discs and the six-leg Opico Vari-tilth.

Hazel let a few more of the ex-layers trickle out of the pens. They seemed to be settling down a bit, and the pens have resisted any predator attack, although there was little sign of anything trying to get in.

I tested positive again.

July 16th

Too hot, too ill.

July 17th

Hazel took the two younger flatcoats out for an early morning swim/training session somewhere way down the A272, in the River Rother. Definitely the place to be. I took another Covid test and came up negative. Mind you, I still felt like shit. It was enough of a spur to make me think that some harvest preparation was in order.

The combine was serviced and ready to go – I assumed, although the recent puddle of oil under the front axle didn't fill me with confidence. All that needed checking was the fuel level. A frenzy of barn owls greeted me when I reached the top of the steps, and I had to stand quietly for a couple of minutes while they worked out the best way out of the barn. I suspect that they were youngsters, judging by the way they crashed stupidly into skylights and grills. Two of them then perched on the woodwork over the old wet grain pit, shaking heads as if slightly stunned. Once they'd gathered their senses, they set off safely outside, and I could continue.

Diesel was at about 40%, Adblue somewhat higher. I thought I'd top up the diesel with what was left in the bowser, and that would see us off to a good start once the weather cools down a bit.

Hazel has sold all the straw in the swath (which will save a bit on diesel), so I spent half an hour resetting all the chopping systems (last used with beans last autumn) once I remembered how. After 25 years with New Holland, it's a bit of a bugger trying to remember how the Claas system works.

The bowser had just enough to do a good top-up, which left only a few more pre-harvest jobs to do: fit the lifters (even though the winter barley is still standing tall), fit the header – and clean the owl poo off the flux capacitor (aka the Adblue regen box).

We took Tigger down to North's for its MOT tomorrow, and I enjoyed a really warm wallow in the pool. Maybe I am feeling better after all.

July 18th

Another dreadful night's sleep. In the small hours, a mosquito decided he was hungry, and for the next four hours was swooping and diving on me, noisily. He had one or two successful hits, leaving lumps on my arms and shoulders. I finally got back to sleep just before six, and slept through till nine. Good thing there's nothing else on at the moment.

I'd only been up for ten minutes when the garage rang with news that Tigger had passed its MOT. One iffy tyre and a slightly rusty chassis were the only advisories. I'd spent much of the wide-awake session in the night pondering vehicle replacement plans if it had failed – but that can all be forgotten for a bit. Again.

As a result, I was a bit late with getting the next FonF approved, but we got there by late morning. It was a bit of a mess to start with, but then again, it was sent while I was still a bit Covid-y. That's my excuse, anyway.

The Cheyney bend was next on my list of hedgetriming jobs, and sitting in a tractor with the aircon on full blast was definitely the right option. It was so hot that there were no walkers to get in the way, and only a handful of cars.

A wallow in a rapidly warming pool rounded off the first day for ages that I've felt remotely human – and the first in ages in which I haven't had an afternoon snooze. And bearing in mind how little sleep I got last night, that is a result.

The big bedtime mistake was to get one of our new brilliant (as in very bright) torches to check what was buzzing in the ivy as I stood on the lawn, watching the stars. Two fucking great hornets promptly zero-ed in on the beam, and, worse, followed me indoors. There was a terrifying frenzy of door slamming, light switch flicking, dogs crying, newspaper flapping, and, finally, two stunned hornets that needed a size ten stamped on them before they would die. Utter, utter bastards.

In another attempt to cool down for the night, I dug out Jonathan's tower fan – the one he bought some years ago when he was still living at home. It was rather noisy, but it did send a blast of air my way, and it did feel slightly cooler. It also disrupted the flightpath for the many mosquitoes trying to land on my nose. I heard one go swooping past my ear crying 'mayday mayday', but I think my arm flailing failed to get it.

July 19th

Finally, it's here. The hottest day ever. So hot that multiple houses caught fire spontaneously all over the country. That strikes me as very odd, but there we go.

I did office stuff until it was too hot to sit indoors, and then went and did some more hedge trimming – a wise move in case our house spontaneously caught fire, too.

A band of thundery rain slid in and decided to ignore us, which was a shame, but by the time I got hold of neighbour Robert for a beer, it was already much cooler. Very lucky – we didn't want the Pots to spontaneously burst into flame, too.

July 20th

The ex-Editor tuned up for a long coffee mid-morning, keen to hear how ill I was (answer: much better, thank you) and even keener to discuss shoot plans now that we have a farm full of ex-layers strutting their stuff and getting used to their new home. He was all for deciding dates then and there and allocating slots and spaces – but we agreed that that would have to wait for a bit until harvest had got going.

We did a bit more preparation: I backed the combine out of the barn (which Hazel then swept) and hitched it onto the header. The combine was new last year (halfway through last year, actually; the delivery wasn't until August, by which time we'd had to summon neighbour Robert Jnr to get the winter barley in) and it's all still a bit strange. I'm trying to warm to it, too. It may be infinitely more sophisticated than the old New Hollands, but much of the sophistication is completely unnecessary.

Another afternoon of hedge trimming beckoned: I did the roadside bits outside the house, and the start of the Dutton Memorial Walk where it runs alongside the Back Meadow. Not the easiest job, what with all the trees now hanging low over the path, and all the walkers merrily setting off to enjoy the walk.

Just as we were contemplating an early night, our Dictol was delivered by hand, and the deliverer wasn't going anywhere until several unnecessary coffees had been had.

July 21st

We're really running out of excuses not to go combining, so we had a morning getting the hedgetrimmer off, finding grain trailers and checking tyres, and getting the Massey all togged up with weights and front bucket, ready for loading duties. And after lunch, we got going in Drier Field, in the later of the winter barley fields. We had a good run in the dry conditions, with a nice swath of straw (sold, of course). I'm not sure there was a great deal of barley out there, but we'll see.

Our last harvest has started. Good grief.

July 22nd

I made an early start to get the next Flindt on Friday written while neighbour Glenn (fully signed up as harvest help) got the first lorry of barley away. Trinity Grain classified it as 'shite' (too much wheat in it), which wasn't an ideal start to harvest. We had some light showers which may have done more good than harm, pushing the moisture content up a bit, and we finished Drier Field. One field done.

Back home, the pest control man came and made the hole in the wall inhospitable for those pesky hornets using some evil-smelling powder, and Hazel single-handedly gave the calves their Dictol. I looked at the heap of barley, hoping there was more there than I thought there was. Oh well.

July 23rd

Glen loaded two lorries of barley, only one of which was shite (too much wheat again) and Hazel and I had a long session transferring the combine to the Folly. We'd decided that as we were going to drive through it to get to more winter barley in White Hill, we might as well get it combined while we were there. The wheat certainly felt ripe enough.

First impressions were good; I was sending a trailer away every couple of acres, and Glenn reported that it felt pretty heavy as he hauled loads up to Godwin's Yard. I rang Trinity Grain to book lorries tomorrow, only to be told that there were none, which is frustrating. I persuaded Hazel to take a bag up there in the evening to see if there's any quality. The report was mixed: the protein was very low, which might back up my theory that there's a lot out there. It was weighing well, at 80 kg/hl.

We got two-thirds of the Folly done before whatever makes me flag far too early made me flag again. Long Covid? Or the hideously uncomfortable ride in the combine?

July 24th

Plans to jump out of bed and refuel just as the sun was rising were scuppered by a deer, who spent twenty minutes barking loudly just outside the window just after half past two. And there I was enjoying a cooler night with minimum insect interference.

I was up late as a result, and the ex-Editor arrived for a coffee to discuss some suggestions I'd sent him about the website for the all-new gun he's involved with. I pointed out that there's no actual picture of the gun, and the drop-down menu for choosing chokes (despite there being no pic, you can still place an order) described choke choices as being in fractions of an inch, rather than just fractions. I mean, honestly. He was very grateful for the feedback. But I really should get out more.

When I did finally get hitched onto the fuel bowser, it was empty, and it needed to have the Adblue tank re-attached with the ratchet straps. And then the Adblue tank needed filling from the big 210l drum in the tractor barn – by hand. The combine was only parked in the entrance to the Folly, but it was twelve thirty before it was all done – both combine tanks full with no spillage. I texted Glenn and said we'd be starting at two.

It all got very busy. We finished the Gleam in the Folly, and moved into White Hill to re-start on the winter barley. There were balers and trailers going ninety-nine to the dozen behind us in the Folly, and another straw buyer arrived in Drier Field and had that done by evening. I'm assuming that everyone out there had a right to be out there; it wouldn't be impossible to furnish yourself with a bale trailer and a loader tractor and drive round the countryside at this time of year just helping yourself. It would be a bit like a wedding; "I thought that chap was with you!"

July 25th

Yet another broken night. I couldn't sleep for being too hot (although the weather has cooled a lot) and my heart rate was well above 120. Bloomin' long Covid? Mind you, measuring it only pushed it up further. I got up and watched the end of *Fury* (tank-based hokum) and nearly got hooked by *All the President's Men* (just about as far from tank-based hokum as you can get.) A mosquito then started buzzing me just after three, but some stalking round the room with my swat and a torch sorted him out. His friend then continued the assault. Not a good night.

It isn't often that you look at the rainfall radar mid-harvest, praying for a sturdy shower to come through, but I could have done with some more sleep. Some were promised, but they hadn't shown up yet. Glenn loaded another couple of lorries of shite barley, and I greased up the Claas.

I could grease up the New Holland TC combine in my sleep (if I got any, of course); after twenty-five years, it became a well-oiled (see what I did there?) routine. Lots of old-fashioned grease points, but most of them were easy to find. The Claas is different; there are a lot fewer, they're almost impossible to find, and you need a ladder to get to most of them. I'm not warming to my new machine at all.

Still, it looked like we weren't going to have a day off, so we had a long session in White Hill, with only Rough Field to do by evening. The showers did show up, but decided to avoid our bit of Hampshire. It was only when I was doing the evening combine cooldown routine that it dawned on me we'd done the haunted bit of the field without incident. Although two lifters had gone missing.

July 26th

Blimey, a proper night's sleep. What a joy. It was much cooler, and the fact that I finally ordered a proper mosquito net probably scared all the bugs away.

We had a power cut just after seven, and it sent me off down a memory lane. In days gone by, I would have been down at the grain drier, using all the equipment to clean and dry incoming grain – even at seven in the morning. A power cut was the worst thing that could happen (except a fire, of course). Everything would stop, including the massive burner, and an eerie silence would ensue. There was then a huge panic restarting all the elevators and conveyors, hoping that the fact that they were full wouldn't mean they were jammed up.

This is winter barley time of year, so the restart procedure would have been to run over to the Conder bins (where we stored early barley) and then work backwards from there: top conveyor, elevator, pre-cleaner (which we'd use for a final pre-storage clean). Back across the yard to get the 3-phase Kongskilde blower going again (hoping that its silver pipes weren't full). Then back to the main switchboard for the top conveyor, clearer extract elevator, the three bits of the Turner cleaner (brushes, motor, fan), cleaner feed conveyor, cleaner intake elevator, drier conveyor, intake elevator and intake conveyor. Once all of those were successfully going, the two monster fans on the drier itself, one for the burner and one for the cooling fan, and, finally, the drier bed itself. And all while in a sweat, in a dust mask and earmuffs. I don't miss those days at all. Hurrah for Trinity Grain storage.

All we had to worry about today was a couple of computers.

Two more lorries of winter barley went out, and I met up with the Claas rep to discuss the combine's problems. I was fully expecting to show him the lack of 'suspension' in the table and then be told 'it does that' – which is the stock reply under these circumstances, but Andy agreed that there was an issue. He'd dug out the book and was looking up pressure settings in the accumulators on the hydraulic circuit. Twenty bar is the setting for my little 5.6m header, and for a grown-up 8m one it would be pumped up to thirty-five bar. Andy reckoned that the latter was the default pressure, and it hadn't been changed. Tempting as it was to dive in with a bit of stick and find the Schrader valve to let it down, we decided to leave that to the experts.

We finished Rough Field (except the late sown spring barley patches) and shuttled over to Cheyney, which took no time. Bev the nanny (from a lifetime ago) arrived unexpectedly in the field with her two massive lads, and everyone was rude to everyone. Some things never change.

We had enough time once we'd finished Cheyney (and the winter barley) for a dismantle and a long drive back to the Drier, then up over Rick and Clump to reach the wheat in Big Broom. I cut my way along the top of Big Broom and Middle Broom, and shut down for the day in the south-west corner. I was on the point of shutting the lids down when I remembered that the fragile mechanised lid system should not be shut with anything in the tank, and I had half a tank already. Oh well – the lids will have to stay open for the night.

I'm sure I should be getting more emotional as we finish each field for the last time. Especially Cheyney, which was my first ever combining job in 1988. Ernie, who normally drove the Claas Protector 6, had retired on health grounds, and after a quick briefing, I was given the task of driving the beast. I was on my own up there with only a Ford 6600 and an eight-ton Warwick trailer for company, with instructions from Dad to fill up the trailer and bring it down to the drier myself (he was still doing drier duties back then).

My day didn't start well; I'd only done three quarters of the first turn of headland when the little grain tank was full. I had to walk round the rest of the headland and fetch the tractor and trailer. Back then, of course, we had a 'sterile strip' around every field, made by a Howard Rotavator, which would go round the outside of every field – twice. Those were the days when you had enough cash to pay a man to do that job for weeks at a time. The strip was just wide enough for the tractor and trailer to get round to the combine, and that's how my day continued, constantly being in the wrong place for the trailer every time I filled up.

I did have one interruption: Dad arrived in the field shaking his head and doing a 'thumbs-down' signal. I stopped and asked what had happened. A key pair of belts had shredded – the ones that drove the top conveyor. There was then one of those 'things we did then that we don't do now' moments. The huge farm ladders were carefully propped up against the conveyor – probably thirty or forty feet up in the eaves of the roof – and I shimmied up clutching two new belts. Dad stood on the bottom rung to act as a very substantial anchor, but even so it was bit hairy up there. I got the job done and was back on the Protector in moments. These days I can't do more than three or four rungs of a ladder before the world starts going round and round. I miss being twenty-six.

July 27th

We're settling into the harvest routine nicely. Glenn loaded a couple of lorries of Gleam from the Godwin's barn, and I did a bit of office work and drove round wondering where we'll go next once we've finished the Godwin's block. The spring barley is still green (it's July, FFS) and that only leaves the two big blocks of Skyscraper. Both of them look ready, but also look like a few more days ripening wouldn't do any harm.

Middle Broom didn't take long, and it filled the barn up again. I think there's a serious bit of wheat out there.

208

July 28th

I tried and failed to write the next FonF. Curiously, they seem to be getting harder and harder to write, as the days of doing them come to an end. Very odd.

We got three more lorries of Gleam away (again, perfect quality except for dismal protein) and did most of Big Broom. Again, we had an early finish thanks to the barn being chokka. Blimey.

July 29th

My plan was to have a day away from the combine. First, write the next column. Second, take delivery of the Dacia Duster test car. Third, jump in it and drive up to Ragley Hall for the Game Fair, getting there just after lunch, ready for an afternoon's gun porn and then *The Field*'s drinks party in the evening. Then drive home very late with a stinking headache and sleep for the weekend.

That's not quite what happened, of course. I wrote the article and took delivery of the car but cried off the Game Fair in favour of another day in the combine. The Duster was delivered by a couple of unbelievably cheerful Chinese chaps, whose pick-up was delayed in traffic. I sent them over to Hinton Ampner House to find the tea rooms for a cuppa while they waited. I hope they weren't asked for membership cards.

Once two more lorry-loads of Gleam had gone, we continued in Godwin's – or would have done if the combine hadn't flashed red warning lights about 'loss of coolant'. I knew that the dealers were on their way to have a look at the pressure accumulator in the header, so I rang them to ask that they bring some coolant as well, and we stood down. I wasn't happy; it's the third time in twelve months that I've sat and waited for a mechanic to get the new Claas going. When it finally arrived last harvest, it managed three-quarters of a turn round Blackhouse Road before the chaff spreader disintegrated. And in BML's the 'regen' system went into red-hot overdrive, resulting in another visit from the dealer and another lost couple of hours. And here I was again, sitting indoors, grinding teeth, losing harvest time.

The Claas mechanics were here just after three and were finished half an hour later; they'd topped up the coolant, and we should keep an eye on it. Meanwhile, they'd found that the pressure in the front accumulator was over 100bar, and it should have been 25bar. I avoided – just – going off on one about the lack of a PDI. But I suddenly had a combine with a table that could be raised and lowered without feeling someone had kicked you in the small of the back. Hurrah.

We finished the little triangle at the top of Big Broom, took the table off, and did Child's Broom – which was the thickest wheat I can remember combining. If we had a whole farm like that... It's a bit late for that sort of fantasising.

July 30th

Two more lorries were booked for the dregs of the winter barley. I had hoped that there would be more than two lorries' worth, mainly because it would have meant a slightly better yield than we thought, but also so it wouldn't have cleared the barn ready for us to have another long day combining. And I felt distinctly second rate – I almost went off and did another Covid test.

The lorries did indeed clear the barn, but the second one may have crept away a tad overfull. So the final yield was definitely moderate. Ho hum. As for rushing out to do more combining – that was abandoned. I did fuel it up and top up the Adblue while it was right on the doorstep (the south-west corner of Middle Broom), and then Hazel and I did the huge trek up to Stanmore – out of Middle Broom, along the edges of Big Broom, Chalks, Rick and Clump, Drier, Folly, and through White Hill up to the (the other) Broom. I hitched on the table, parked up the combine and came home in the tractor. We'll have a go up there tomorrow. The sofa beckoned and I was out like a light.

A good snooze, a swim and an early tea all meant I felt better, and I took the Duster out for an evening spin. Trouble is, it had only been delivered with a quarter of a tank of fuel, so I'm going to have to ration my journeys – or buy my own fuel. I feel a grumpy email coming on.

July 31st

Two more lorries of Gleam went, both of them feed. There's still a big pile of it in the Godwin's barn, so yield should make up for quality.

We finally called in brother-in-law Noel to help with corn cart, now that we're doing the long-distance haulage from the Stanmore block. The afternoon didn't last long; the Skyscraper up there was a bit of mess, littered with fresh green stalks. It went through the combine OK, but the sample was pretty green. I was really hoping that one of the heavy showers coming in from the west would hit us and I could adjourn to decide what to do. Very late Roundup? Go and find something else to combine? The showers refused to hit us, but I called it a day after we'd finished Broom. It's turning into a funny year. Mind you, they all are. I decided we'd send a lorry of Skyscraper in tomorrow and see what they think of it.

I had an early swim and a shower, and went into Winchester to pick up Jonathan, coming down from London for the night – part four (or is it five?) of his big move back up to Newcastle after his year with the Bank of England. He and his flatmate are moving from their idyllic flat in Kentish Town back up to Jesmond – a bit early in the academic year, and he's going to do a last month at the Bank remotely, but the tenancy runs out on the London flat, and the Jesmond house is ready. Anthony very kindly booked a van and offered to drive up and back in exchange for a night out and a bed. Jonathan then caught the train down here for a brief catch-up and a huge plate of home-produced lamb. His plan is to repossess 'his' i20, and head back up to Newcastle in the morning. God, I miss being 22. I get knackered from five hours in the combine.

August 1st

The House Rule is that the first to find a pile of dog poo in the morning gets to clear it up. That'll teach me to leap out of bed feeling positive and upbeat on a Monday morning. One (or more) of the dogs had had a rough night and there was a kitchen full of violent emissions from both bodily ends. Bother. It's time to grab the dustpan and the paint scraper (for lifting the bulk of the solid matter) and the mop and bucket. Half an hour later, all the affected dogbeds were on the lawn drying out, and the kitchen was spic and span, and smelling of Flash.

Neighbour (and ex-employee and soon-to-be ex-tenant) John called in for a cuppa and a long chat about our plans – and those of the Trust. His house will soon be moving from being under our control (and I use the word lightly) to under the Trust's control (ditto.) He was dead keen to exchange notes about the Trust's plans for the farm, and, like all old-school hardcore farming types, can't believe what the Trust are planning. "A thousand acres of ragwort," was his prediction. I scolded him for being weedist. Ragwort – I pointed out – is just a misunderstood plant that identifies as wheat.

He also brought news of local parish councils demanding meetings with the Trust about the Big Plan. There's a great deal of huffing and puffing going on, as all the wealthy locals seem to think they should be dictating what happens to the land. I think I know what's going on: they've seen how much fencing is going to be erected and are horrified to see that their self-proclaimed right-to-roam is actually going to be physically curtailed. Joy.

The Bat Policeperson was back, this time to inspect our 'voids' (oo er missis). Her self-belief was once again unshakeable, as she tried to instruct me on the layout of the house I was born in. I escorted her round, making sure that I kept things moving along nicely, but she was still delighted to find plenty of evidence of bats. That'll stop anything happening ever. Apparently she and her fellow Bat Nazis are telling the Trust that no scaffolding can be erected near the south-facing hanging tiles, and all work will have to be done by a cherry picker. I laughed until I realised she wasn't joking. The Bat Police don't joke.

Jonathan was up late, with a face full of mosquito bites. He hadn't got the memo about the hordes, apparently, and merrily slept with his window open. Poor chap. He spent much of the morning packing a few things into the i20, checking tyres and fluids, and then he was gone, off to Newcastle for another student year. It'll be good for him to get back to Uni – he's had a very intense year in the City.

I rang Trinity Grain to see what they thought of the first load of Skyscraper. Was it too green? "No," said Bill. "Keep going!" So we did. I drove the Claas through the gap into the north-west corner of Long Field and we had most of it done by evening. Noel and Glenn were still shuttling down to the Drier barn the long way – mind you, the yield wasn't anything special, so there was no hurry. When Hazel came up in Pig with tea, she brought assorted clipping tools, and set about the ride that goes from Pipeline into Drier Field. It'll be common sense to go through there when we start in that field.

August 2nd

My new mosquito net – the latest tool in the battle against the bitey bastards – is perfectly and delicately set up over the bed using string, clothes pegs and a selection of old ropes from the family's riding days. It all looks a bit pervy. But it seems to work. It's nice and secure.

Or it was secure until this morning, when Cain the cat leapt on the bed to say hello, discovered the netting and went into a kitten frenzy. It's all going to need rebuilding before bedtime tonight.

The two lorries were both very late – Hampshire's yields appear to be overwhelming the store – so we kicked our heels. I gave the combine a grease up and decided it was time the cab air filters were given a clean. Unfortunately, it's not a simple job; Claas, in their wisdom, have decided that two Torx screws have to be undone first. I'm sure I've got some Torx drivers somewhere, but God knows where. It's the classic set of specialist tools that you buy and then lose within days. It was quicker to jump in the Duster, drive up to Rod Gaskin's and buy a new cheap 'n' cheerful set.

By then I'd had my post-grease-up wash, so didn't fancy getting filthy all over again, and decided we'd crack on with combining once the lorries had gone. There was only a sliver left in Long Field, and we got most of Pipeline done in a long-ish afternoon. In places it was good, in other places not so good. Hazel's lopping work through to Drier Field was worth the effort, though. The combine didn't have to stop once.

Actually, that's not quite true; a semi-familiar face came wandering out of the woods at one stage, obviously angling for a chat. It was one of the arable team at *Farmers Weekly*, who has called into the farmhouse in the past. He and his wife were doing the Trust walk and thought he'd say hello again. It made a welcome break from the combine, even if it did hold us up for twenty minutes.

Pipeline looked stunning in the evening sunshine. Will I miss it?

August 3rd

Cain's demolition job of my mosquito net somehow let a midge in, and I was given a good going over during the night. Bites from top to toe. With very little sleep, I confess I was quite relieved to see steady drizzle when we got up. I rang to check we still had two lorries, and gave the pool a good hoover, thinking that a quiet day would be handy. It did mean I could concentrate on writing up the Duster for *The*

Field. They dropped me a 'cough cough' email to remind me that it was overdue. And there's me thinking *The Field* would know about the countryside and what goes on at this time of year.

But the drizzle stopped, the sun arrived – but the lorries didn't. A late morning phone call of not inconsiderable grumpiness revealed that we'd, ahem, fallen off the list. But two were hastily rescheduled to come our way.

With all excuses not to go combining gone, we headed off to finish Pipeline. It didn't take long – even after all these years, I still can't judge areas. We finished the last bit right where the old original Stanmore Farm was (demolished by Dad shortly after arriving here in 1959) and was the thickest bit of wheat you ever saw. I suspect it was where the old thrashing yard was, which always produces a stunning few square yards of stuff.

It will never do so again, of course. The Trust have got this bit of land down as 'natural regeneration', so our mediocre crop of Skyscraper is the last arable crop to come off it. Ever. I'm not even going to be helping the Trust with their plans up here – it's a simple 'walk away and fence it all in' plan. I hope we'll be up here with our little shoot for a few years, but it really is the end of me driving farm kit up here. Blimey. I had yet another little moment, thinking about the implications.

There wasn't much time to pontificate; I was meeting Noel in Broom Field to hitch off the front of the combine and head back to the Drier via the Folly, and Glenn was off to move telegraph poles so that I could use the north headland of Blackhouse Road to get to Joan's Acre and start on that block of Skyscraper.

It all went very smoothly until it came to driving the combine – without its header – over the slight bank into Joan's Acre. One huge tyre started to spin on the grass, and that was it; all traction lost. It got worse. The huge machine started to bounce violently and uncontrollably. There was stuff flying around the cab – phones, wetwipes (unused, thankfully), Makita battery-powered blowers (for cleaning the engine and flux capacitor at the end of every day), Makita batteries, Thermos flask – I can say with full confidence that the resonant frequency of a bare Claas Tucano 420 is 3hz. It took some time for Noel to stop laughing, and we could finally get the header back on.

We knocked off after a good late afternoon run, with only a triangle in the south-east corner to do.

August 4th

Scary stuff: the RPA Inspector arrived on the dot of nine o'clock. OK, he's not doing anything as horrific as a whole farm inspection, but instead he's coming out to do a check on the acres we've entered into the SFI Pilot Scheme. In other words, only about a hundred acres (i.e. Dead Dog Farm) and the associated paperwork. The other good thing is that his work is all 'experimental', just like the Pilot Scheme itself. Everyone is trying out a new concept, and that includes those inspecting it.

He was definitely a country type – check shirt, bit of a West Country accent, and a natural affinity with dogs, who were all over him (in a good way) as soon as he stepped through the door. In a previous life, he was a pest controller. That explains a lot.

He and Hazel (the SFI Pilot is her project) sat down with paperwork and laptops, and got to work. I made myself scarce. Two lorries came and went, and I hit the phones to order more diesel. I ordered another batch of 2,500 litres for a whisker under £1/litre – a nice 20% drop on the last order.

I did wonder if I had ordered too much. Are we going to go through that much before Michaelmas? Mind you, I've agreed to do a lot of cultivation work for the Trust, so it was probably a good idea.

We finished Joan's Acre, flew though sweet little Dell Close, and then threaded our way through assorted banks and ditches left by the pipeline team to get to Hurst Down. Not a bad bit of wheat at all.

August 5th

In what is turning into the most atypical harvest, it was a typical Friday: write FonF (late again), got two lorries out (both of which went as Gp 4 soft – which is good, even if there will be no premium for it), and had another good afternoon in Hurst Down on the Skyscraper second wheat. The fact that the barn filed up again pretty quickly was good news, too.

The hosepipe ban started. I'm not sure we've had one here since 1976. That was the year Dad dug down into the lawn to find the old Victorian brick bell chamber that collected rainwater – the very same one he'd covered over with concreted-in harrows to make the opening safe for a house full of small children in 1959. He also connected the bath outlet to a tin tub on the lawn, and all to collect water for his courgettes. Which, if I remember rightly, no one liked.

In somewhat less good news, I tweaked my lower back getting dressed. There's always a few minutes of waiting to see if it means three days out of action, or three days just on painkillers. It seemed to be the latter, and Hazel picked up super-strong ibuprofen when she was at the chemist picking up my wheelbarrow-full of repeat medications. Let's hope that keeps me going.

August 6th

Two more lorries away from the bottom barn, and then a short afternoon in Top of Hurst Down to finish the Skyscraper – the last bit of wheat and my last ever bit of wheat. Once again, it was an odd moment, but still no great sadness. These little moments are arriving so thick and fast that it seems easier to just give each one a nod as it passes.

It would have been a shorter afternoon had it not been for the fact that I had to subdivide the field further (bearing in mind that the new pipeline had already cut a nice 66-acre field in half) by cutting a headland next to the drooping electricity cables, sagging further in the heat. They've been 'low hangers' for years, but the old

214

combines, with their flip-over grain tank lids, sailed under them with feet to spare. The new Claas had one of the silly flip-up jobs, and I really didn't fancy taking a chance. A windy day, every square inch of the south of England bone dry…

It meant a long session of cutting triangles and short work. Still, there's no hurry. Next year it'll all be back to one field. Except it won't be me combining it.

Anthony and Diana came down for a flying visit, both looking well. He had a bit of contract gardening to do in Bentley, and she was down for a school reunion bash. The four of us polished off a monster bit of beef for tea. I reckon a quiet day will be in order tomorrow.

August 7th

The top barn has still got a pile of very early Gleam in it, the bottom barn has a big heap of Skyscraper, and all we've got left to cut is 300 acres of spring barley. I did sweep the dreaded left-hand lean-to (with its dodgy walls and nuisance poles) in case we did need some tipping space, but without any muscle available, we really don't want to use it if possible.

Two lorries cleared the top barn perfectly – always nice to keep sending full lorries, and not have nuisance half-loads to sort out. When I retire, I'm going to buy a little lorry and drive round farms clearing up small loads at cheap rates. Of course, being at the back of the barn, it was the very first bit of Gleam that we did some weeks ago. It was a bit warm, not in the best of condition, but it went on the lorry OK, and obviously came back out OK, and that's what counts. Even better – both loads made Group 4 hard. A good result, even if Bill at Trinity doesn't hold out much hope for a premium. Oh, and the Gleam reached a splendid (for us) 4.11 t/a.

I decided we'd have a day off. Hazel took Anthony and Diana back to the station and I tried to have a snooze. I failed, so I had a drive round looking at all the many fields of spring barley, trying to make a plan. If we combine tomorrow, we'll just have to use the left-hand lean-to.

My attempt to have a nice polite farmer-friendly chat with two walkers at the top of Big Field went downhill after a promising start. She was veggie, he was a Remainer – and as soon as we'd established those facts, it crashed and burned.

My swim was lovely. I often lie very still at the west end of the pool, watching the swallows line up and approach the water for a scoop. An exciting new development is a sparrowhawk (looking like a kestrel that's been painted matt grey) which has worked out that there are rich pickings to be had by lurking on the swallows' approach path. I had a wonderful pool-top view of several aerial battles. The swallows survived the ones I saw.

The ex-Editor was home alone, and rang suggesting Beer on the Lawn. We lit the brazier, filled a watering can ready for the inevitable grass fires as embers fell out, and summoned neighbour Robert. We don't usually have Beer on the Lawn on a Sunday, but it was none the worse for it.

August 8th

A couple of very important calls to make as soon as the world surfaced. First, to summon wasp control man. He'd only been here a few days ago to pump some 'dissuader' into a hole in a wall that the hornets were busy making their own. We found ourselves under wasp invasion over the last couple of days, and a stroll round the house with what's left of my eyesight found three wasp nests – one over the falling-down French windows was the busiest I've ever seen. He promised he'd be here this afternoon.

The next call was the NFU insurance team, to cancel the insurance on the i20, which has vanished off to Newcastle. Another easy job, if you ignore being told that your name is "perfect", and the reg number is "no problem at all" and your home address is "fantastic". Why these expressions of utter joy have to be made beats me.

Two more lorries went – both getting quality again – and I set off to Hurst Down for a big grease up. You need to take your own stepladder to reach some of the nipples on the Tucano, which seems utterly bonkers – but I think I got them all. The handbook isn't much help, either. In my next life, I'm going to rewrite technical documents so that they make sense.

Wasp man arrived just as we were setting off after lunch, which was good timing; it's a good idea to be somewhere else while the wasps get angry and eventually decide to move on. 'Somewhere else' was the spring barley. Hazel dropped me off at the combine, and I threaded my way through the bunds and banks (again) and met her at the exit of Joan's Acre, where she'd been trimming away at the hedge to make entrance easier. Stop giggling at the back. I cut along the bottom of Big Field and Rick/Clump, and dropped into BOMS. It was one heck of a crop of spring barley – if it's all like that, we'll be laughing. The only downside was that we were using the left-hand lean-to after all. Oh well, just once more.

August 9th

Yet another night of ferocious and bizarre dreams – and a car speeding past the house faster than you would believe possible at 4.30 – didn't make for a settled sleep, and when diesel man rang to say he was imminent it was already five past seven. A high-speed climb out of jim-jams and into shorts and shirt meant I was on my way out in moments, but the landline rang as I was passing. At ten past seven? It was the new family in our first house, Manor Cottage, who were thrilled to find all the sheep in their garden. I think they were genuinely pleased. Unlocking the diesel barn was shelved temporarily while I tried to raise Hazel (who had set off at dawn in Pig with Tim to water the pheasants, but with no phone) and then Shepherd Ella. Like all da yoof, she was on Facebook already, and I managed to send her a message. Phew.

The cheery diesel lorry driver was in on schedule, and we were finally fuelled up and ready for the last big harvest push. I could go and make my porridge.

Pig puttered its way up the orchard, and Hazel's report from round the feeders and strips was very positive. It helped that the morning was stunning, with the first dew of the season. Just a hint of autumn appearing. And all made much more pleasant by the fact that the wasps have indeed taken the hint and buggered off.

Two more lorries cleared the last of the wheat. One went with a bit of quality, one didn't. The second would have been yet another proper full load if the keeper hadn't requisitioned six buckets' worth for her pheasants. It's a curious thing to think that from now on, we'll have to go and buy wheat from our neighbours. And straw. After a lifetime of limitless supplies of both, we're going to have to rethink a few strategies.

I did another combine refuel and even climbed inside the grain tank to give the double-glazed viewing window a polish. After an early-ish lunch, Hazel dropped me off at New Pond to pick up the combine and I drove it up the track, into Chalks at the top, and got stuck in. It was another unbelievable bit of barley, especially on the flat bit at the bottom.

It was the perfect field to show off the combine to some potential buyers. The man who services my sprayer deals with someone who had bought 700 acres up near Basingstoke, but it has always been farmed by contractors – so there's no kit. Sprayer Service Man pointed out that we're about to give up about 700 acres of arable, and wouldn't be needing our kit. That's why, this afternoon, I had a farmer and his two sons in the field, all keen as mustard on the combine. I gave them rides up and back, and then Hazel turned up with tea and biscuits – and all four dogs. It's a good thing that there's not much hurry on harvest (yet) – we wasted about an hour nattering. That's my excuse for not finishing Chalks in a day.

Darkness brought an awesome display of coloured lights piecing the sky from Cheesefoot Head, a sharp reminder that the dreadful Boomtown Festival is about to start. Four nights with no sleep. Not that we're busy or anything.

August 10th

Yet more early morning excitement. Some builders had arrived at Godwin's Cottages and were merrily installing posts and gates which would have meant no more access to Godwin's Yard. It was a bit like the Vogon Constructor Fleet – they said they were only following plans, and hadn't we seen them? I think I had, somewhere on the South Downs Planning pages, but can't remember seeing the stupidity of the proposed gate location. If I had, I probably assumed that wheels would turn so slowly that we'd be out of the Godwin's Yard by the time anything happened. I certainly wasn't expecting a load of builders mid-harvest.

I'm afraid I told the builders all that, and went off on one in the middle of my speech. I must find out who they were and apologise. Still, I felt much better for an expletive-filled rant. George the Trust's building man arrived at speed and in a bit of a panic, and immediately told the team to move the site of the gate back to the start of Glenn's drive. Much more sense. We could get on with farming.

The first two lorries of Planet spring barley went, and both as Grade One malting. Hurrah. Let's hope the yield over the whole 300 acres matches that quality. Maybe a good year to have too much spring barley.

My next test 'car' – a Polaris UTV – arrived on the back of a small lorry. I just about had time to sign a computer screen and send him away. It's all getting wonderfully busy. We finished Chalks and moved into Rick and Clump. The top of Clump immediately sent my yield optimism crashing, but Rick was much better. Another very low electricity cable meant I'll be cutting false headlands in that field, too. There no point waiting for cooler weather to shrink the metal a bit.

August 11th

This morning's excitement was up at Trinity Grain, where a 'software update' meant lorries couldn't be weighed in. That meant our tiny quota of two lorries was very late, and we didn't get them away until one-ish. It did mean that my next FonF went in nice and early, though.

It got seriously hot again. I set about the Claas' air filters and radiators; it had been running consistently at 83° yesterday, but we're all beginning to get into a bit of a panic about the heat and dryness. We finished Rick and Clump and did about half of Big. They're now talking about a change in the weather next week, and I think I'm going to look a bit daft for not going more flat out.

The good news was that there was no noise from Boomtown, but that may all change tomorrow. The bad news was that there was a funny noise coming from the hydraulic pump on the combine. I'd already had to send for a top-up of hydraulic oil, so whether they're linked I don't know.

Hazel very kindly spent much of the day doing an online HSE course – one of those ones that is 'voluntary' but hideously threatening at the same time. There will be inspections this autumn (the letter said) and it would be wise for us to do the course. This sort of stuff gets right up my nose; Hazel, being a grown-up, is happy to jump through the hoops. Bless her.

August 12th

With a break in the weather looming next week, I thought I should push on a bit today. I was refuelling the bowser with diesel and Adblue very early (for me, anyway), and had the 5l drum of hydraulic oil that the Claas man had dropped off. It was bit of a battle working out how much oil to put into the combine's little tank – shiny new oil on a shiny new dipstick didn't seem to be making much of a mark. I ended up fetching a dry twig from the hedge and using that. It showed that the real level of oil was way below the end of the metal dipstick. All five litres had to go in. No wonder the pump had been making funny noises last night. It was tempting to call off the visit from the Claas mechanic; he was due to come and look at it as soon

218

as he could, but I thought he ought to have a look anyway.

The two lorries were late again, and it wasn't until one o'clock (again) that we got going in Big Field. And we didn't get very far. There was a 'bong' meaning that the dreaded 'regen' was happening in the DPF, followed by another 'bong' and a series of alarms and red flashing lights. The error message was trying to tell me that the DPF is too bunged up for regeneration to take place, and that I should switch to 'automatic' at once. This seemed odd, not least because it was already set to automatic.

I stopped the combine, but kept the engine running, and rang the dealer for advice – although the same bloody thing happened last year, so I know what's going to happen. He said he'd ring me back in a few moments with a plan.

He didn't of course, and when I finally got hold of him again, he'd already got an engineer on the way. Gee, thanks for keeping me in the loop. I told Glenn and Noel that we were calling a halt, and drove back down to New Pond. Do I stop the engine? Do I keep it running in the hope that the regen somehow happens? Do I turn it off and on again? I turned it off, but grabbed the garden sprayer (ten litres of water and a hand pump, which – funnily enough – I fished out of the barn only this morning) and climbed up onto the top of the combine to supervise the DPF unit.

It was still up to something. The diesel pump could he heard ticking away frantically, and the heat coming off the silver box was terrifying. I sat there in the scary sunshine watching a scary burn-off taking place in the scariest drought for decades. There I was enjoying harvest until today.

A Claas van came hurtling into New Pond and a tech-looking type jumped out with a laptop. He'd had no briefing, of course – just been told to get here ASAP. I told him what appeared to be going on and left him to it. I stood everyone down and hit the sofa in a huff.

A couple of hours later, feeling no better, I went back down to see how he was getting on. The combine was parked up doing a stand-still regen, engine blasting away. He said his plan was to finish that, and then he'd start poking around to see what the problem was. I told him I'd be in the farmhouse. It was nearly five o'clock when he drove into the yard; he'd finished the regen and then recalibrated the two pressure sensors either side of the filter itself. It appeared that they were getting confused about the level of blockage (as shown by the pressure difference) and having a hissy fit. He asked if we were going to use it tonight, but I said we were all done for the day. I didn't tell him that I was in a monster huff, too. I'd already texted the team saying no more to be done today.

I'd also told Team Corncart that we're going to have the weekend off. Everything is too dry, we've got a combine that thinks it's Keith Flint and I'm generally fed up. Boomtown is due to kick off in earnest tonight, so there will be no sleep to be had.

The best part of a fairly dodgy day was having a long evening wallow in the pool, which is now officially hot.

August 13th

Not a squeak from Boomtown. Not a squeak, not a beat, not a thump, not a 'big up massive yo yo', not a 'smack my bitch up' – nothing. It was delightful. I woke cheery and refreshed, full of enthusiasm to crack on with combining. The forecast suggested a bit of hurry-up might also be in order. Thank Goodness Team Corncart were happy to change plans again.

I changed our daily lorry 'order' to just one (not enough in yesterday) and we restarted in Big Field after an early lunch. It was still scary; there were an awful lot of flints out there just begging to hit a combine section. We were carting to the Drier barn, and at first it seemed extravagant to have both trailers out there. But as I got over to the far side, and near the heavier land up near the spring, the barley got better and it was worth it to stop the combine from having to wait.

We finished Big and moved into BML's, with its garish pipeline gash through the middle leaving two awkward triangles of crop. Everyone was happy to push on a bit later than normal, and we finished that one just before seven. It helped that BML's is the chalkiest on the farm, and that I got it rolled nicely back in the spring (unlike most of Big). I could put the table down properly and push on.

August 14th

Odd. Still no noise from Boomtown. I checked the news to see if it had been cancelled. No – it all seemed to be going on. Still, another good night's sleep.

I rang Bill to check on this morning's lorries. "You didn't want any. You said you were standing down for the weekend!" He was absolutely right, of course. Even so, he said he'd find me one to be going on with. It helps that all the proper farmers have finished and are off on holiday. It was dear old Trevor who steered his huge artic down to the yard. Trevor, who has been coming here as long I can remember, and claims to have seen me as sweet little prep schoolboy in Stockbridge, where his lorry yard is. Hazel and I called in to see him for a chat on the way to the combine, but he was too busy monitoring his weigher and sipping a skinny latte from a fancy paper cup. He's not as ruffty tuff as he used to be.

I picked up the combine and brought it up the track, into Chalks and parked up over at the corner nearest Godwin's Park, where Hazel picked me up again. We had a very early lunch, called the troops and had a proper long day cutting spring barley, doing both Godwin's Park and Roe Hill. It helped that Roe Hill appears to be mostly shooting strip now. The barley wasn't brilliant, and it'll be too dry, but we need to get on. It's a bit late in the harvest season to adopt that attitude, but there's nothing like the threat of rainmageddon to spur you on.

Bill rang mid-afternoon to say he'd got another lorry. I told him to sod off.

With the change in wind direction, Boomtown finally managed to permeate the house for several hours, although it did quieten down enough at bedtime for Classic FM to smother it. I read recently that the Boomtown Team are desperately trying to get permanent planning permission rather than having to reapply every year. That explains perhaps why they've been a bit more considerate this year. God help us all if they do ever get the permanent go-ahead.

August 15th

The weather changed dramatically. It was cooler, misty and rather lovely. I had the Monday morning writing jobs to do – check proofs for *Farmers Weekly* and *The Field* – and then set off with the bowser for a big refuel. It was another 'moment'. The combine is doing three days to a refill, and we've got three days of combining left. Will this be the last ever fill up? All those decades of cans, funnels, hand pumps, electric pumps, all those gallons of diesel.

I was interrupted by a machinery dealer I'd emailed the other day. I'd explained the Big Plan, and asked if he'd be interested at the very least in valuing all the kit we're going to sell, and at the most, handling the whole thing. He was dead keen to come down and have a look – but we agreed we'd get the last few days of harvest out of the way first.

After taking the bowser back to the barn and having a bit of a wash, I walked down to pick up the combine and drove it down to New Pond, then carefully along the short bit of road and into Blackhouse Road. We had a good day with all the long turns (not to mention the huge headland) and had done just over fifty acres by the time we called it a day. We dodged a humungous thunderstorm just as evening started, and my evening swim was cool and short.

There was a bit of a spooky moment as I passed the Drier barn on one of the headland turns. I looked over the hedge, fully expecting to see Dad on the concrete ramp, hands on hips, khaki trousers, green cotton shirt darkened with sweat. Behind him the burner was roaring, and dust was being blown from the cleaner via the huge exhaust pipe. But those days – and he – are long gone.

It was a relief to see the Mazda test car had been safely delivered. So many press offices are dropping *The Field* like a hot potato, and it's becoming blooming hard work to get test cars out to the farm. That should see me another month, anyway. And the Polaris is here too. That's another month.

August 16th

Another cool and misty morning, but the rainfall radar suggested something lively was on the way. Nothing was likely to be dry enough to be combined, so it was time to get some car testing done. I started with the Polaris UTV, which was a very odd machine. Whereas Pig (Kubota 400) is small, nimble and lively, the Polaris felt clumsy and awkward. It also felt utterly gutless. I did a huge tour of the farm nonetheless, meeting up with one of the pipeline team in BML's. I casually suggested that if he had any spare chalk, we could find somewhere to suit it. He took my number, just in case.

We got two more lorries away before some serious rain came in, and the world immediately felt better. A spare afternoon, a lovely red Mazda in the yard, and a few more shooting strips needing some work all combined into a lovely drive over to Fovant to pick up some 'Autumn Promise' from Bright's. The Mazda was lively, although it was a bit depressing to see that every man and his dog has finished harvest between here and there. I came back with far too many bags. Can you have too many pages of 'repair' shoot cover? Probably not.

The next job was to convert the old CO3 from maize (which was its last job fourteen months ago) to small seeds (the Autumn Promise). It was a bit of a marathon, and I didn't get it all done. I reconnected all the pipes to the 'mushroom' distributor, changed the roller and got connected to the tractor. That was quite enough for one day, so I went to the Pots with a brace of neighbours. One of them was a bit grumpy, which sort of squashed the mood. Let's hope a couple of days wildfowling in Norfolk cheers him up.

Bedtime saw Tim trying to come to terms with his first hedgehog on the lawn. And the first I've seen for ages. The badgers round here make short work of the poor helpless things. The worst noise in the world is a hedgehog being unrolled by a badger and eaten alive. Tim was making noises too, but they were just funny. The tiggywinkle scuttled off into the shrubs, probably not long for this world.

August 17th

I did some late-night research into the Polaris. It is speed limited to 15 mph unless you plug in the seatbelt. Right, that explains it. I decided to have another run round. It very quickly became very quick, and the seat belt was much needed. It seemed a tad ironic that the whole vehicle only became dangerously fast once the seatbelt is plugged in. That should make for one good paragraph, anyway. It's fortunate that I didn't scribble 520 angry words about how gutless it is. Still, it's my own fault. When they rang with the booking confirmation, I got all sniffy about doing a 'Teams' meeting to learn how to use it. "Look here, my man," I huffed, "I drive farm vehicles for a living, and anyway, it's harvest and I'm a busy man. I have no time for 'Teams', whatever that may be." Twit, Charlie.

Everything was still soaked, there were no lorries (Glenn was away), so I got back to work on the CO3 for the late shooting strips. A quick grease up of the row of rear wheels, a quick pump up of every tyre (only about half of them would hold any pressure, though) and, finally, a proper calibrate. Perfect. Everything ready to go.

Pipeline is a long way away – a very long way to go and find that something in the aged electronics has given up on the CO3. And the problem with solid state electronics is that there's next to nothing you can do to sort it. I played with cables, doing disconnections and reconnections, but to no avail. I could make the feed rotor turn by waving my hand in front of the radar, but when I lowered the whole machine – which is the cue for it to start taking signals from the radar – it did nothing. It went 'beep boop', which is code for 'no seeding required at the moment' instead of 'beep beep' which means 'let's go!' All very frustrating.

I made an assortment of phone calls but no one could really help. I decided to bring it home and swap a few control boxes around, and see if that helped. That was the plan, anyway; in reality, I fell asleep on the sofa as another heavy shower came in.

August 18th

Everything was soggy after yesterday's rain – perfect for my faltering mission to get the late cover crop in. I sat in the Deere and played with the malfunctioning control box. Curiously, after a 'configuration error' message it started to behave itself again, or seemed to. I was on the point to driving to Petworth for a new pressure switch (one of the favourite solutions that had been suggested during yesterday's phone calls), so I was very relieved not to have to.

Full of enthusiasm, I did the long drive to Pipeline to find that the old drill still wouldn't drill. It was back to where I'd started yesterday: it refused to acknowledge that I wanted it to drill, and assumed I was raising and lowering it without seed being fed, as if marking out a headland. I swore at it for ten minutes, called Tom the Horsch man again, who was as baffled as anyone, and then gave it up as a lost cause. It would have to be a job for the old Sulky box drill.

A bit of cultivation would be needed first. I've foolishly sold the 3m disc/subsoiler unit that would have been perfect, so had to put on the aged Terradisc instead, and as usual, it didn't do anything like a perfect job. It left ridges, broke shear bolts and really needed a complete change in metal – but it'll have to do. I did a selection of existing strips that had failed, ones that hadn't been sown, and even marked out a few new ones just for the sake of it. I'll be praying for rain on them soon.

August 19th

Curiously, as the end of my farming career looms large, and the end of writing columns for *Farmers Weekly* looms even larger, it has suddenly become awfully hard to write those columns. I came up with something this morning – a day late (again) – but it wasn't vintage. It'll have to do. From here on, I'm doing dramatic farewell pieces, and they should, I hope, be a bit easier to write.

The last paragraph was just being polished when a very noisy Jimny puttered into the yard. It was the ex-Editor coming up to check dates for the next shooting season, and wanting to tweak his allocation. He needs to get his guest list sorted out very early, otherwise all his pish-posh chums will have had better offers. Most of my guests are sorted on the Wednesday before the shoot – which is on Thursday. We hurried him through the allocation chart and told him to drink up his tea – another minibus full of trainee RPA inspectors was imminent.

Sure enough, only minutes after the noisy Jimny (exhaust is falling off, apparently) had chugged away, the Sparsholt College minibus arrived. Out got Graham – normally our ACCS inspector, but today with his training hat on – and a gaggle of slightly nervous looking trainees. It didn't help that Hazel was already heading across the yard with Sasha straining at the leash, and she (Sasha) makes an imposing sight. As soon as she knew all these strangers were supposed to be there, she was fine, and could be unleashed. Cue lots of cuddles and hugging. With the dog, I mean.

They all came in for coffee and our usual "this is us, we're a bit of a shambles" routine. They had already been to a couple of grown-up farms, where you meet in an office and you could eat your dinner off the grainstore floor, and it must be a bit of an eye-opener to visit a farm like ours – in a good way, of course. We spent an hour looking at machinery and then headed out into the Back Meadow to look at what little livestock we've now got.

"Is this your key?" asked one of them, holding up – miracle of miracles – Tigger's spare key. It was the one that Hazel had lost on November 4th last year, during a shoot. I'd been to Southampton to try and get a spare sorted, and driven to Basingstoke for the same thing, but two independent auto-electric experts had been comprehensively beaten by Tigger's security system. In the New Year I had made provisional bookings at the Hyundai garage in Basingstoke, where they said it would be no problem, but not cheap. They estimated about £300. It was some relief to see that spare turn up.

We waved goodbye to the trainee inspectors (who must now be referred to as 'advisors', apparently), hoping that they were now much better informed about real farming than they had been only a couple of hours earlier.

Glenn loaded two more lorries of barley, and I checked the standing crop in Blackhouse Road. It was just about dry enough, so I summoned the troops and we got stuck in, finishing it in good time. We'll do the big transfer for our last ever field tomorrow.

August 20th

Not a good night's sleep. Probably all the weird dreams brought on by the significance of the day. I reckoned there was about seventeen acres of spring barley in White Hill and Rough Field, so I had time to get the little Sulky drill set up for sowing Autumn Promise, and even went out and did a few strips. They went OK, but really could do with a deluge.

But not just yet. We had a bit of combining to do. It didn't take long, and the flapjack-heavy tea break at the top of Rough Field/Barracuda wasn't really needed. In places, the south end of White Hill was brilliant, and Rough Field was, well, Rough Field, but we did it anyway.

And there we are. That's the last bit of combining… I had a flashback to the Langdon map of the Kilmeston estate in 1616, on which you can make out strips of land being farmed by humble serfs. That's a lot of years of food production. And we're the last ones. That bit of England is destined for trees because Greta. Blimey.

There wasn't much time to dwell on the implications – we had a drinks party to go to. Neighbour Robert's lovely wife is having a significant birthday in a day or two, and there had been a general summons put out for us all to meet down at their Tichborne farmyard for some home-produced fizz and nibbles. We sat in the smart courtyard, sipping and nibbling, and exchanging farming rudeness with dozens of neighbours. And all the while, barn owls swooped in and out of the huge 14th-century barn only fifty yards away.

Also there was John Primmer, the patriarch of the famous Tichborne clan, and retired farm worker for the Youngs – of many generations. Tall, smart in dress and smart in mind, and of a very good age, he listened intently to our retirement plans. "Well done you," he said, after a moment's thought. Somehow it was the most authentic endorsement I've ever had. Very reassuring.

August 21st

I'm sure I should have woken with a sore head after last night's bash, but I felt fine. It helped that I had a pile of tractor work to do, which in itself was odd. Yesterday was supposed to be the end of my arable career. I went out with the little drill again and finished as many strips as I could find with Autumn Promise, and Hazel went out in the afternoon and rolled them all. They couldn't have gone in any better. A bit of fert and bit of rain, and it'll be as good as one could hope for.

I kept waiting all day for some sort of meltdown moment, but none came. Probably because we were all still watching the weather forecast, this time hoping for rain. One day I won't bother with the weather, and that really will be a turning point.

August 22nd

There was no time for an emotional 'last harvest evah' session; it turned into a very busy Monday. There were books to post, articles to proof, and technical queries from *Field* subs who don't seem to try and find out stuff themselves anymore. Once all that was done, I had a last drive in the test Mazda, which is growing on me, and left Hazel to oversee pick-up. I put the sprayer on the Deere and headed off to the fertiliser tank (for the last time) and drained it. Just over two cubic metres came out, and I did some in-cab sums to work out how to spread that over eight hectares of strips and have a bit left over to give the Back Meadow a bit of a boost – although the recent rain is doing a good job of that already.

Land Agent Chris came round for a chat on progress with the Big Plan. Is silence good news? Should we be doing anything? Will the Trust be honouring their side of the agreement – especially the bit about getting the barns fit for reletting – which, in theory, is how we're going to pay our own rent? Chris was calmly optimistic, and even made a few calls to relevant solicitors to check on paperwork progress. No one answered, though, but Chris remained calm and confident.

Last job was to pick up Anthony from Winchester station. He's coming down for a bit of a break from London, and I suspect, a bit of think about life. His plans to do one last bit of corn cart had been scuppered by the early end of harvest, but we assured him that there was lots of shovelling into lorries to be done. He didn't look terribly thrilled at that news.

August 23rd

Just for a change, I managed a bit of a lie-in. Very nice it was, too. But there was still half a tank of fertiliser to go on the Back Meadow, and the forecast was for very suitable rain. I set the rate to 130l/ha and guessed some 24m tramlines in the Back Meadow; it worked out perfectly. Who'd have thought I've been doing it for all these years? I hitched the trusty and slightly rusty sprayer off (possibly for the last time) and gave the Chafer/Yara rep a ring when I got in. "I suppose you're ringing to say you don't need your tank anymore," he said. That took the wind out of my 'dramatic announcement' sails. He was another one who couldn't help but agree with what we're doing, but can't get his head around the madness of ending food production in the UK. I explained we were doing our bit to hasten the day when the agrifolly becomes obvious to all.

We got two more lorries away – Noel at the controls of the Massey now that Glenn is back to Sparsholt after the summer break. The crud from Rough Field scraped through as Planet 3. The lorries had to wheedle their way past an assortment of SSE lorries and generators; another huge limb had split from a tree in Bob's Wood and come down on the line to New Pond. It made a right mess of a pole and left cables dangling everywhere. Thank goodness it didn't happen a few weeks ago at the height of the heat and dryness. Doesn't bear thinking about

August 24th

Chaos this morning. The building team who had won the contract to get our windows sorted out (before they all fall out) arrived for a site recce. There was the head man, his foreman, a joiner and the scaffolder. I was relieved to see a scaffolder involved – the Bat Nazis obviously haven't managed to stop the whole project, or insist that everything is done from an airship.

The Trust's own pest controller turned up, too, confused as to what was going on with our barns. I tried to explain that we were giving up a couple of yards, and had asked our present pest controllers to end our contact at Michaelmas. I had suggested to the Trust that they should find a replacement. This new chap got very confused – insisting that he had to give me a quote. I tried my best to correct him and sent him off to Godwin's and the Drier Yard with a map. Something makes me doubt he ever got to either of them.

SSE drove into the yard, asking permission to take their repair stuff into BOMS to get to the mangled poles. Of course they can, I said, but leave any old poles behind, please. Still useful, even on a much-reduced farm.

Finally, two grain lorries arrived. The first cleared out the Godwin's barn and needed topping up down at the Drier Yard, the second cleared out the Drier barn and made a good hole in the left-hand-lean to. One more lorry, and that will be that. One more lorry.

Hazel and Anthony did the lorries; I had a quiet day, snoozed and had a lovely swim in the odd heat and humidity. It feels like a break in the weather is imminent.

August 25th

We had a really good, proper rain for four or five hours. I rang Trinity Grain to put the last lorry EVAH off, but they were one step ahead of me; they'd already cancelled him.

The first of the many machinery gurus we're planning to consult with arrived in the yard in the steady rain. I've asked him to have a look at all our kit, and then advise us what to do with it all. We had a long cuppa to start with, and by the time we set off with clipboards, the rain had eased off. We did a thorough trip round everything, clutching the list I'd compiled the other day, each machine getting a comprehensive inspection.

The summary was that we've got a yard full of stuff that will be much in demand. We've got a dilemma in that we're not actually sure what we're going to sell. The combine and the sprayer, obvs, but the rest of the list doesn't have a tick against it as 'go now'. If I'm keeping going with the Trust's contracting work, I'll need the big Deere and the cultivation kit, and if we're keeping and establishing grass on Dead Dog Farm, we'll need the grassland kit. In many ways, it would be simpler if we flogged the lot and re-bought as we needed. Simpler, but probably not very sensible. He went off with lots of notes and a promise to be in touch.

A large orange Openfield lorry crawled past the house soon after lunch. It had come to pick up our last ever load of stuff. Good grief – there's a thought. Hazel and Anthony set off to do the last ever sweeping and shovelling, but I was very soon summoned by phone to make it a proper full house – with Noel at the wheel of the loader. Cameras were busy as we swept and shovelled, and the heavy rain meant that 'lower shithole' (as the drivers christened that yard many moons ago) lived up to its name.

We even made a good lorryload – 25 tonnes, as opposed to the 14 or so that we'd all predicted. More photos were taken, and the huge orange Openfield lorry squelched its way out of the yard. It was a thoughtful cup of tea that followed that. Mind you, I was just glad that I hadn't put my back out.

August 26th

Today's machinery guru was auctioneer Tom. We've known him for decades; back in the golden days of the mid-nineties, when Hazel's suckler herd was roaring, he was in charge of selling at Guildford market, ensuring that the fat-as-butter calves went for a small fortune each. That was all before March 21st, 1996, of course.

His machinery inspection was a bit less detailed than yesterday's, but his verdict was also positive. This is a great time to sell lightly used kit. Get some more 'guest' stuff off all our surrounding neighbours, clear the Back Meadow for a day in early October, and we'll be laughing. And he wanted to know when I was going to have a go at actually standing on the rostrum at a sale? Me? Auctioneering? With my shy and retiring personality? Actually, it sounds like fun.

There was a lot to think about as I put the combine and one green trailer (after sweeping our the nicely fermenting barley lodging in the front corners) away in the main barn.

Talking of future plans – niece Sarah descended on the farmhouse with assorted husbands, sisters and children, and there was a fantastic cake-fest. Cattle were fed, dogs were cuddled (Sasha in heaven at the hands of small people) and several children couldn't resist the lure of the pool. There was much talk of our plans, the implications and opportunities, and (more specifically) the idea being mooted by *Farmers Weekly* that Sarah might take over Flindt on Friday. We all agreed that this was a tad optimistic, but it would be fun to do some sort of joint column. I could ask some awkward questions about regen farming, and she could answer them. Or not, as the case may be.

It took ages for the two sisters to gather their herds and then pile them into just the one car, ready for a sleepover tonight. I hope the sugar high wears off at some time.

August 27th

A quiet Saturday – at last. Anthony did lots of gardening, carting vast heaps of cuttings round to the bonfire site, and Hazel spent most of the day at the Alresford Show ground. It's back after two years of not happening, and she is back in her old role as Trade Stand Secretary. She handed the job over just before lockdown in March 2020, but the new girl who took over chucked it in early this year, leaving everyone in a bit of a panic. Hazel, of course, agreed to step in.

I listened to more suspiciously one-sided cricket and did some well-overdue writing invoices. I also set about the insurance claim form for our 'two-tone Crusoe'. In autumn 2020, we ordered 13 tonnes of Crusoe seed, perfect for filling the barn with top-quality milling wheat. We drilled about 160 acres with it, not in the best of conditions (it was yet another challenging season), but it looked a lot better by the time spring came round.

But then it started to look odd: there seemed to be two types of wheat in it. It was definitely part of the mix, as proved by the occasional bits of wide drilling, which were still bare. In other words, there wasn't a residual bank of volunteer wheat coming through. Phone calls were made, reps were summoned, complicated tests were done, and in the end it was agreed by all that our Crusoe seemed to be about 40% Skyscraper. I got a couple of articles out of it, which prompted a few phone calls from other farmers round the country. It wasn't just us, then.

It was agreed that the seed company would compensate us by paying the price difference between what we got from Trinity Grain and what we would have got had the Crusoe all gone for Grade 1 milling. Which it would no doubt have done, oh yes. It did mean we've had a bit of a wait on our hands since combining it and sending it off to Trinity twelve months ago. We had all the (dismal) tonnages, but the final 'long pool' prices only came through (with a handy cheque) a week or two ago. That meant I could finally sit down with the seed company's claim form and fill it in. Once I'd done the maths, it came to a very handy £14.5k. We wait with interest to see how quickly the insurance team will act. The trouble is, my column will cease in a few weeks' time, and my handy platform for making a fuss will be gone.

We popped down to the ex-Editor's shed in his garden to moan about everything over a couple of beers. And we were very good at it.

August 28th

The racing stables where Hazel does part-time book-keeping isn't far away, but it's a different world. We went up there this afternoon for 'owners' open day'. We had drinks and nibbles, and then settled down on bales and deckchairs to watch a parade of racehorses. It was a dream-like scene: highly bred animals being lead round the little square parade area, with the head man chattering away about each horse's pedigree and form. There were even one or two at the end that were for sale. I know we've retired, but our pension funds would only buy half a leg. There were plenty of familiar faces (in the crowd, at least), and none of them Qatari billionaires; these were folk who had got together with a bunch of mates and bought a beast, perfect for a retirement hobby, and a chance to enter the owners' enclosure at assorted racecourses – even, perhaps, the winners' enclosure. But no one was in it to make money.

The stables occupy a hilltop just east of Winchester, and it was as much fun watching the aircraft, big and small, looping over us and then settling down for their long approach to Southampton Airport, following the M3. The swallows were gathering on the cables, too, suggesting that summer is done.

One of the big-name owners up there is the man who bought the Krispy Kreme Donut franchise when it was a piddling little company. He is now worth a few bob. He had donated a vast box of his product for the day – you bought half a dozen for a tenner and the cash went to the multitude of stable staff, who were all far too skinny to have ever gone near a donut.

One of the owners was a machinery salesman from the days of SCATS. I jokingly complained about the Terradisc we'd bought off him in the late 1980s. He looked at me as if I were mad. I'm not sure he recognised me. The daft thing is that we are still using the Terradisc.

Reality barged its way back as we drove home. Just north of Owslebury, two dodgy cars were blocking the road, side-by-side, gesturing out of the windows at the lovely open fields – perfect for, ooh, I don't know, a spot of hare coursing. They reluctantly returned to single file as we drove up behind them, and then sped off in a hideous cloud of diesel fumes. Something told me that an MOT centre hadn't been troubled for some time. We jotted down numbers as we followed them down the A272 to Cheriton. I put the numbers through the very handy MOT checker on the internet, and found that one was untaxed and had no MOT. I sent a message to Policeman Ian, and even fetched the dashcam from the car. It had captured perfect shots of the two cars, so I sent him those, too.

August 29th

There was a time when the August Bank Holiday Monday was the only busy traffic day of the year. Even back in the late 70s and 80s, Dad would try and organise harvest so as to minimise road work. Mind you, we were driving Super Majors with no brakes in the mid-seventies. These days, every day is as busy as a 70s bank holiday.

We're done and dusted, and at a bit of a loose end. I had a long drive round the farm, enjoying the stubbles, and thinking how I probably won't be needing a 4x4 in a couple of months. That'll be a shame, as mud-plugging is one of my favourite hobbies. The recently sown strips looked good, having had rain and fertiliser on a hot seedbed. I tried to memorise all the bales of assorted looseness that were littering the fields. It would be a good job for Anthony to go for a long trundle and gather as much valuable straw as possible.

Hazel teamed up with her gang of dog chums for a training session up in the woods, and I set about the review of the Deere 6155M that I promised I'd do for the machinery pages of *Farmers Weekly*. I hope they like it – it would be another handy little job to pick up, post retirement.

The pool was cool – but we shouldn't complain. We've got our money's worth out of it this year.

August 30th

What a productive writing day. I proofed the FW harvest review (complete with 'last one ever' teaser in the last paragraph) and, while the mood was right, flew through the two-page 'this is why we're downsizing' FonF. I finished the review of the 6155M, too, and sent in a selection of relevant photographs. The force was truly with me.

Tractorwork proved a bit more problematic. We are done with loading lorries and unloading huge bags of seed, so the big block of Ford wafer weights is now spare to act as front weights for the Deere. I thought the time was right to have a go with the enormous folding 4m Proforge discs. I'd picked them up with the Deere's rear linkage a few weeks ago and the front wheels nearly came off the ground, so I know the weights would be needed. And if I'm going to be ploughing this autumn (as the Trust requested), they'll be needed for that, too.

As usual, it took far longer than it should have done to get the weights on, and even longer to get the discs on; it didn't help that the balls for the latter are category three (or is it four – I can never work it out) which means the hitching points are wider than on all the other machines. A certain amount of adjustment and fiddling was needed, but I got them on in the end.

The Trust's first batch of grass seed arrived, in a van and in lots of 20kg bags. I opened up the container to make space for them (the only really rat-proof venue on the farm) and left the man from Cotswold Seed to manhandle them in. I don't want to put my back out at this stage of the year.

My treat in the pub was to explain the concept of Krispy Kreme Donuts to neighbour Robert – Cheriton's finest winer and diner. His face was a picture.

August 31st

I set off for BOMS with my shiny new folding 4m discs, keen for a long day's cultivation. As soon as I reached New Pond, there was a problem. An X-Trail was parked sideways across the entrance to Rick and Clump, blocking the way. Also there was Debbie, who only moved out of No. 1 a few weeks ago. It turned out that she was back to do a final clean-up before handing the cottage back, and she, too was blocked. I suggested she park in the Drier Yard.

Meanwhile, I had a closer look at the X-Trail. What made me laugh was that if you compiled a list all the red flags you could think of on a suspicious vehicle, this Nissan had them all: high mileage 4x4, 210 litre oil drum in the boot with a couple of five litre cans, lamping kit in the front passenger footwell, crowbar behind the front passenger seat. It couldn't have been dodgier if it had a big 'arrest me!' sign on the roof. Debbie's neighbour emerged from No. 2 and said the Nissan had been there for a day, which was a small relief; I really didn't want to come face to face with a quartet of violent hare-coursers. She also said she'd done a bit of interneting and it wasn't taxed. I took the tractor home and rang Policeman Ian.

He was out about 20 minutes later, and the recovery truck not long after that. He'd taken one look at the X-Trail, and its contents, and said, "We'll have that!" He called in for a cuppa with a big grin. He just loves jobs like that.

The big 4m disks made short work of the nice soft ground in BOMS when I finally got out there. I even managed to take a few 'at work' pics for the 155M review in *Farmers Weekly*.

September 1st

It's a completely new situation: I've got a whole bunch of arable-ish work to do – cultivating fields and establishing grass seed – but it's for my new 'boss', the National Trust. The seed is in, and I've just ordered an Opico grass harrow/seeder unit from the Opico MD. He was in charge of the dinner I did in Stamford last winter, and was very helpful with a deal. I'm going to miss having such powers – bwah ha hah!

But I need to check if the Trust wants me to push on regardless. Should I keep ploughing, or cultivating, as we agreed I should, back before the drought kicked in? Should I try to get the seed in while the weather is suitable? I know what I'd do if it were my land, but it's not anymore – well, Kilmeston Road and the Hangar, anyway. But no one is available to answer my queries. They're all on holiday, as the bounced-back emails show. All of them. And I appear to have four 'bosses'. Oh well.

Anthony and I fired up the chainsaw and went log cart instead. Even that wasn't a great success, though. The new transport box went on the back of the Massey nicely (unlike the Fleming one I bought ages ago, which was only fit for hobby tractors) and we headed out to Big Field to tackle what I was sure was an enormous ash. It turned out to be less bounteous than I thought. The chainsaw misbehaved (it's getting very long in the tooth) and the chain jumped off once or twice as I tackled horizontal trunks the wrong way. And it was very hot indeed. We knocked off earlier than I'd planned, and I had to pull over on the way home to get rid of a short spell of dizziness. Anthony went up to the top of BML's and picked the wood that the pipeline gang had left when clearing a path for their huge project. That made the trip out slightly more worthwhile.

September 2nd

Hazel vanished to the Alresford showground again, getting ready for tomorrow. I sat around and felt sorry for myself (I'm not as fit as I used to be) and Anthony was despatched to shovel the wheat we've held back after harvest into one of the green trailers. We thought we'd saved enough to just about fill a trailer, and we were absolutely right. Well, Glenn should get the credit; he was the one who carefully bucketed just the right amount of dry (and therefore safe to store) wheat into the right-hand lean-to.

September 3rd

If it's five fifteen on a September morning and the kitchen is already full of people getting ready to go out, that can only mean one thing: it's Alresford Show day. Anthony and Hazel were gone by quarter to six. I went back to bed, failed to get back to sleep, and decided to get up.

They were back for breakfast and a cuppa once the vast majority of traders (Hazel's department is Trade Stand Secretary) were in, and it was time to effectively stand down, but that wasn't until well past nine. Once refuelled, Hazel was off again, ready to deal with any complaints.

I had an early lunch and set off just before twelve. The queue of traffic started just before Cheriton, which was fantastic news. And once I finally got in, it was heaving. Mind you, it was the perfect day for it. Not too hot, no rain, all the farming community done with harvest, prices good, everyone wanting to get out and about in a post-Covid mood, and, of course, there has been no show for three years. I did see one mask, though.

Halfway down the bulging machinery lines was the Ineos stand, and they'd brought a Grenadier. This was a huge coup for the Alresford Show, which isn't a big event. I'd emailed the chap I know at Ineos a few months ago, suggesting they came along, more in hope than expectation. After a long delay, they announced that they'd be up for it, and brought a working prototype to do the 'new machinery' parade. Their stand was very busy all day, so I hope it was worth the effort. The Grenadier is still a long way from being delivered to the tens of thousands who have placed orders, and I do hope it isn't going to be the De Lorean of the 4x4 world.

I somehow got the job of commentating while lots of new machinery drove into the ring in convoy – including the Grenadier (the first time I've seen one moving) – and did a couple of laps. Blimey, that was a hard job, trying to read the last-minute notes that I'd been given on each machine while squinting into the distance to see which machine was next in the queue. It didn't help that the air was full of dust from the car parks, which were beginning to empty, and diesel fumes and smoke from the massed ranks of historic tractors that had just, reluctantly, left the ring.

It was a fantastic day. Everyone was talking about the number of people who were there. I was getting ready for my stint with the microphone when the radios crackled with news that all the car parks were officially full and were shutting their gates. I hope my efforts with the Grenadier helped.

Hazel and I did a couple of loops of the field, catching up with friends, and having two completely unnecessary ice cream cones each. Hazel was getting lots of congratulations for her organisation, and I was getting lots of 'good call' comments from people who had heard of our farm plans. It was that sort of mood. Anthony very kindly went and got fish and chips from the Alresford chippie once we staggered home, and we watched the final of the Hundred (the cricket version of a double cone with strawberry sauce). Well, I did; Hazel was snoring as soon as she hit the sofa.

A wonderful day. A real 'all's well with the world' day. It probably won't last.

September 4th

A bit of a calm day. Hazel only spent a couple of hours at the showground and checking emails for any complaints and comments. Most of it was overwhelmingly positive.

Another early night was wrecked by a stunning two-hour thunderstorm and vast quantities of wonderful rain. Good thing it didn't arrive 48 hours earlier.

September 5th

"What about that thunder?" I said to Hazel first thing.

"What thunder?" she asked. Blimey – she was tired. The world seems to be returning to work after the long summer break. I finally managed to get hold of some of my new bosses at the Trust, to discuss the grassland establishment I'm supposed to be doing for them. They were happy to persevere with the September sowing of what was delivered the other day in the Hangar and Kilmeston Road, but my suggestion of cultivating most of the rest of the farm as a hare-courser deterrent wasn't so well received. 'Erosion' must be avoided. I pointed out that in thirty-eight years of ploughing, cultivating and overwintering stubbles, I have never seen soil erosion. I'm not sure that empirical evidence will trump green agri-dogma.

There was a flurry of emails with *Farmers Weekly* discussing my future there. It was all a bit of a mess. The machinery editor was dead keen for me to do stuff for him, although I pointed out that my days of heavy machinery investment are, in theory, over. He said a chat down here was needed. As did Emma, who looks after stuff I send up there at the moment. She kindly invited me to return to the rotation of opinion columns; I suggested a monthly chronicle of how things turn out, but she said that wasn't possible. She couldn't say why – a meeting down here would be needed. Interesting.

And the FW editor forwarded to me a lovely email saying how wrong it was that I was retiring, and how I just have to keep writing for FW. He had replied that one way or another I would be still writing for FW. All very good for the future.

Not such good news was an email from the Trust about the huge external repairs and decorations that are about to start. The price would be phenomenal, and we are obliged to pay two-thirds of that, as per our tenancy agreement. She did agree that she would be happy to negotiate, as decorations had slipped behind schedule somewhat. What she should have said was that the house has only been touched twice in the twenty-five years that we've lived in it, and both time it was done by complete cowboys. That's why all the windows are falling out. I avoided the temptation to email her a message in that vein, but forwarded it to land agent Chris instead. I hoovered and then jumped in the pool to calm down, and it was as warm as it has been for weeks.

Another fantastic thunderstorm arrived just after it got dark. Good news for everyone trying to sow stuff in the next few weeks. I just hope I get my grass seed sorted out – and there's me thinking I could stop watching the weather forecast.

September 6th

Working on the assumption that Kilmeston Road and the Hangar would now be soft enough to plough, and that my new grass seed sowing machine would turn up in the next ten days, I hitched off the discs and put on the plough. It has gone a bit rusty (some silly sod failed to grease it up after all that work in August) but hoped that some firm chalky soil would soon shine it up.

Our landlord came round for a chat about our plans to plant trees on the new shoot. The bill for the window work came up, of course, and she was the first to admit that much of the size of the bill was down to the Trust's failure to keep up a regular redecoration schedule, and that our contribution was negotiable. That was good news, and it kept things nice and cheerful. She suggested that Hazel and I go over to Hinton Ampner House on the 29th for a cuppa as a little 'hand over' ceremony, which was a nice thought.

The Hangar was indeed soft enough to plough, and I had a long afternoon out there, enjoying the job. It went well, with occasional thunderstorms skimming past, and I had the wonderful satisfaction of ploughing up lots of paths that locals had already made. I was hoping that someone would be out to remonstrate with me for it, and I could just say I was doing my job, but none came. One of the Trust's rangers popped out for a chat, and asked how to turn off the water trough that's been leaking for as long as I can remember. It was bit of an odd moment: a 4x4 coming along Dark Lane, a figure – in theory, one of my new bosses – strolling out into the field and stopping for a chat about progress. Just like the old days.

The Trust have cut and cleared a couple of new gateways from the north-west corner of Kilmeston Road into the Hangar, and a beautiful cone of smoking ashes was all that was left of their chopping and burning. Ploughing it in was hugely satisfying, as the hot ash met damp soil, and a few square yards of soil proceeded to steam gently for half an hour.

I had a quick shower and tea, and Anthony gave me a lift to the Pots to meet Robert. Anthony is planning to head back up to London this week, so this will be the last lift I can scrounge for a bit.

September 7th

We've only got Anthony home for a couple more days, and we haven't made much of a hole in the long list of jobs we were going to do using his muscle. Hazel decided that a couple of runs to the plastic recycling centre would be in order. It's been a long time since all the carefully bundled seed bags and chemical drums were cleared, so there was quite a heap. And these will be the last seed bags and chemical drums to leave the farm.

The old and somewhat knackered twin-axle car trailer was just about roadworthy – the tyres hold their air for 24 hours, but they all go round, which was a bonus. And most of the lights work. The bags aren't heavy – they're just bloody awkward to manhandle onto the trailer and strap down. Or so I'm told – I was indoors recovering from last night's beer. By lunchtime, there was a lot more space in assorted barns and lean-tos.

We then set off to Fovant, to visit Bright's Seeds. I was only there a few weeks ago, picking up late game cover seed, and today was their official open day to launch the smart new offices and warehouse. Very smart it was too, although their trial plots of game cover were suspiciously good. "Why don't any of our strips look like these?" I asked Arthur as he took us round. He confessed that the soil there was something special, greensand heaving with nutrients after many decades of dairy farming. That's cheating, that is. I think they should open a satellite branch on a cold bit of Hampshire clay.

Our evening thunderstorms were a bit lighter, although they're promising another week of it. Too wet to plough, and that's a tad ironic after all the dry weather.

September 8th

More phenomenal rain, and it started coming through the ceiling into the hall where the back stairs are. I managed to get hold of the Trust's building manager, who sounded as stressed as ever, and he promised someone would come and have a look. My inspection from the top of a ladder suggested some broken tiles in the bottom of a gully. Actually, there were broken tiles everywhere, so it could just as easily have been coming through anywhere. We put towels and newspaper down and hoped the rain would stop soon.

The gang who came out to look at the combine when we were doing the spring barley in Chalks arrived on masse again, waving their virtual chequebooks. Within five minutes, the deal was done. It was another one of those deals which must be kept hush-hush, but it's safe to say that I've had two seasons (one-and-a-half, if you take into account the fact that the Tucano was delivered very late last year) for very little depreciation. I've no doubt that the accountant will kick up a fuss, but I'm simply trying to raise lots of retirement cash.

Hazel took Anthony to the station, and he set off back to London, having had a three-week think about life, the universe and everything while down here. He didn't get to do any corn cart, but he spent many hours reclaiming areas of the garden and walking dogs. He enjoys that, at least.

I was showing the combine buyers round everything else (their shopping list to equip a 700-acre bare farm is long and amazingly similar to my 'for sale' list) when Hazel got back, so we had another lengthy round of tea and biscuits. We were all making phone calls to assorted Claas reps to find out if the precious five-year warranty would still be valid, but they went on their way with that question unanswered.

Then the Queen died.

It was quite surreal. I'm no Royalist (I used to be), but I'm certainly no Republican, and liked to think I was completely neutral when it comes to matters royal. I despair when they make eco pronouncements but love them when they are simply everyone's family. But it hit me amazingly hard – and Hazel, too. After all, we're both sides of sixty, and we've known no one else.

September 9th

Hazel went round the farm in the Massey putting all the telegraph poles back in the gateways. It seems an odd thing to do on fields that we're on the point of saying farewell to, but life is easier for everyone if the hare coursers are somehow kept off. I suspect that it will soon take more than just telegraph poles, once the word gets about that these fields are absentee farmed. Hazel said that she got quite melancholy.

A post-harvest haircut was needed, so I went into Alresford for a trim and a gossip, picked up yet more pills at the chemist and popped my head round the door of Oxley's bookshop to see if they needed any more copies of Books One or Two. The good news was that he was down to the last copy of Book Two, and asked for another half dozen.

The plough beckoned again, but I only managed a couple of hours in the Hangar this time. While trying to get a gargantuan flint from between a skim and a mouldboard I noticed that the tractor's back axle was covered in oil. One of the aged hydraulic pipes had split. Bloody typical; I was miles from home, too. I drove back as fast as I could (bearing in mind how many gates I have to get through because the sheep are still in Springshot) to make sure I could get up to Rod's before five o'clock and get Dave to knock up a couple of nice new pipes. Which he did. I treated Tigger to new wiper blades while I was waiting.

The funny thing was that my two-page Flindt on Friday appeared today. I suppose I was hoping it would cause a bit of a stir, but Her Majesty put paid to that. I managed to sell a dozen books today, though, by plugging them in the article.

September 10th

It's really official now: autumn has started. It was cool last night, the dawn was late, and Hazel was off at some silly hour for a full day's dog training with Tim. I took the rest of the dogs for a walk, ate too much, fitted the hydraulic hoses to the plough and then briefly considered more ploughing. I decided against it.

Curiously, the mood has changed from sadness at the Queen's death to cheerful recollection. You can't turn on the television or radio for funny stories and personal memories. And crowds are gathering to cheer the new King and sing the updated national anthem. I'm back to being a royalist.

September 11th

I'm not sure what I did while wrestling with hydraulic hoses yesterday, but I had a stiff neck that was as bad as anything from rugby days. Bloody agony. The trouble is, there's a new boss insisting I get lots of cultivation done. They want sixty-five acres of grass seed established, and there are only a couple of weeks left to do it. Ooh, a new Channel Four programme. "And today, Charlie has woken up with a cricked neck…" I took some ibuprofen (blimey, it is just like rugby days) and headed out to the Hangar for a long hot afternoon.

I've forgotten the last time the Hangar was ploughed – it may have been at the same time as Kilmeston Road, eleven years ago, but I'm not sure. All I know is that there was a whole underground culture being wrecked by the mouldboards, with mice scurrying in all directions. It seemed sad to be ploughing in all the cowslips that have suddenly blossomed out there while the field was untouched.

The radio stations were tentatively cheering up, with the music becoming a bit more upbeat. I couldn't find the cricket on my new radio (really should have got that sorted by now), which was a shame. It sounds like it's another 'blink and you miss it' Test match.

The land work went really well, and I reckon it will only need a roll before it's a seedbed. I had one too many jolts when starting the headband (ploughing in) and suddenly felt that I'd done enough. I came home for a not-too-cold swim.

September 12th

It all kicked off this morning – in a very positive way. There were builders and scaffolders en masse in the yard by seven thirty. We made sure all the gates were open in time and tried really hard to look as if we weren't just out of bed. There was then that curious tradesman half-hour where everyone sits in their vans and does whatever they do while they're sitting in their vans. Next was that 'getting to know you' stage, where introductions were made and dogs were greeted. Everyone seemed happy to be mobbed by a pack, and Sasha showed her approval by presenting nearly all of them with something to throw so she could retrieve. One particularly ruffty-tuff scaffolder was thrilled, and we lost Sasha for some time while he played fetch with her. It didn't seem to slow down the execution of the scaffolding, which rapidly surrounded the house in a cacophony of pipes, brackets and air spanners. The hanging tiles on the south of the house remained unenclosed; the Bat Nazis has decreed it so.

Meanwhile, the builders/carpenters have moved into the old estate workshop, and I made a point of telling them the significance of where they were now working. I warned them to look out for the ghost of Bob Thornton, the old boy who spent his whole life in that shed, making doors, windows and gates for the whole village. The Portaloo arrived, too, which was one thing Bob never had; there was a primitive hole alongside one of the sheds, with a telephone directory acting as the Andrex of its day.

My neck was a bit better, so I persevered with ploughing. I had a long hard look at the 'Quick Fit' points on the Kverneland and pondered whether to replace them. I'm going into Kilmeston Road next, which is much tougher than the Hangar, and the points will need to be a bit sharper. I was hoping to sell the plough with brand-new points fitted (always a good marketing strategy), but I'm wary of wearing down the point holders. I was full of confidence that some or all of the new points I bought the best part of a decade ago would have vanished. But a quick rummage in the old calf pens revealed all ten. And the unused toolbox that came with the Tucano last year revealed a sturdy club hammer and a drift. Now there was no excuse.

Luckly Rod Gaskin rang, wanting to talk about changing Pig for a newer but near enough identical model. Kubota have spotted that small UTVs are still wanted (unlike the horrid Polaris I drove the other week), and the new model's changes extend to a different engine, and that's about it. Funny to think that we first met Rod when we were in the bungalow, and he was keen to sell us a Massey combine. That was probably thirty years ago.

I got the new points on the plough in hot sunshine (I felt sorry for the scaffolders) and set off for the Hangar. There was a digger hard at work next to the water trough. Well, he was sitting in the cab of his Land Rover – but that sort of counts. The Trust's plan is to tap into the water main at that trough and take a line along the valley for a new trough in Kilmeston Road, ready for when they graze eco cattle. I had a chat with the man, promising to leave him a bit of headland so he could get in and out, and started to head off to Kilmeston Road once I'd done all I could do. I was interrupted by Digger Man calling. He'd managed to nick the water pipe while digging and his hole was rapidly filling up. He asked if I knew if the pipe was plastic or metal. I had a bit of a think. The trough was installed in the late 70s, possibly early 80s, as part of Mr Dutton's plans to stop Dad overwintering cattle on the permanent pasture in the Park (which we still had as part of the farm back then).

Mr Dutton (the landowner at the time, of course) had built Dad a barn (the 'cattle barn', just down the hill from the farmhouse) in the 60s as somewhere to keep the cattle over the winter months, but that didn't work. The next idea was to spin turnips into the Hangar's arable crop late in the summer, and then strip graze the luscious greenery over the winter.

That was the theory, anyway. It never worked, either. The big store cattle had never come across electric fences, and merrily walked through them. The green mushroom-shaped energiser was useless, too. The turnips never grew to any size. And the storm of January 1990 felled all the poplars next to the source of the Itchen onto the boundary fence and the cattle arrived on a grumpy neighbour's daffodil lawn. A hideous time.

We took over in 1991, and never put cattle out there again. The water trough stayed, but I think it has leaked ever since – until the weekend, when someone appears to have had a good rummage in the mud and found the stopcock. It was now leaking again, but once we'd decided that it was plastic, Digger Man set off to his LR for some tools. I left him to it.

Kilmeston Road went well, but it was pretty hot. I had the back and side windows open, so no air-con. I ended up opening the left door and letting cool air in that way. But I had to keep shutting them all as the phone kept ringing. The Toyota delivery man rang to say that he'd be here with the Hilux at seven thirty tomorrow morning and had to get a train from Winchester at eight thirty. There was then a long pause. It was tempting to say 'bugger off!' but instead I suggested he book a taxi company to be here to meet him in the morning.

The Claas dealer then rang to say they had to fit a 'software update' to the combine, and did we still have it? I told him we did, but its departure was imminent, and he'd better look lively. It does seem odd that a combine should need a 'software update'; it's a combine, FFS. My Protector 6 never needed one.

The pool was as warm as it has been for weeks, just right for a pre-rehearsal wallow. The band's first get-together since the Covid gig at the ex-vets wasn't brilliant – too much messing about like children back at school. It was still fun, though. You can't beat 'Hush' – the Kula Shaker version – for clearing the tubes. Best of all, the agonising tendonitis in my right hand didn't make a reappearance.

September 13th

The scaffolders were full of the news that an old couple from Lancashire had arrived in the yard yesterday bearing copies of Book One and Two, hoping to get them signed. "Woss all that abaaaah?" they asked, as per *Harry and Paul*. I explained my literary fame. "I look like Steven Gerrard's bruvver!" said one. I nodded in agreement, although I have no idea who Steven Gerrard is.

The Toyota Hilux arrived as promised, and the delivery man set off down the road to meet the taxi I hoped he'd managed to book. I never saw him again, so I assume all went well.

The rain curtailed what was intended to be a long day in Kilmeston Road. The tractor started slipping too much, and the wireweed refused to go through the plough, messing up a quality bit of ploughing. I might drop the skims a bit before I go out there next.

There was a strange message on the phone from an Indian gentleman, claiming to be from Experian, wanting to go through our business details for a credit check. I've no idea what this is all about. I have managed to wangle a keenly priced Opico grass-seeding machine from their MD, and they're supplying it through a local dealer that we've not used before, so that might be something to do with it, I suppose. I'll ring them back tomorrow.

Poor old neighbour Robert was a bit sorry for himself in the Pots. He'd gone arse-over-tit in his bathroom a few days ago, and had a damaged shoulder and bruising down his left side. I told him to be grateful that that was all he'd suffered. Folk of his, ahem, vintage usually don't get away with as little damage as that. And he's lost a lot of weight and, therefore, padding in the last few months. He agreed and got stuck into bag of crisps.

September 14th

It's a good thing I don't have a proper job. I lost most of the morning not feeling too good – nothing to do with the beer and peanuts of course. There was a lot more rain. The ex-Editor dropped in for tea and a scan of our cartographical plans for the small shoot – a highly detailed set of drawings with copses, hedges and strips. It was all completely wasted on a man who is hard pushed to find London or the Arctic on a map. Still, he got very excited about it.

It was all very sticky after the rain, which gave me the chance to try out the Hilux with a trip to APM for a new plough skim. One had shattered in the Hangar, joining the centuries' worth of YL42s and horseshoes that some metal detector will find in the centuries to come. Or perhaps some arable farmer of the future will find it when he's ploughing the land when the cry goes out for wheat production. Perhaps I might still be alive to see that happen. Who knows?

I topped up the tiny order with two cans of WD40, because that's what you buy when you need to make a trip worthwhile. Not sure I'll be needing it as much in my new future, but there we go. It's still useful when rain has got into the aerial connection.

There was a detour to Halfords to get some Velcro tape, used to stick my simple Teejet guidance system's receiver on the roof of the tractor. If and when the wide grass seeding kit gets here, I'll be needing it to judge six-metre distances. It was flipping expensive for two short lengths, but there were countless staff all talking loudly at the desk, and they all need their wages. "Can I send you a receipt by email at all?" asked the teenager who finally got round to serving me. ("At all"? Why "at all"?)

"No need," I said. "I'm standing right here." He looked a bit grumpy at this logic; I think they're paid to harvest email addresses. Mind you, he wasn't as grumpy as the man from Experian, who I rang to ask what this 'credit check' was all about. He quoted some odd worldwide credit agency. I said I hadn't a clue what it was about, and had no intention of giving lots of financial details to him. I also suggested he get a proper job rather than scamming people.

September 15th

It's all very well having an expensive German Army mosquito net rigged up carefully over the bed, but when the mosquito is on the inside with you, it's all been a bit of a waste of time. In the small hours, I was lying flat on my back, phone on my chest with the bright LED lighting up the whole of my little net tent, waiting to catch a glimpse of the little bastard who had already bitten me a few times. I found I could keep him from settling down by gently pulling on the netting, and he finally whizzed past a foot or two away. I clapped him flat. Hurrah.

It should have been a doddle to get back to sleep, but the late fry-up we'd had wasn't sitting too well, and it was well past three o'clock when I dozed off. Trouble is, a house full of builders won't allow a lie-in to catch up, especially when they're merrily dismantling the upstairs windows and climbing in. Could be a bit embarrassing.

It turned out that the scaffolders weren't making up the story of the two old farmers wanting to drop in to have their books signed. They rang late last night and arrived this morning. We called them in for a cuppa and a chat, duly signed their copies of Book One and Two, and they were on their way again. I'm going to miss these random drop-ins from best friends we've never met before.

Ploughing beckoned again, and the job got better and better. I cracked the right speed to give time for the wireweed to get through the skims (6.2kph), although the fact that everything was drying by the hour probably helped. That's the joy of ploughing – the almost infinite variables. Great band name.

September 16th

There's one thing I'm not going to miss when I give up farming: idiot delivery companies. My phone buzzed at ten past seven, with a cheery text from a driver. He'd be here with a large load of grass seed at eight. I replied with a dig about notice being a bit short, but got out of bed anyway. He was here a bit before eight, and the jolly building team (who have wonderfully occupied the old carpenter's workshop) pointed him to our kitchen window.

The last load of grass seed was hand-unloaded into the container, but this was a slightly bigger load: two huge pallets and a much smaller one. I had to do some on-the-spot planning. I'd need the loader tractor to get them off, but probably not the weights on the back. (Lucky, because they're on the Deere.) I dug the old bale trailer out of the hedge, hoping the tyres were in a fit state, and carefully lifted two very tall pallets of grass seed off – and then one tiny one.

It was all done in a few moments, and the driver seemed totally unconcerned about the short notice arrival. "Nuffin' to do with me, mate! I only found out my destinations this morning." Ho hum.

Once he was sorted – and Hazel very kindly offered to take to the trailer down to the Drier and park it there (it's the second-best ratproof area after the container) – I could get on with the penultimate Flindt on Friday. It's hard to know how to judge these last few columns; cheery? Sad? Philosophical? I went for a rant about regen farming instead. It might get sent back with 'again?' metaphorically red-inked across it.

Another long afternoon in Kilmeston Road went really well. I kept the Deere in its sweet spot for allowing wireweed and ragwort to filter through the skims, and on the flat ground at the bottom it was ploughing as nicely as any ploughing I've ever done. Shame I'm giving it up, really. I had done all the long work and the top headland when it was time to come home for a quick shower and an evening trip to the Pots with the ex-Editor and Mrs ex-Editor. The Pots was heaving and not terribly nice to relax in – a far cry from a wet Tuesday night. Mind you, it's the busy evenings like this that mean neighbour Robert and I can have the place to ourselves on a wet Tuesday night in November, so we shouldn't complain. We still did, though.

September 17th

We hadn't been up long when we realised a dodgy pick-up was trying to get into the yard. It tried our gate, and then the double gates round the back – both of which were still locked, as you expect at eight o'clock on a Saturday morning. I managed to scoot around the back just in time to see it make off; it was from the building company who are doing our windows. It was of course the rubbish monkey, the poor soul who goes round at the weekends tidying up the rubble and offcuts.

He was back half an hour later. The poor fellow hardly had a word of English, and hadn't got a clue where he should have been. We found a pile of rubbish, stacked up next to the Portaloo, and on top of the old whetstone. I told him to leave that – it wasn't rubbish.

It was only while I was helping him out that I realised how cold it was. Hazel reported back from Cheriton that ice had been found on some windscreens down there. Cold, but very beautiful. A drop more rain wouldn't go amiss, though.

I finished ploughing. Kilmeston Road went a treat, although there was a lot of reversing and faffing, having decided to plough the headlands in. And the bottom headland was pretty hard. The knock-on points I fitted only a few days ago are already well down, and the plough was struggling to penetrate. I'd left a tiny headland next to the trough in the Hangar for Digger Man to do his stuff, and once that was done, so was ploughing.

The mouldboards were finally shiny and clean. I went down the Drier in the test Hilux, which I'm liking less and less with every drive, to get the can of wax and an old spray applicator (originally for window cleaning) with a view to getting the plough looking as good as possible for sale. A wipe down with an old T-shirt and a generous spraying of wax made it look perfect. I made sure I was upwind of the wax spray – it's nasty stuff.

September 18th

Flipping cold again. Hazel was off very early for a long yomp with picker-up Suzi and two brown flatcoats. Tim and Sasha were left behind, and sulked while I ate my porridge.

There was a text from Team Toyota, saying they'd be in to pickup the pick-up on Tuesday. It dawned on me that I hadn't been able to get out and about in it much. I decided I'd go shopping for cars.

You see, there's the small matter of my retirement present, and I've got my eye on a Mazda 3 saloon in red, with the snicketty manual gearchange. Oh, and black leather. It's quite rare, with only a couple of dozen of them on Autotrader, and before I come home from the pub one night and foolishly click on 'buy now', it would be wise to at least have a sit in one.

There's a Mazda garage down in Eastleigh, only a few miles drive though the lanes and roads of south Hampshire. I set off in the Hilux, through Twyford and Colden Common, and it became pretty obvious, pretty quickly, that the 'lanes' of south Hampshire were solid. This is, of course, an unusual bank holiday, and everyone is out and about. The short stretch of road as you enter Eastleigh proper – Allbrook Hill, I think it is – was solid. It's effectively a narrow residential street, but it was mayhem. Drivers were ignoring the 'priority' signs, refusing to pull over, swearing and hooting at each other; in the middle of it was a poor learner who could only just see over the top of the steering wheel. I gave her extra space and a thumbs-up. It was the least I could do.

The Mazda garage was part of cathedral of car showrooms, with Kia, Mazda and Honda all together in a sequence of modernist glass cubes. I found somewhere to park the Hilux (easier said than done) and strolled down the lines of used cars, looking for a 3 to sit in. A bored salesman leant against a wall in the 'Used Car centre' and ignored me. His phone was far more interesting. In the main showroom I found a loo and a salesman, in that order. He was happy to show me to a demonstrator he had outside, even though it was a hatchback rather than the saloon I crave. It was a relief to find I could climb in and out of it easily. I asked if I could take it out for a spin.

"We'll need your licence, you National Insurance Number, another form of ID such as a passport, and then we'll be able to make a booking," he recited robotically. You can fuck off, I thought to myself.

What I actually said was, "I'll see if I can get that organised. In the meantime, can I have a brochure?"

"We only do e-brochures," he said. "But I'll see if I can print one off for you." I wandered round the showroom, inspecting the assorted machines, most of them electric now, of course. 'Range of 135 miles' claimed one proudly. I'd have kept quiet about that if I were them. "I'm trying to find some paper," apologised the salesman, scurrying back and forth. Finally, I was handed a dismal copy of a brochure in black-and-white, which is no use when the main reason for buying a Mazda these days is the red they use. I thanked him and left.

The idea of taking on all those lanes again didn't appeal, so I turned left out of the showroom car park and headed for the M3 north. It was solid. I sat in the queue and pondered the time when a ten-mile trip to Four Marks via Cheriton and Alresford would have passed garages that sold Saab and Subaru (New Cheriton), British

Leyland (Cheriton), Proton (Hankins in Alresford), Volvo (Lentz in Alresford) and Peugeot/Citroen in Four Marks. I bet each of them would have sent you out with a test car without a murmur. And you could have had a pint between each garage, too, when there were plenty of pubs. The traffic crawled up to Winchester, where it finally freed up. God knows why I'm thinking of buying a car. When was the last time driving was fun?

The Hangar, thankfully, was traffic-free. The new 4m discs made short work of my ploughing, and by the time I'd finished, it looked an absolute treat. Just right for the grass seed, if the machine turns up on Tuesday. There's the small matter of a funeral between now and then, of course.

September 19th
The Queen's funeral. I watched it in the office so I could focus on proceedings, and blubbed all the way through it.

September 20th
It was all very exciting; my new machine was on its way. You might think that imminent retirement would mean an end to buying new kit, but this toy – grass harrows with an airseeder on top – is going to be a vital tool in the next few months. The Hangar is all prepared and ready to go, and I spent the early morning taking the huge discs and the weights off the Deere. I put the transport box on the front, thinking it would be the best way to carry lots of bags of seed out to the field, and then waited for the mob.

There's a very good reason for buying simple second-hand kit: you don't have to endure the 'set up' involving reps and company experts. I'm very happy for a pre-loved bit of machinery to arrive on the back of a lorry, and then I sit down and read the book. Nine times out of ten I know what I'm doing when I set off to the field, and on the tenth time, it takes a field or two to get the hang of it.

Because this grass seeder is a new machine, it came with a bit of a crowd. There was the man from the dealers who were 'supplying' it (although I'd ordered direct from the MD), the man from the company, and a freelance photographer/writer who I know via *Farmers Weekly*. It turned into a very jolly day. These three knew each other very well, and it was quickly established that no grannies needed to be taught to suck eggs, and the whole thing could have taken a lot less time if we hadn't been gossiping and messing about.

The morning was spent getting it attached and wired into the Deere, and then there was a long lunch break. We piled into the house and drank tea for another hour. Then it all got a bit complicated. The four of us set off in three vehicles: I went first in the Massey with the pallet forks, clearing the poacher barricades in and out of Folly. The dealer followed me in the Deere with the seeder all set up and ready to go, and the rep and the photographer followed in a pick-up.

All three took one look at the seedbed and said it needed rolling. Right. I got back in the Massey and drove all the way back home to pick up the rollers, hoping that the tyres weren't flat. They were just about hard enough, and I could head straight back. The photographer (it was turning into that sort of day) jumped into the Massey and set off rolling, while the rest of us continued to get the seeder sorted.

Eventually, I got going, trundling across the field at a steady 7kph, engine barely above idle. The first two bags cleared almost exactly as calibrated, and the multitude gradually left me to my own devices – but not before the photographer had got back to his day job and spent half an hour clicking away with his fancy SLR.

I caught up with the edge of the rolled land, switched back to the rollers and did the rest. I rang Hazel to get her to walk out and bring the Massey home, leaving the rollers folded up under the trees. And I came home in the Deere, slightly knackered. Not too knackered for another Tuesday night in the Pots, though.

September 21st

It was probably a mistake to discuss the new grass-seeding machine with neighbour Robert in the pub last night. I had just about got my head clear and was ready to set off to the Hangar again when the distinctive rattle of an utterly knackered Defender signalled that he was on his way into the yard. I think he was expecting something a bit more impressive than a grass harrow with a hopper on the top, so I tried to impress him with its fancy GPS metering. By then he was casting his eyes round the yard, as farmers do, and he seemed most taken with my 1986 Sulky drill – £300 off eBay – that does my game strips.

He was just out of the yard in a cloud of diesel fumes when neighbour John arrived to talk through the future of the cottage he lives in; it used to be 'ours' but is now going back to the Trust, of course. John had heard nothing from the Trust, so I promised that I'd give them a prod. There's a lot of technical issues to be sorted before they become problems.

Inevitably, talk turned to the philosophy of what we're doing, and a long debate about farming's future. John sells vast quantities of grass seed and has been my sounding board for the Trust's ideas on what we're sowing at the moment, but even he was dismissive of the nation's rush away from food production. He raised the very important point that food crops after grass suffer from pests like wireworm, and the authorities have done away with all effective methods of control of these nasty little critters. When the cry goes out for food, there will be a mad rush to rediscover some handy if somewhat nasty insecticides.

While all this was going on, I was exchanging cross texts with the Trust about the Bat Nazis, who want to come and check the house – yet again. I dug my heels in and said I was very unhappy about this – I'd only had a day's notice, and that was by text. It was about time (I texted pompously) that our privacy was respected. It may be a Trust house, but it's our home. Harrumph. I then got a very formal email from the building manager ("Dear Mr Flindt...") making an appointment for them to come in a week's time. That's better.

Finally, I could head out to the Hangar. I finished the first pass with the new seeder – once I'd asked the Trust's huge team of archaeologists to move all their 'find' flags. I think they're getting a bit fed up with us cultivating ground they're working on; the photographer had to ask them to move yesterday, too. But it's a glorious insight into the way the Trust works, with lots of different branches supposedly all working for the same organisation completely failing to communicate with each other. I did laugh at the brilliantly enquiring minds of an archaeology team failing to spot that a field was in the process of being worked down and sown. I stopped for a long chat with them anyway and got a guided tour of their work. There were lots of bits and pieces they'd found out in the Hangar itself, and they showed me the Saxon bank that they're cutting through to make public access into the Park. They did laugh that they'd found a .22LR case, and I pointed out that my best ever long-range shot from the passenger seat of Dad's Land Rover 108" using a silenced BSA Supersport 5 with 4x28 Nikko Stirling sights was taken from this very spot, down the hedge that separated the Hangar from Cheriton. That could have been the very bullet's case. God, you wouldn't do that now.

Once that was all sorted, I could do the whole field again, at a slightly different angle, of course. The Trust had ordered enough seed for two passes of 20kg/ha, and assumed that the hangar was 8ha. The new seeder measured it at 9.1ha, so for the second pass I nudged the seed rate down. I have no idea how many bags I actually used, because I forgot to keep count of the number of bags I loaded into the new transport box which fitted neatly onto the front of the Deere. I don't think it was far off the target rate in the end.

September 22nd

There was a slightly worrying exchange of emails and calls about the Big Farm Surrender. We've been leaving it all to the experts – mainly because all the assorted paperwork is way beyond our pay grade – and one side wasn't sure that the other side (won't say which) weren't up to date with the relevant forms. It turned out that it was half-true, but not an issue. No need to panic. That's lucky, because it's only a week away.

Hazel went out to the Hangar and rolled it, and then left the rollers in Springshot ready to be used in Kilmeston Road. I gave the new seeder a clear out and a blow off with the compressor. The fins on the fans are very important, apparently. They pick up dust and then lose their impetus. I hitched it off in the barn in case tonight's rain really does arrive. Then it was back on with the discs and the heavy front weight for another session in Kilmeston Road. It really could do with a good rain. Some of that ploughing at the top is pretty baked out.

September 23rd

We had a rain, but we could have done with more. What we did get was an invasion of builders, carpenters and decorators. Mind you, we could have done with even more of them, too – the quicker this monster house renovation project gets done the better. They asked if they could continue to use the old carpentry workshop for the foreseeable, mainly because they've won the contract to do lots of other cottages in the village as well. I said I was happy, as I'm sure we will sort out who owes who for what in the long term. I reckon if we're really nice we might get some high-speed installation of log burners while all the expensive scaffolding is up.

While all this was going on, I was trying to get my last ever Flindt on Friday done. Blimey, it was a challenge. Odd, because the previous 250-odd have mostly been easy-peasy. But how do you sign off from a weekly column that – apparently – is very popular? An overnight idea grew in the writing, and wasn't too morose or sad – and Emma at FW agreed it was about right. It ended with the promise that I'd be back in the middle pages soon, which was an upbeat finish.

Next job was trip to the doctors in Medstead for a bit of review. The surgery is the last bastion of mask wearing, which means a lot of scrabbling for one I'd stuck in my pocket on the way out. But things were running on time up there, so I didn't have to endure too much mid-morning grief telly ("I fell in love with him online and he ran off with all my savings…") There were blood samples, pee samples (worryingly clear after a morning drinking tea), a session on the scales (112kg; oops) and on the height measurer. Hope I haven't shrunk. Blood pressure was reasonable, and no change from the last visit, which is a result. "Do you want your flu jab?" asked one of the nurses cheerily.

"Only if it's only the flu jab; I'm not having any Covid booster, thank you," I replied sounding a bit tinfoil-hatted. Funnily enough, they seemed perfectly happy with this, although I suspect that I was given the booster anyway, without being told. That's what the world is coming to. If my heart gives up in the next few weeks I'll be proved right.

Back home, there was one bit of paperwork that needed attention. In 1994, Hazel and I started farming in partnership. All the paperwork was drawn up by our solicitor at the time, and then, when children started arriving (January 1995), got put in the safe, unsigned, and forgotten. The deal we're about to do with the Trust is heavily dependent (for reasons I can't possibly go into here) on us being partners in the farm. And while it's true that we have an infinite pile of evidence we could show to those who might want to know that we've been working as a partnership for thirty-eight years, there's no actual paper agreement. Our new solicitors had sent through a draft of one a few days ago, and pointed out that there's a bit of haste needed. So we had a Teams meeting with one of their team after lunch, going through mundane things like the name of the partnership and the name of the bank, and slightly more curious philosophical stuff like what happens to the voting rights of one partner when s/he dies. That stuff sort of went over my head. He said he'd send it to Agent Chris for perusal, and if we could sign it with a witness, all would be well.

It was a bloody relief to get in the tractor again, and have a short afternoon in the rapidly drying mud of Kilmeston Road.

September 24th

The run of fantastic weather continued, and the builders were dead keen to make the most of it by all turning up on a Saturday. Hazel did the right thing by grabbing a couple of dogs and setting off to Oxford for a flatcoat training day. I endured a very long day of banging, hammering, whistling and joshing. Still, it all contributes to getting the job done.

There was a slightly awkward moment when a very urgent dump was needed, and both loos had no windows. None at all. They were already out and being fettled in the workshop. There was no time to make alternative arrangements, and I think using the Portaloo that was brought in for the building site would have killed it. I drew the big heavy curtains upstairs and got on with it. At least there was plenty of fresh air.

Trying to catch up with some writing was all but impossible with all the activity, and it was quite a relief when I got a phone call from someone desperate for some bits for his Horsch CO3. I know him through a speech I did some time ago, and from recommending that he bought a CO3. We occasionally bump into each other at quizzes and meetings. He had just started drilling his patch down near Botley, and one of the CO3's duetts had lost its baseplate. The local Horsch dealers were shut (odd, for a busy Saturday) and he was keen to crack on. I'd mentioned to him that I had a barn full of duetts, thanks to my habit of buying all the ones on eBay that are being sold by Horsch owners who have fallen for the latest trendy replacement points.

He wanted to know if I had a spare baseplate, but we very quickly agreed that the simplest thing would be for him to take a whole assembly. Two big chunky bolts, and he'd be back in action. That would be far simpler than trying to disassemble one just for the baseplate. Any sense of urgency dissolved when I put the kettle on, and he was here with a dead keen youngster – a nephew I think, c/w John Deere cap – for over an hour.

Hazel and two dogs got back from Oxford knackered but very happy.

September 25th

There's another lone mosquito who has worked his way inside my mosquito net, where he lives quite happily, and can help himself to blood as easily as he likes. He woke me up just after one o'clock, and I was damned if I could get back to sleep. The television beckoned, and I spent a surreal couple of hours watching something called 'LeoVegas', which is semiautomated casino show, and *The Patriot*, which is possible the biggest heap of cinematic cack I've ever seen. Mel Gibson gurning his way through a series of implausible atrocities inflicted on plucky Yanks by dastardly comic book British baddies. I couldn't take my eyes off it. No wonder it was four o'clock before I finally slept.

Hazel arrived back from getting the Sunday papers at a crawl. The Skoda had a flat tyre. When we bought it in April 2019, I went onto eBay and picked up a full-size spare wheel, a jack and a 17mm tyre lever. It seemed extravagant, but it's at times like this you're pleased you did it. There's no resorting to glue or a silly space saver. Twenty minutes of grunting and the Skoda was ready to go. And I didn't put my back out. The flat and the spare are both on their last legs, so a call to North's in the morning will be in order.

Plans to get out to Kilmeston Road and keep on discing were scuppered by Mac arriving in the yard with his enormous Fendt with a teeny tiny 800 litre Allman sprayer on the back. He's doing more pony paddock work for the White Settlers, and wanted to chat about using our rotavator again. That was the theory, anyway. It turned into another lengthy coffee break. I promised I'd order a new set of 'L' blades for the rotavator.

Sister-in-law Heather was in next for coffee and a briefing on housesitting for us when we go on our first holiday for 11 years. It's how we're celebrating Hazel's Significant Birthday and the conclusion of the Big Deal – which is only a couple of days away, and still doesn't seem real.

I took Sasha out for long late walk, loving the view across fields that will soon not be ours. But it still doesn't seem real.

September 26th

"Drop it down when you've got the chance," said Gary at North Motor Company. "We'll get it sorted." It wasn't long after eight when we got down there, and it promptly turned into a social gathering, with several people we knew down there all keen for a chat. It reminded me of Owen's, the welding shop just along the A272 from the bottom of Hinton Hill, where farm kit was brought for patching and repair by the multitude of farmers who didn't have the skills or kit to do welding themselves. You couldn't take a bit of stuff down there to be welded without an hour's nattering with everyone who was down there.

I was out in Kilmeston Road mid-morning, finally getting the last bits of discing done. A couple of heavy showers came through, which made the job go better. We've got a huge rain on Friday, apparently, which could be handy. Funny how I'm caring about it; it's not my field and not my grass.

Hazel rolled Kilmeston Road in the afternoon, and I hitched off the discs and the weights. Once the grass seeder was on and I'd loaded up the front box with fancy grass seed, I was ready to crack on. I went for a long walk instead.

The tyres were done on the Skoda by late morning, and we brought it back in the evening, with two smart new Falkens on the front. Less than a hundred quid each, too.

September 27th

There was something different at the dentists. I hammered on the front door and it swung open. I realised you could just walk in. All the screens had gone. The 'virus killing' (yeah, right) air conditioning unit in the corner was gone. It was back to normal. Even the hyperactive receptionists had gone, and the new one's vocal register was within my range. She still said 'perfect' a lot, though.

A brief check-up (£79, FFS) revealed nothing of concern, and there was no lecture on how to brush my teeth, which makes a change. I was still instructed to make an appointment with the hygienist. Yuck.

On the way back from Alresford, the heavens opened. A real deluge, and an unforecast one. When I got home, I found Hazel and four dogs all drenched. They'd rushed out (she had, and dogs followed, of course) to cover up the grass-seed bags I had stacked, uncovered, in the front box of the tractor. I hope those plastic sacks are as waterproof as they look.

There would be no grass-seed sowing for a bit after that rain, and it got heavier while the National Trust's comms team arrived for a cuppa in the kitchen. Not quite a 'team'; it was one girl who is putting together some press releases about our Big Plan, and wants to make sure everyone is happy with what she says. As is now traditional, it turned into a very jolly hour, and I was able to insist that I'm not referred to as some green convert; I'm very sceptical of what the Trust are going to do with our land, but it's not up to me to tell them what to do. I will watch with interest what rewilding and regen farming achieves. But it's quite hard saying all that without swearing too much.

It rained more, and suddenly got very cold. I emailed my several bosses at the Trust suggesting that we abandon sowing Kilmeston Road, but got no answer. I adjourned to the office instead. Hazel lit the log burner for the first time, and it all suddenly felt very autumnal.

The pub trip with Robert was shelved as we had an unusual Tuesday band rehearsal. It was unusual because of the day, and also because we all played very well. It was the last rehearsal before the gig on the October 8th – the gig that I agreed to do because Hazel was adamant she didn't want to do anything for her big birthday, and a quiet night at home would suffice. It now turns out that the picking-up team have decided that they are all taking Hazel out to the pub for her big birthday, because that rotter Charlie is doing a gig. You can't win.

As the day of our surrender gets closer, we needed a day like this – one where nicely organised fieldwork plans were scuppered by inept weather forecasting. It's nice to be reminded what we're not going to miss.

September 28th

There was a definite 'no more drilling' feeling in the air. Everything was sodden from yesterday's rain, and the forecast didn't suggest much of a break in the next few days. After I'd sent an email to the Trust saying that that was probably the best decision, we decided we'd work our way round assorted drills, giving them an end of season – and end of era, of course – clear-out. There was still a bit of 'Autumn Promise' in the CO3, left over from the trip up to Pipeline when the old drill refused to work, and some dregs in the faithful Sulky box drill, left over from when it had to step in and do the job that the Horsch refused to do.

The grass seeder took a bit more work, as it had two bags of seed in it, and grass seed doesn't flow. But with the farm's most useful bits of kit (a stick and a Roundup can halved longways) we prodded all the seed back out, bagged it up, and locked up the container. Phew. All done. Bring on the autumn gales.

The trip to the doctor's surgery for a chat about my tests the other day was interesting. It was done with another squeaky-clean nurse, and she was the only one there wearing a mask. And that change has taken place since I was there a few days ago. Most of the results were very good – blood pressure, liver and so on. She asked if I was aware that they do a 'weight-loss clinic'? I pointed out that I find 'not eating so much' to be a very useful weight-loss concept – no clinic required. And I suggested she should have just called me a fat bastard and moved on. Probably just as effective. Of course, at my age, prostate is the big one (if it becomes a big one) and I asked if she could do a blood test for that – and a vitamin D one, too. My life-saving Questran powder is a miracle, but it does play havoc with vitamin D levels, and the days are getting shorter.

She was very happy to do both of those, but wanted to know, before she did the prostate test, if I'd been on a bicycle today, and if I'd had intercourse. "No," I said with utmost seriousness. "No bicycling, and no intercourse, not even one-handed." I fully expect to be reported to the thought police.

Hazel set off for Cambridge in the Scout to pick up Diana, who is coming down for the final Big Surrender tomorrow, and commandeer Diana's cast-off computer. I checked emails to find a series of long pleading messages from the Trust: could we please please *pleeeaseease* keep going with the grass seed in Kilmeston Road? Even if we only get one pass in, even if it makes a mess? It sounds like getting some cover of some sort is vital – I suspect they've already signed up to some scheme that insists on it. Funnily enough, the morning had been a vintage drying one, and I was already getting itchy feet about calling off all drilling.

There was only one thing for it. Fill up the grass seeder again, fill up the front box, leave all the lonely dogs behind, and set off for Kilmeston Road. Life was made easier by the fact that Shepherd Ella has taken all her sheep away (the last commercial livestock in Springshot ever) and dismantled the electric fence. There was far less annoying jumping in and out of the cab.

The sowing went beautifully – far better for a load of rain yesterday. I ran out of seed after about fourteen hectares, which was the majority of the land work. It was just getting dark when I came home and gave the dogs a much-needed spin round the Chalks dell. Hazel and Diana got back just after half past eight, having had a very smooth drive round the M25.

September 29th – Michaelmas Day

Good God. It's finally here – 'Surrender Day'. The good news is that it's due to be a frantic day, perfect for not getting into a stew about it. Big rain is forecast tomorrow afternoon, and I have started Kilmeston Road; I must finish it. Bizarre, really, because it's not my field and it's not my crop. It's my work, though.

I was out there ludicrously early (for me) and got the first pass of drilling finished by about ten. I had just started all over again (two passes with half-rate seed at a good angle to each other is the way, I'm told) when a posse of Trust employees arrived. They started off by inspecting the work being done by the Digger Man at the bottom of the field. He is slowly and methodically working away at digging a 'scrape', perfect for some sort of wildlife haven. The trouble is, no sooner has he worked his way through what the Trust has marked out for him, than another set of posts is driven into the ground to show where his new boundary is.

The same happened this morning. A senior Trustie could be seen from a distance addressing the throng, and then out came the club hammer and new set of posts. A new area was defined, much of which I'd drilled earlier. I mentioned this point to the Trustie when we all got together for a chat, and he got quite cross, as if it was my fault. I said that it made no difference to me what he dug up; I'd drill what I could, and he could bury/dig up what he wanted. He was probably upset because I'd pointed at the vast heaps of earth and asked if that's what they meant by 'nature recovery'.

One of the Trust team then took lots of photos of me in the tractor, and then leaning on a gate, and then leaning on a gate looking thoughtfully into the distance. They'll all go to make up the big press release about today's events that is due to be released soon. Eventually, I could get back in the tractor and keep going with the grass seeding.

Another interruption beckoned. The Trust had laid on a little gathering on the lawns of Hinton Ampner House to celebrate Surrender Day, and it was very sweet. We had cake and fizz, and were all very rude to each other, which suggested that everyone was very happy with events. Diana chatted away happily with the Trusties, they made a short speech, I made a short speech, I made my excuses that I had to get back to work for my bosses (i.e. them) and we walked back to the farmhouse. We took a short detour into Hinton Ampner churchyard and visited Dad for a moment or two. I think he'd approve of today's events.

Amazingly, the usual crushing post-lunchtime drinks headache stayed well away, and I was able to have another long run in Kilmeston Road, stopping as it got dark with only a bit of second-pass land work still to do.

A really lovely and significant day was only spoiled by news that the chief Bat Nazi had arrived unannounced at some stage in the day, and had been wandering around our bedrooms, rummaging in Hazel's clothes for the long key that opens the loft hatch in her room. Now that did give me headache, and the emails I sent out reflected my fury.

We persuaded neighbour Robert to come down to the Pots with us to celebrate an end of an era. He didn't take much persuading, mainly due to the fact that a century ago today, his grandfather took on the tenancy of Grange Farm, Tichborne. We sat and toasted everyone we could think of. At least I think we did. You could hardly tell over the din of the Pots on a Thursday, as vast quantities of yoof laughed twice as loudly as they needed to. But we cleared the place by ten, and went home, well toasted. And that was that. Farming's End.

Bonus Day – September 30th

Despite last night's beer, I was out in Kilmeston Road again shockingly early. The forecasters are convinced that there was big wind and rain on the way, although you wouldn't guess it from the stunning morning. I got the last corner of short land work done, then did three turns of headland, and the seed I had in the little hopper ran out just right. There were three 20kg bags left over, perfect for patching up come the spring. I was quite pleased with myself, using a new drill in a field that kept changing size every time you turned your back.

I dropped the drill off in Springshot and picked up the rollers, still down there after rolling the Hangar. They did a fantastic job. I started over by the road and worked my way back. Hazel came and took over after dropping Diana at the station, and I used her tractor to bring the Opico seeder (now officially my favourite bit of kit) home. I gave it a clean out with the airline and parked it up in the barn, and then went and had a sit down.

You could tell my mind was elsewhere because it took me ages to notice that two dogs had vanished. Tim and Evie were nowhere to be seen. A search round the house turned into a search round the garden, which turned into a search round the yard, which turned into a slightly urgent call to Hazel, just finishing the rolling. The building team hadn't got them, and hadn't seen any white vans crawling around and seizing dogs after checking that they were breeding stock – both Evie and Tim are 'entire'. That scenario is the worst one of all.

Hazel came back from rolling at some speed. By then, Tim had appeared, looking slightly flustered. I jumped in Tigger and set off along the back track, hoping to find that a walker had inherited a friendly flatcoat, and had somehow forgotten to return her – but there was no one to be seen. Just as I was beginning to feel a bit sick, my phone rang. Hazel had set off with three dogs, all barking madly, and that had been enough to draw Evie out from her hiding place. The builders had left the gates open, and Evie, feeling a bit lost without Hazel at home, had made her way to her favourite place: Pig, parked up in the calf pens. She'd been sitting there for hours, with Tim as company for a bit, ignoring my calls and whistles, and only emerging when she realised Hazel was home and appeared to be setting out for a walk. Bloody dogs.

Once that was sorted, and our nerves had calmed down a bit, we hitched off the rollers, shut and locked the barn doors and headed indoors. A gale had got up, and the Beauworth horizon vanished in the incoming deluge. For once, the weather muppets got one right.

POSTSCRIPT
On a hotel balcony, St Brelade's Bay, Jersey; October 3rd, 2022

Our first holiday for eleven years - a two day, three-night break in the posh hotel that Dad used to frequent twice a year, every year, for forty years. He used to treat us and our small children to a few days over there every so often, and we thought we'd go back to mark our retirement. We think we've found a waiter who remembers him, although he may have been being polite.

On arable farms all over England, the seed drills are flying, the rollers are improving seedbeds and saving moisture, and the sprayers are busy stacking pre-ems to control grassweeds.

When we get back home (probably feeling a bit ill by the sound of the weather forecast), there will be none of that. Dead Dog Farm is arable-free, and will soon be grass and livestock only, with a smattering of environmental schemes to pay the rent. We'll be custodians of only about a hundred acres (The Back Meadow, Chalks, Roe Hill, BOMS and the Folly – and many of these are to be reduced by tree planting.) Life will be very different.

What's next? There's a pile of valuable machinery to sell, although now that I've agreed to help out the Trust with fieldwork, much kit will be staying; the farm sale has been shelved. It was remarkable how all that September grass establishment put a stop to what could have been a post-harvest month of morose navel-gazing. *Farmers Weekly* are insistent that there's work to be done for them. Neighbours are dropping hints about how handy a man with a tractor is at busy times. Hazel keeps gathering small book-keeping jobs to fit around her livestock – which will remain, of course.

It could be a lot busier that I'd thought. There might be enough material for another book. Maybe not.